FOLLOWING GOD
CHARACTER SERIES
BIBLE STUDY

An inform
of life princip
and the Christian's walk.

The Acts of the Holy Spirit

GUIDANCE FOR THE CHRISTIAN WALK

BOOK 2

AMG

PUBLISHERS

EDDIE RASNAKE

Following God

THE ACTS OF THE HOLY SPIRIT
BOOK TWO

ISBN: 978-1-61715-530-7

Manuscript editing, text design, and layout by Rick Steele Editorial Services
http://steeleeditorialservices.myportfolio.com

Cover illustration by Daryle Beam/Bright Boy Design

Printed in the United States of America
2019 First Edition

This book is dedicated to my
late brother,

Ron Rasnake,

who went to be with the Lord shortly before this
book's printing. His faith has now become sight.

ACKNOWLEDGMENTS

This two-volume work constitutes the fifteenth and sixteenth installments for me personally in the series I was privileged to launch with AMG Publishers and my fellow authors, Wayne Barber and Rick Shepherd, two decades ago. Though the publishing industry has changed much since then, the enduring nature of these studies is a testament to the fact that God's Word is an inexhaustible ocean, with neither beach nor boundary, and God's people will always look for ways to study these living Scriptures more deeply. I am especially grateful to the body of believers at Woodland Park Baptist Church in Chattanooga, Tennessee, who have walked through this and many other studies I have written and have been a continual source of encouragement as we continue to develop new ministry tools together. Thanks to all the folks at AMG, especially Steve Turner and Amanda Jenkins, and to my long-time collaborator, Rick Steele, who always does a great job with editing, layout, and text design. Most of all, I remain grateful to the Lord Jesus, who saved me and continues to teach me and lead me in what it means to follow Him with a whole heart.

THE AUTHOR

Eddie Rasnake

EDDIE RASNAKE graduated with honors from East Tennessee State University. He and his wife, Michele, served 7 years with Cru at the University of Virginia, James Madison University, and the University of Tennessee (as campus director). Eddie left Cru to join Wayne Barber at Woodland Park Baptist Church, where he still serves as Senior Associate Pastor. He has authored dozens of books and Bible studies and has published materials in Afrikaans, Albanian, German, Greek, Italian, Romanian, Russian, and Telugu. Eddie and his wife Michele live in Chattanooga, Tennessee.

PREFACE

The book of Acts is a pivotal book of the New Testament, yet sometimes it gets neglected in study because of its length and narrative nature. This is unfortunate, for these accounts of the first-century church show how by the power of God, the early believers impacted the culture around them despite their minority status. Now more than ever, the church needs such examples and reminders as we seek to turn our world upside down (or perhaps a better way to express it is turn our world "right side up"). Like the early church, we believers must live our mission in the context of an antithetical and sometimes antagonistic culture. Like the early church, we do not have social leverage, political clout, or military might to change society by force, but we do have the name of the risen Christ, the person of the Holy Spirit and the life-changing power of God the Father on our side. It is my prayer that as you study this impactful New Testament narrative, you will do so with faith that God can do in our day what He did in theirs!

Following Him,

EDDIE RASNAKE

CONTENTS

WEEK 1 • THE MISSION OF THE CHURCH (Acts 13–14)   1

WEEK 2 • THE MESSAGE OF GRACE (Acts 15:1–35)   17

WEEK 3 • WHATEVER THE PROBLEM,
GOD HAS A SOLUTION (Acts 15:36—16:40)   33

WEEK 4 • THE BASIS OF BELIEF (Acts 17:1–34)   51

WEEK 5 • JOINING WHERE GOD IS WORKING (Acts 18:1–22)   67

WEEK 6 • CHANGING THE WORLD (Acts 18:23—19:41)   87

WEEK 7 • PASSING THE TORCH (Acts 20)   107

WEEK 8 • WHEN GOD'S WILL IS HARD (Acts 21:1—22:29)   125

WEEK 9 • THE FALSE SOLUTION OF FOLLOWING
OUR FLESH (Acts 23)   143

WEEK 10 • THE FRUIT OF PATIENCE (Acts 24)   167

WEEK 11 • A DEFENSE FOR THE HOPE WITHIN (Acts 25—26)   177

WEEK 12 • PRISONS BECOME PULPITS (Acts 27–28)   195

LEADER'S GUIDE   213

LESSON 1

THE MISSION OF THE CHURCH
ACTS 13—14

Have you ever reflected on why the church exists? Is it designed to be a holy huddle where believers insulate themselves from this sinful world? Is it to be a social club without drinking and dancing where moralists can interact comfortably? While these may be ways some churches function today, it is not the plan God has for His people. While there ought to be safety and community within the walls of the church, it is not meant to be a place of escape. Our refuge is heaven, but why are we not there yet? Since heaven is the best place why do we not go there upon becoming Christians? The answers to these questions, at their core, relate to the mission God has given the church. We are the body of Christ. We are the visible manifestation of His work and passion on planet earth. What He wants done, He does through us. His mission is our mission. What is that mission? Luke 19:10 answers that question for us: *"For the Son of Man has come to seek and to save that which was lost."* The purpose for the church and the reason we are here instead of in heaven is to gather lost sheep into the fold. We are created to be a rescue mission. This task cannot be fulfilled by staying within the walls of the church.

> *"For the Son of Man has come to seek and to save that which was lost." (Luke 19:10)*

The entire book of Acts is a record of the mission of the church, but chapter 13 begins a whole new era of ministry. Jesus foretold at His ascension, *"...you will receive power when the Holy Spirit has come upon you; and you shall be My witnesses both in Jerusalem, and in all Judea and Samaria, and even to the remotest part of the earth."* The early church grew rapidly among the Jews and over time began to reach beyond them to the Samaritans and even to the Gentiles. But it wasn't the mother church in Jerusalem that was responsible for most of the spreading of the gospel. It was actually a Gentile church in the urban metropolis of Antioch that became the real catalyst for fulfilling the last part of Christ's vision. This week we want to look at the birth of the ministry of world missions. We want to see how the church came to define itself in living out the mission of Jesus, *"...to seek and to save that which was lost."*

DAY 1

THE MANPOWER OF MISSIONS: ACTS 13:1–4

C. T. Studd gave up a lucrative career in professional athletics to take the gospel into the dark interior of the African continent. He was the Peyton Manning of his generation and sport, excelling in the British game of cricket. Many thought he was wasting his life and talents after he chose to become a missionary. There is a short poem, attributed to him, which seems to capture why he made the choice:

> *Some wish to live within the sound*
> *Of church or chapel bell;*
> *I want to run a rescue shop*
> *Within a yard of hell*

 IN THEIR SHOES
Leadership Team

Acts reveals some significant details about those in leadership at this church. We already know from earlier in Acts that Barnabas is a levitical priest from Cyprus (Acts 4:36). Simeon is known as *"Niger,"* which is Latin for "black." Most likely he is a black-skinned African. Lucius is from Cyrene and may have been one of the church's founders. Manaen, we are told, was *"brought up with Herod the tetrarch"* (Herod Antipas). This indicates that he comes from high society. Some have suggested he is perhaps a cousin of Herod, but in any case, is probably of the same age and is a close companion to the leader. Finally, we have Saul, who is a former Pharisee and citizen of Rome. The leadership team of the church at Antioch is a testimony to diversity and to the universal appeal of the gospel message.

Studd was not content to dwell in safety and comfort when there were others standing in need of rescue. He is also the source of the famous quote, "Only one life, 'twill soon be passed; Only what's done for Christ will last." He gave his life's labors to the purpose of world evangelization, recognizing that the task of taking the gospel to the *"remotest part of the earth"* (Acts 1:8) takes people—and not just any people, but the best the Lord has to offer.

📖 What stands out to you from the information we are given in the list of church leaders in Acts 13:1?

Barnabas is mentioned first, and the list is probably given in order of priority with Saul (Paul) falling last. This means that Barnabas is the key leader, the "senior pastor" if you will, and that Saul is the elder with the least seniority and significance. Barnabas was the official representative sent by the mother church to help establish this church when it first formed (Acts 11:22) and he continues to play a key role. We know little of the three men mentioned after him, but we can suppose a few things. Simeon, *"who was called Niger,"* is probably African. Lucius of Cyrene may well have been one of the founders of the church since he is one of the key leaders, and Acts 11:20 tells us the church was birthed by men from *"Cyprus and Cyrene."* Manaen is apparently an aristocrat with close ties to the politically powerful family of Herod Antipas. Last on the list is Saul, whom Barnabas brought in to help with the teaching ministry (Acts 11:25–26).

Read Acts 13:2 and answer the questions that follow.

What is the Spirit's message to the church leadership?

What were the leaders doing when God called out Barnabas and Saul?

It is worth noticing that the great thrust of world missions is born in a season of prayer, not a planning meeting. The leaders are worshiping and fasting. The Greek word translated *"ministering"* here is *leitourgeo*, from which we get our English term "liturgy." It is in the present tense, indicating ongoing action. The emphasis seems to be that they are in a season of seeking the Lord as the ministry continues. We don't know the catalyst for their fast, but it is during that fast that God chooses to speak. His message is clear and unequivocal—He wants to reassign two of the key leaders in the church.

Identify from Acts 13:3 the church's response to God's message.

After finishing their fast, the leadership of the church at Antioch prays and then sends Barnabas and Saul out as missionaries in the cause of Christ. This group of five leaders probably represents the elders of the church, and although it is a costly obedience to release such prominent leaders, once God has spoken there is no hesitation. They lay hands on the two men, identifying with their call and ministry and commission them to the task which God has called them.

 Looking at Acts 13:4, why do you suppose the men choose the route they take?

WORD STUDY
Sent

Although in our English Bibles, both verses 3 and 4 of Acts 13 use the word "sent," there are actually two different Greek words employed here. In 13:3 when the Antioch leaders "sent" Barnabas and Saul, the word translated sent (apoluo) means "to loose or unbind, to release." In 13:4 when it says the Holy Spirit "sent" the men, the word (ekpempo) means "to send out or send forth." It is God, not the church, who has called Barnabas and Saul. The church's role is to affirm God's calling (by laying on of hands) and then to "release" the men to do what God has called them to do. It is always important to remember that though a man's ministry may be to a church, it is God, not man, who calls him.

The most obvious reason for the direction of travel Barnabas and Saul choose is the fact that they are *"sent out by the Holy Spirit."* We trust that not only is the task divinely initiated, but the process as well. We know that Barnabas was originally from Cyprus (Acts 4:36) and would have been familiar with the culture and area. Seleucia was the seaport of Antioch and is the logical route to Cyprus.

The first major thrust of world missions has begun, and it comes at great cost to the thriving church at Antioch. The two called out are not laborers who can be easily spared. Both are central to the teaching ministry there. Yet to reach the world takes people. Sadly, today some wrongly believe that the standards for a missionary are less than those for a pastor. But it takes more than a plane ride to make someone an effective minister. The cause of Christ deserves the very best people we have to offer. Barnabas and Saul are leaders of proven worth who would be effective wherever they went. They helped build the Antioch church to a place of stability, and it would continue without them. Their skills and passion are now needed by the Lord elsewhere.

DAY 2

THE METHOD OF MISSIONS: ACTS 13:5–12

Church is not something we "do" but what we are and what we build. One reason many local assemblies are ineffective and have little impact on their community is that they are stuck simply "doing" church. They are busy keeping the form of church instead of focusing on the function. A successful church is not defined by *services* but by *service*. It takes more to be effective than just to gather and fulfill the expected rituals. The world is not changed by committees but by laborers. In many respects, when the church gathers on a Sabbath, it is like the huddle at a football game. The huddle is not what people pay money to watch. It is necessary, and it is tolerated. Fans want to see an effective huddle that makes a difference on the playing field. When the church huddles, it is necessary but not the whole game. When the church breaks huddle and scatters onto the field, the real game begins. The church should do this with a plan and strategy progressing toward the goal. Today, as we continue looking at the first missionary journey, we want to try and identify what is revealed of the strategy and methods those early laborers use.

Read Acts 13:5–6 and make note of any principles you observe of the strategy of Barnabas and Saul.

Their ministry begins in the town of Salamis, a port city on the eastern coast of Cyprus and the initial stop on their journey. They go first to the Jewish synagogues and proclaim the word there. These local gatherings had two aspects that made them a strategic place to begin preaching the gospel. First, these were people who already believed in God and hopefully were spiritually sensitive to the message of the Messiah. Second, it was an open forum that allowed men with Barnabas' and Saul's credentials (a Levite and a Pharisee) to address the audience from the Word of God. It is a consistent pattern throughout the missionary journeys that the first stop in each new town would be the synagogue if there was one. Another principle we observe here is that Barnabas and Saul have a helper—John (also called Mark—author of the second gospel). This may not seem significant, but one does not learn to minister in a classroom only. Taking an apprentice along shows a plan for the future, not just the present. We see in verse six that the team is thorough and systematic. They journey through the whole island, apparently village by village. Paphos was a port city on the western coast of Cyprus.

DID YOU KNOW?
Proconsul

In those days, a "Proconsul" was a regional governor sent in by the Roman Empire to rule a particular province. With the abolition of kings, this was the highest-ranking official in the area. Because of their great influence, his conversion to Christianity is a tremendous boost to the cause of Christ in Cyprus.

It is worth reminding ourselves that all of this strategy is supported by the principles found in the first four verses of the chapter. Effective strategy can accomplish nothing unless it is carried out by experienced and trained laborers who are called by God. If their leaving Antioch is at the Spirit's initiative, we can assume they follow His lead in each town. True ministry is initiated by God. It is "received" not "achieved."

📖 Look over Acts 13:6b–8 and record what you learn of the opposition they face at Paphos.

In Paphos a tremendous opportunity greets the men when the proconsul of the province expresses interest in the gospel message. It is not surprising that ministry to this strategic potential convert would be opposed. In those superstitious days it was common for political leaders to keep sorcerers and astrologers as advisors and fortune-tellers. This man Elymas is not a follower of Jehovah, but rather, one who dabbles in the occult. No wonder he opposes Barnabas and Saul. He has enough sense to recognize that if the proconsul comes to Christ his job is in jeopardy.

📖 As you examine Acts 13:9–12, write down what stands out to you from Paul's dealings with the magician's opposition.

Perhaps the most significant principle in Paul's dealings with his opponent is the phrase mentioned first: *"But Saul...filled with the Holy Spirit..."* We cannot do battle with spiritual opposition in our own strength. But we have the promise of God's word that "greater is

He who is in you than he who is in the world" (1 John 4:4). When we are yielded to the Spirit, we have both the power and the wisdom we need to confront our opposition. God reveals through Paul that His power is greater than that of the magician by striking him down with temporary blindness. As a result, the proconsul believes.

Barnabas and Paul operate from an intelligent plan, but they subordinated that plan to the Lord's leading. There is tension that exists between the two and balance that must be found. We need to have a wise strategy in our approach to ministry, but we must also be sensitive to the Lord's lead. The wisest human strategy is no substitute for seeking the Lord any more than commitment to following God does not exclude planning and preparation. Both must work together.

Barnabas was the main leader of the church at Antioch and initially leads the mission team. He is mentioned first by the Lord when the two are called to the task. An interesting thing happens at this juncture of the missionary journey. When the team is confronted by the magician, Elymas, it is Saul who speaks. At this point it appears that the leadership structure begins to change as Saul comes to the forefront as spokesman in the missionary journey. Instead of *"Barnabas and Saul"* (13:2), it now becomes *"Paul and his companions"* (13:13) or *"Paul and Barnabas"* throughout most of the rest of the missionary journey (13:42, 43, 46, 50) until they return to Jerusalem. Back in Jerusalem it is "Barnabas and Paul" (15:25) again, for there, Barnabas has the greater respect and credibility. In Acts 14:14 though, we see that Barnabas is mentioned first again. His name is given first in reference to tearing their robes (a sign of humility before God) at the thought of being worshiped by the people. The suggestion is that Barnabas may have taken the lead in doing this. It is worth noting however that Paul, not Barnabas, is stoned in Lystra.

DID YOU KNOW?
Saul Who Was Called Paul

In the days of Acts nearly every Jew had two names—one Jewish which they used with other followers of God, and the other Greek which they used in secular matters (e.g. Cephas was the Hebrew name for the apostle Peter [his Greek name]). It is significant that from this point on, Saul chooses to be known as Paul—apparently identifying with the Gentiles to whom he was called to minister.

Think about what has happened here: Barnabas is in charge of the mission journey, and then Paul takes over. How would you have handled that? Is there any evidence at all of Barnabas struggling with this? Most people would be hurt and offended; many would rebel, but not the one who was called the *"Son of Encouragement"* (Acts 4:36). It would seem that he has transitioned to the point that his primary ministry is to Paul directly and working through Paul more than directly ministering to the crowds. He leaves that to Paul. You see, one who is characterized by encouragement is not so concerned with who gets the credit, but that the work gets done and God gets the glory. That is all that matters. Barnabas is secure enough in himself to allow Paul to bloom. We are beginning to see the petals of that blossom unfold.

DAY 3

THE MESSAGE OF MISSIONS: ACTS 13:13–41

The purpose of missions is to communicate the message of Christ. While many missionaries use charity and community service to gain a hearing for their faith, the message should always be the most important part. If we go to a remote community and dig a needed well or provide food and clothing or set up a medical clinic but do not share clearly the message of Christ, we have not helped people at all regarding eternity. We may have improved the quality of their temporal existence, but it is better to go to heaven hungry than to go to hell with a full stomach. For this reason, the message must remain central to the cause of world missions. As the men traveled from Cyprus to the mainland, getting the message out was their main objective. Once again, when they arrive at Pisidian Antioch (a different city than the Antioch that sent them out), they go directly to the synagogue to begin ministry and are given a chance to speak. With today's passage from Acts we are given our first glimpse into what Paul preaches when he presents the gospel. By studying it, we can clarify the message of missions. The outline of Paul's sermon is easy to identify. It is broken into three divisions, each beginning with a salutation of sorts where he speaks directly to the audience as either *"Men of Israel"* or *"Brethren."*

 DID YOU KNOW?
The Letter to the Galatians

Not so very long after the events of this journey, Paul wrote a letter to the people of Pisidian Antioch, Iconium, Derbe, and Lystra. It is the letter we call The Book of Galatians, for all these towns were part of the Roman province of Galatia.

📖 Read the first section of Paul's sermon (Acts 13:16–25), and summarize the main points in your own words.

Paul begins his sermon by reviewing what his audience already knew about the history of Israel leading up to the Messiah. Obviously, these Jews were familiar with the ministry of John the Baptist, who was recognized by all as a prophet. Every devout Jew accepted that the Messiah would come from the descendants of King David and that a prophet would announce his coming. Paul is helping them make the connection between John the Baptist and Jesus. Although not all would have been ready to recognize Jesus as Savior, there was little in the preparatory phase of Paul's message for them to disagree with. This part of the sermon can be summarized by the word "foundation."

📖 Now look at the second section of Paul's sermon (Acts 13:26–37) and make note of the main points and theme.

Paul moves from the past to the present with this part of his sermon. The key points here begin with the guilt of the Jewish leaders over the death of Jesus. They put Him to death because they didn't understand the prophecies nor recognize their Messiah when He was in their midst. Along with this, Paul makes note of the fulfilled prophecies and the death, burial, and resurrection—reminiscent of Peter's sermon at Pentecost. Paul repeatedly quotes from the Old Testament and climaxes his argument with a reference to Psalm 16—a psalm all the Jews considered to be a messianic psalm, since it is clear the promises do not refer to King David. Paul has built a compelling case for them to recognize Jesus as the Messiah.

📖 The third portion of Paul's sermon is Acts 13:38–41. Study what it says and identify the applications Paul calls for.

Paul points out to these Jews that faith in Christ could give them two things the Law could never provide. First, Jesus offers forgiveness of their sins. The Law could reveal sin but can never take it away. Second, Christ can not only forgive them but justify them as well. The word translated freed (*dikaioo*) is the root word for "justified" and speaks not just of forgiveness but freedom from having any charge against them. In closing his challenge, Paul moves from the benefits of accepting Christ to the consequences of rejecting Him, reminding them that the prophets foretold judgment for those who scoff at the work of God.

As we study the book of Acts, we must remember that Luke has not told us everything that happens during this time period, but rather, those things which he deems of greatest importance. If we catalog the contents of Acts, we discover that Luke spends an inordinate amount of time detailing the sermons and messages, often spending whole chapters recording what is said. He wants to make sure we recognize the message each apostle preaches and the harmony in what they say. Though the messages are adapted to the individual audience, they all come back to the same basic components. Each sermon speaks of the promise of Christ, the prophecies fulfilled in His life and death, and the power of God manifested in His resurrection. Each sermon calls on the audience to come to Christ for forgiveness and right standing with God.

DAY 4

THE MOVEMENT OF MISSIONS: ACTS 13:42—14:28

The prophet Isaiah writes, *"How lovely on the mountains are the feet of him who brings good news, who announces peace and brings good news of happiness, who announces salvation, and says to Zion, 'Your God reigns!'"* (Isaiah 52:7). It takes those lovely feet to get the gospel to the far reaches of the earth. The first missionary journey of Barnabas and Paul is almost a geography lesson in itself as they traversed Asia Minor, preaching from town to town. Jesus says in Acts 1:8, You shall be my witnesses *"...from"* and *"...to."* Missions is the movement of the message from where it is to where it is needed. Luke mentions thirteen specific cities on their journey but makes it clear they minister in many more places than that. Not only does this passage record the movement of the gospel from town to town, but also from the Jews to the Gentiles. As we will see today, all that matters to Barnabas and Paul is finding people open to the gospel.

Read Acts 13:42–52 and summarize the differing responses to the gospel in Pisidian Antioch and what motivates them.

DOCTRINE:
Appointed to Eternal Life

Acts 13:48 gives us the divine side of evangelism, for even though each person has a choice to make, onc having made it he or she cannot take full credit for it. The word translated appointed (*tasso*) means "to place or to arrange" and is in the passive voice. This emphasizes God's part. The word *"believed"* is in the active voice and emphasizes the individual's part. The human role is further highlighted by verse 49. Without preaching there can be no belief. People must spread the Word of truth.

The first response we see is a very positive one. The people *"kept begging"* them to speak these things again. After the meeting *"many"* follow Paul and Barnabas. Amazingly, the next Sabbath *"nearly the whole city"* turns out to hear the Word (13:44). Wouldn't that be exciting if it happened in your town? What seems to motivate those who respond positively is that they are already *"God-fearing"* (13:43). They have a heart for God and are ready to respond to further truth. Not all respond positively, however. Some Jews react quite strongly to the large crowds that follow Paul. They contradict (13:45), instigate persecution (13:50), and even blaspheme (13:45). The motive of those who become antagonistic is rooted in pride. When they see the attention Paul and Barnabas are getting, they become jealous (13:45). They are more concerned with their own reputations than with truth.

📖 Look over Acts 14:1–7 and make note of the different responses of the people in Iconium.

After Antioch, Paul and his companions travel about ninety miles to Iconium. As usual, they begin at the synagogue, and, as usual, many believe, but others are antagonistic. Verse 2 is very revealing about the source of opposition to the gospel. Notice that first some disbelieve, and then after making their decision about Jesus begin to oppose the gospel. Paul and friends are not hindered though and continue to speak truth boldly and give evidence of God's power. The *"people of the city* [are] *divided"* in their response, with some believing and others opposing. We can expect the same today. It isn't until the crowds become violent that Paul and company move on to another city.

📖 Examine Acts 14:8–20. Consider how they get the gospel out and how the people respond.

Lystra is located about eighteen miles southwest of Iconium. There is no mention of going to the synagogue, though this alone does not mean there are no Jews there. God manifests Himself through Paul performing a miracle, healing a man lame from birth. The audience appears to be pagan, and instead of starting with the Scriptures, Paul begins the gospel with nature and then looks to the Creator behind it all. Their lack of knowledge about God is evident in the fact that they want to worship Barnabas and Paul as Greek gods. In the end, however, opposition from Antioch and Iconium catches up with them and the crowds are won over to violence. Though some became antagonistic, others became followers. The message of the cross divides based on a person's heart toward God.

Look at Acts 14:21–23. How do the missionaries follow up with those who believed?

DID YOU KNOW?
Zeus and Hermes

To understand why the people at Lystra mistake Barnabas and Paul for Zeus and Hermes, we must look to the legends of Lycaonia. A common story in the region was that Zeus and Hermes had once come to earth in disguise. None in all the land showed them any hospitality. Finally, two elderly peasants, Philemon and his wife, Baucis, took them into their home. In anger the gods wiped out the whole population except for these two and made them guardians of a splendid temple. When Paul heals the crippled man, the crowds do not want to make the same mistake attributed to their ancestors.

Although Paul and Barnabas travel from town to town birthing people into the family of God, they do not leave them to fend for themselves. We see here that they return to the cities and are *"strengthening the souls of the disciples."* Their mission is to make disciples not just converts. This pattern began back at the sending church of Antioch in Syria. In Acts 11:24 we learn that as a result of the ministry, *"considerable numbers were brought to the Lord."* But that was not the entire ministry. In 11:26 we see that they also teach *"considerable numbers."* Paul and Barnabas help these new believers get established in their relationship with God and help organize their churches by appointing elders.

The chapter closes out by mentioning that Paul and Barnabas preach the gospel in Perga on their way back to Antioch. We can assume that there is a similar divided response here. After a very successful campaign, the team returns to their sending church to bring a report and to minister there. Make certain not to miss that point. When we consider world missions, we know that missionaries must go, but they cannot go unless they are sent. Someone must supply the finances and prayer to back their ministry. One circumstance that hinders world missions is that many churches do not develop a relationship with missionaries they support. Missionaries are not given time to report what God is doing. As a result, the congregation is robbed of the encouragement from seeing the fruit of their investments. A church that does not know its missionaries will have a difficult time convincing its people to give sacrificially and pray faithfully. It takes all of us to reach the world.

DAY 5

FOR ME TO FOLLOW GOD

Sadly, not all in the church today share a proper concern for the salvation of others. In his book *Growing Strong in the Seasons of Life*, Chuck Swindoll tells a parable of a lifesaving station that really drives this point home.

"On a dangerous seacoast notorious for shipwrecks, there was a crude little lifesaving station. Actually, the station was merely a hut with one little boat...but the few devoted members kept a constant watch over the turbulent sea. With little thought for themselves, they would go out day and night tirelessly searching for those in danger as well as the lost. Many, many lives were saved by this brave band of men who faithfully worked as a team in and out of the lifesaving station. By and by, it became a famous place.

Some of those who had been saved as well as others along the seacoast wanted to become associated with this little station. They were willing to give their time and energy and money in support of its objectives. New boats were purchased. New crews were trained. The station that was once obscure and crude and virtually insignificant began to grow. Some of its members were unhappy that the hut was so unattractive and poorly equipped. They felt a more comfortable place should be provided. Emergency cots were replaced with lovely furniture. Rough, hand-made equipment was discarded, and sophisticated, classy systems were installed. The hut, of course, had to be torn down to make room for all the additional equipment, furniture, systems, and appointments. By its completion, the life-saving station had become a popular gathering place, and its objectives had begun to shift. It was now used as sort of a clubhouse, an attractive building for public gatherings. Saving lives, feeding the hungry, strengthening the fearful, and calming the disturbed rarely occurred by now.

Fewer members were now interested in braving the sea on lifesaving missions, so they hired professional lifeboat crews to do this work. The original goal of the station wasn't altogether forgotten, however. The lifesaving motifs still prevailed in the club's decorations. In fact, there was a symbolic, miniature lifeboat preserved in the *Room of Sweet Memories* with soft, indirect lighting, which helped hide the layer of dust upon the once-used vessel.

About this time, a large ship was wrecked off the coast, and the boat crews brought in cold, wet, half-drowned people. They were dirty, some terribly sick and lonely. Others were black and "different" from the majority of the club members. The beautiful new club suddenly became messy and cluttered. A special committee saw to it that a shower house was immediately built outside and *away from* the club so shipwreck victims could be cleaned up *before* coming inside.

At the next meeting there were strong words and angry feelings, which resulted in a division among the members. Most of the people wanted to stop the club's lifesaving activities and all involvements with shipwreck victims...("it's too unpleasant, it's a hindrance to our social life, it's opening the door to folks who are not *our kind*"). As you would expect, some still insisted upon saving lives, that this was their primary objective—that their only reason for existence was ministering to anyone needing help regardless of their club's beauty or size or decorations. They were voted down and told if they wanted to save the lives of various kinds of people who were shipwrecked in those waters, they could begin their own lifesaving station down the coast! They did.

As years passed, the new station experienced the same old changes. It evolved into another club, and yet another lifesaving station was begun. History continued to repeat itself... and if you visit that coast today, you'll find a large number of exclusive, impressive clubs along the shoreline owned and operated by slick professionals who have lost all involvement with the saving of lives.

Shipwrecks still occur in those waters, but now, most of the victims are not saved. Every day they drown at sea, and so few seem to care...so very few. Do you?" (from *Growing Strong in the Seasons of Life*, 1983, Charles R. Swindoll, Multnomah, pp.98–99).

> *What good is a lifesaving station that no longer*
> *cares about saving lives?*

Years ago, I was privileged to hear John Hannah, the great church history professor from Dallas Theological Seminary, deliver one of the most prophetic and powerful messages I have ever heard while he spoke to the staff of Campus Crusade for Christ. He spent several minutes reviewing some of the successes our ministry had accomplished over the years and most of us were smiling and patting ourselves on the back until he came to the punch line. He made this statement: "Campus Crusade has a glorious past, but a questionable future." We were stunned to silence. For the next half hour, he gave example after example of great movements of God that started out having a considerable impact but ended up insignificant because they wandered from their original vision. His message was crystal clear—it is far easier to stray from your founding principles than it is to stay the course. The same is true of any ministry. Your past is no guarantee of the future. You cannot face tomorrow's challenges on yesterday's victories.

As you honestly reflect on your church or ministry, are your victories in the present or mostly in the past?

Which of the following fit?

- More focused on outreach than just inward fellowship

- Effectively partnering with those taking the gospel to the world

- Sending out missionaries

- Giving missionaries enough support in prayer and finances

- Providing opportunities for missionaries to report on what God is doing

- Creating a vision for the world

- Passionately concerned about those who don't know Christ

*It is far easier to stray from your founding principles
than it is to stay the course.*

What would you say are your church's greatest weaknesses in the area of world missions?

While certainly missions is a corporate activity, and we can accomplish far more by linking arms than by going it alone, there is also a reality that it is for each of us an individual issue. I began supporting my first missionary while I was still a college student. I didn't have much money, but I was challenged and made an initial commitment. The interesting thing is, the more I gave of my resources, the more important missions became to me. I would have expected it to be the other way around. I would have thought that caring would come first and then giving. But Jesus said, *"Where your treasure is* [present tense], *there will your heart be also* [future tense]*"* (Matthew 6:21). Our heart tends to follow our billfold.

There are more ways to be involved in the cause of Christ than giving financially. We can pray for the needs of missionaries (but we'd better be open to answering some of those prayers). We can send them resources. We can encourage them with letters. We can go on short-term trips to help meet specific needs or for catalytic involvement in a ministry. We can commit our willingness to serve long-term elsewhere as God calls.

Who are the missionaries with whom you have a relationship?

What are some ways you are presently involved in world missions?

___ Giving

___ Prayer

___ Encouragement

___ Letters

___ Resources

___ Short-term trips

___ Surrendered willingness to long-term service

What application points do you sense the Lord calling you to?

"Where your treasure is, there will your heart be also."
(Matthew 6:21)

Jesus said in Matthew 9:37–38, *"The harvest is plentiful, but the workers are few. Therefore beseech the Lord of the harvest to send out workers into His harvest."* Missions begins in prayer. The first missionary journey began as a result of prayer. Our own mission involvement should be birthed in seeking God not just in responding to an emotional appeal. Why not close out this week's lesson with a written prayer to the Lord?

LESSON 2

THE MESSAGE OF GRACE

ACTS 15:1–35

When God rescued His people from centuries of enslavement to the Egyptians, a new era of faith began. After showing His power by parting the Red Sea, God showed His holiness by giving the Law. For forty days Moses met with God on Mount Sinai, and the Lord gave him the decalog—the Ten Commandments carved into tablets of stone. Yet before Moses returned from the mountain top, God's people were already breaking this Law. When Moses shattered the tablets of stone God had written, he gave a visual demonstration of what the people had done in their hearts. The record of Scripture gives unending testimony to man's failed attempts to fulfill the Law of God. What we learn is that the Law is not a means to attaining righteousness, but rather a vehicle to show our need for it. The Law reveals what righteousness looks like and shows us what we ought to be. But if the Law could make us righteous, we wouldn't need a Savior.

If the Law could make us righteous, we wouldn't need a Savior.

The central question of humanity since the fall is "How can a person be right with God?" Just as Adam and Eve tried to hide their sins behind fig-leaf fashions, we, too, look for human ways to attain right standing and to cover our sins. But God could not accept Adam and Eve's feeble attempts at covering sin. He took away the brittle, drying leaves they hid behind and replaced them with leather hides. Innocent animals had to die for the sins of the guilty. This practice continued in the priestly activities of the Tabernacle and Temple, foreshadowing the Lamb of God who would not just cover our sins, but take them away. When Jesus died on the cross, His last words were, *"It is finished!"* Nothing we can do could possibly add to His completed work. That is the message of grace. However, we still try.

This week in our consideration of the book of Acts, we will see yet another example of humanity's misunderstandings of how to become righteous. Clearly it is not the first attempt, and the history of all people as well as our own personal histories make clear that this is not the last time people try to add to the work of Christ.

Day 1

The Problem of the Legalists: Acts 15:1–6

When the apostle Paul writes his letter to the Philippian Christians, he warns them, *"Beware of the false circumcision; for we are the true circumcision, who worship in the Spirit of God and glory in Christ Jesus and put no confidence in the flesh"* (Philippians 3:2b–3). His view of what righteousness looks like is made clear—glorying in Christ and what He did and putting no confidence in the flesh and what we do. By contrast he also paints a portrait of the other view. The false circumcision would glory in self, not Christ, and would put confidence in what people can do. There were many in his day, as there are in ours, who try to add something to the work of Christ. Faith in what He did is not enough. Perhaps it is faith plus baptism, or faith plus legalism, or faith plus church membership, or some other good work. Whatever we add to faith, however, ends up detracting from it. Paul writes to the Galatians, *"I do not nullify the grace of God for if righteousness comes by the works of the Law, Christ died needlessly"* (Galatians 2:21). In other words, what he is saying is that if there were any other way to be righteous but by the sacrifice of Christ, then His death was for no purpose at all. It is frustratingly meaningless. As we will see today, the Jerusalem Council is convened to debate this very same issue.

📖 Look over Acts 15:1. What are the men from Judea teaching, and why is it controversial?

> *"I do not nullify the grace of God, for if righteousness comes*
> *through the Law, then Christ died needlessly." (Galatians 2:21)*

Sometime after the first missionary journey, while Paul and Barnabas are back at Antioch ministering, they face a particularly thorny problem that threatens the whole unity of the early church. Men from Judea come to Antioch and begin teaching that men cannot be saved without first being circumcised. They are calling into question the validity of every male Gentile convert and seeking to require them to not only trust Christ but to also fulfill the Mosaic Law. In essence what they are saying is, "In order to become a Christian, you must first become a Jew." Faith alone is not enough to save.

📖 Read Acts 15:2, and answer the questions below.

What is the first method used to attempt to reconcile the opposing views?

When that doesn't work, what is proposed and by whom?

Clearly the teaching of these men from Judea runs contrary to the doctrine of Paul and Barnabas—men who have built the Antioch church from the ground up. The first attempt at resolving the controversy is apparently a public debate for an undisclosed length of time. It would seem that the inability to reconcile the two teachings leads the brethren (the Antioch church) to send the matter to the mother church at Jerusalem to resolve. They send Paul and Barnabas and others to personally deliver the problem and to represent the Gentile believers. The text tells us that the others are "of them" and uses the Greek preposition *ek*, meaning "out of them" or "from them." Although Paul and Barnabas could faithfully represent the Gentile concern, they are not Gentiles, and it is determined to be beneficial to have some of the Gentile converts represented at the council that is about to convene.

 Take a look at Acts 15:3–4 and summarize how these actions of Paul and Barnabas relate to the question at hand.

DID YOU KNOW?
Gentiles and the Law

Acts 15 is not the first time the issue of Gentiles and the Law comes up. When Peter returned from the first Gentile conversions at Cornelius' house, he was confronted by legalists. Acts 11:2–3 tells us, "And when Peter came up to Jerusalem, those who were circumcised took issue with him, saying, 'You went to uncircumcised men and ate with them.'" After he related his vision from God, and the response to the gospel message the conflict died down, but as we see in Acts 15 it doesn't really go away.

As Paul and company travel through Phoenicia and Samaria, they meet with groups of believers along the way. The Christians in these regions would be mostly Hellenistic Jews (Jewish racially but Greek culturally) and Samaritans who would be more receptive of the salvation of Gentiles than the more hard core Jewish believers of Jerusalem. The response in Phoenicia and Samaria is universally positive to the record of God's working among the Gentiles. Once the group arrives in Jerusalem, they begin, not with the thorny doctrinal question, but with the testimony of God's work in Gentile lands. This is an important foundation to the debate, for changed lives give evidence of true conversion, and these reports are speaking of the fruit of the gospel message.

📖 Examine Acts 15:5, and respond to the questions that follow.

Who takes issue with Paul and Barnabas?

What do these others expect of Gentile converts?

It is not surprising that those who take the lead in demanding that Gentile converts be held obligated to the Law are of those who worshiped the Law—the Pharisees. Before we throw stones at them, we must recognize that these particular Pharisees are among those who have believed. They have accepted Jesus as Messiah and Savior. They have acknowledged salvation by His grace. But they still revere the Law and fear its neglect. They hold it *"necessary"* that Gentile believers be circumcised and directed to observe the Law of Moses.

📖 Looking at Acts 15:2, 4 and 6, to whom exactly are Paul and Barnabas bringing this question and what do we know about them.

Three times the passage identifies the audience for this difficult question as the *"apostles and elders"* in Jerusalem. Jerusalem was the hub of the Jewish faith since the time of King David. With the birth of the church in Jerusalem, it becomes the "home office" so to speak of the Christian faith as well. The apostles spoken of here are those eyewitnesses of the resurrection who are the core leadership of the universal church. The elders are separate and distinct from this group, though some apostles may also be elders. They are the leaders of the local church.

The new church is at a critical juncture. What was at first a body made solely of Jews has begun to draw in Gentiles. The central question of the Jerusalem Council is "how does a Gentile come into the church?" Must he first become a Jew? Certainly, there is nothing wrong with Jews continuing to honor the Law even though they recognize it cannot save. To not do so would offend the fellow Jews they are seeking to reach. But is it right to put the burden of the Law on Gentiles, a burden which Peter says, "neither our fathers nor we have been able to bear?" This is the crux of the issue and key to the message of grace.

DAY 2

THE SPEECH OF PETER: ACTS 15:7–12

Some years ago, I was sightseeing with my wife in the city of Prague at the end of a mission trip to Eastern Europe. We wandered through the beautiful Old Town district as typical tourists looking at shops and souvenirs. Then we made our way across the historic Charles Bridge and up the hill to Prague castle and took a tour of the ornate St. Vitus Cathedral built in the 14th century. It is adorned on the outside with hundreds of gargoyles and intricate parapets. I found the interior equally impressive with beautiful frescos and icons and filled with valuable relics from antiquity.

After seeing all there was to see, we returned to the Old Town square with its statue of persecuted Jan Hus. With no particular forethought, our next stop was Hus's Bethlehem Chapel—the first Protestant church in the world. The contrast was overwhelming. Instead of scores of parapets, it was adorned only with a simple spire topped with a cross. Inside, one was overwhelmed with its simplicity (adversaries of the Reformation movement mockingly called it a barn), yet I found in it a warmth that had been lacking in St. Vitus Cathedral. Instead of icons and paintings, the plain walls are adorned with Scriptural text—emphasizing belief and truth.

After a few minutes in the uncluttered meeting hall, we made our way to the pastor's study, where I was gripped by a small painting on the wall. It featured three men—John Wyclif holding a candle, Jan Hus holding a torch, and Martin Luther at a bonfire. I wept as I recognized the message. These were the men who gave birth to the Protestant Reformation. Jan Hus had been profoundly impacted by the writings of Wyclif, who oversaw the first English translation of the entire Bible. When Archbishop Zbynek ordered all of his books burned, Hus protested and ignored the order. Eventually Hus was executed for his opposition to the sale of indulgences and his break with the Catholic hierarchy. Luther is recognized as the father of the Reformation, but few realize he stood on the shoulders of men like Wyclif and Hus. Throughout the history of the church there have been those who misrepresented Christianity by elevating works as necessary for salvation, and there have always been people willing to take a stand against human-centered spirituality as advocates of God's grace.

As we will see today, not only did Peter risk his life to do that before the Jewish Sanhedrin, he continues to be a persuasive campaigner of the message of grace.

Luther is recognized as the father of the Reformation, but few realize he stood on the shoulders of men like John Wyclif and Jan Hus.

📖 What explanation does Peter give in Acts 15:7 for his authority to speak to this matter of the salvation of the Gentiles?

Once the question is introduced, there is apparently a period of great disagreement as the subject is addressed with *"much debate."* When Peter speaks up, his message is a turning point in the discussion. It is right and appropriate that he would speak to this matter. He reminds the crowd that God had given him the specific call to be the first to take the gospel to the Gentiles. Peter himself had been raised as a devout Jew, and as such, a staunch separatist from all things Gentile. It took a thrice-repeated vision from God to convince him to cross that barrier (see Acts 10). Once he did, God used him as the first gospel voice to the Gentiles. Who better to address the question of the salvation of Gentiles than the first preacher to witness it?

📖 What impact does the information of Acts 15:8–9 have on the question at hand?

Peter makes two points from the conversions he witnessed at Cornelius' house those years before. By his own testimony in Acts 11:15, he saw no distinction between their conversion and the work of God with the Jews at Pentecost. The Gentiles to whom Peter preached received the Holy Spirit just as he had in Acts 2. Notice how Peter emphasizes that God sees the heart. This is an important point since the believing Pharisees are putting the emphasis on external spirituality. Peter also points out that God has cleansed the hearts of the Gentiles *"by faith,"* reminding the Jews of the source of their salvation.

📖 How does Peter's argument in Acts 15:10–11 add to his case?

Now therefore why do you put God to the test by placing upon the neck of the disciples a yoke which neither our fathers nor we have been able to bear?" Acts 15:10

In verse 10 Peter makes perhaps the most defining statement of the whole debate. He challenges the pharisaical devotion to Moses by identifying the Law as, *"a yoke which neither our fathers nor we have been able to bear."* There are a couple of subtle points in his statement which should not be missed. First, he accuses the legalizers of putting God *"to the test."* In other words, their opposition is not with the Gentiles but with God. Second, he calls the Gentile converts *"disciples."* Clearly, he does not consider them in any way as second-class Christians in the manner of Gentile adherents to Judaism under the Old Covenant. The church is to hold no barrier like the "dividing wall" of the Temple, excluding Gentiles from full participation. Peter states emphatically in verse 11 that the Jews are saved, *"through the grace of the Lord Jesus"* and not through the Law. The message has a name—grace.

What changes do you see from Acts 15:12 in the tone of the meeting after Peter's speech?

It is clear from the wording of verse 12 that the debate ends with Peter's words. We are told that *"all the people kept silent, and...were listening."* The character and credibility of Peter is such that his words effectively end the discussion. The focus shifts from debating circumcision and the Law to celebrating God's working in the Gentile world.

It is worth noting the similarities between this situation and Acts 11. When Peter returned to Jerusalem from the fruitful ministry at Cornelius' house, he encountered opposition similar to what Paul and Barnabas face here. Representatives from the circumcision advocates accused, *"You went to uncircumcised men and ate with them."* Peter's vision and the pouring out of the Spirit diffused the concern for a time, but it resurfaced with reports of the Gentile fruit in the first missionary journey. With the twenty-twenty vision of hindsight, it is easy for us to throw stones at the Jewish believers, but we cannot appreciate the cultural revolution in which they are immersed. Lloyd John Ogilvie explains the dilemma well:

"These converted Pharisees and their followers were not bad people; their problem was that they stood with one foot in Moses' Law and one foot in Christ's love. Now the ground was separating beneath them. They would have to leap one way or the other, but not without a frantic effort to hold back the earthquake and the resulting theological fault. Having tried to maintain 'both-and,' they were ending up with an 'either-or' which contradicted the Messiah Himself and His unqualified love for all" (Lloyd John Ogilvie, *Drumbeat of Love*, Waco, TX: Word Books, 1976).

Day 3

The Verdict of James: Acts 15:13–29

> *"For by grace you have been saved through faith; and that not of*
> *yourselves, it is the gift of God; not as a result of works, so that no*
> *one may boast." (Ephesians 2:8–9)*

The Christian life is not me trying hard to be like Jesus. It is me yielding control of my life to the Lord, so Jesus can be Jesus in me. This is the message of grace—*"Not I, but Christ."* The apostle Paul expressed it well in Philippians 3.

> *"I count all things to be loss in view of the surpassing value of*
> *knowing Christ Jesus my Lord, for whom I have suffered the loss of*
> *all things, and count them but rubbish so that I may gain Christ,*
> *and may be found in Him, not having a righteousness of my own*
> *derived from the Law, but that which is through faith in Christ,*
> *the righteousness which comes from God on the basis of faith."*
> (Philippians 3:8–9)

You see, that is the difference between law and the message of grace. Law seeks a righteousness of our own. The pride of law wants to be able to say, "I did it," but the message of grace is not about what we do but what He did. If we could have a righteousness of our own, we could boast. But Paul wrote to the Ephesian believers, *"For by grace you have been saved through faith; and that not of yourselves, it is the gift of God; not as a result of works, so that no one may boast"* (Ephesians 2:8–9). That isn't just the message of how we are saved. It also speaks to how we live the Christian life—by faith in Him, not in ourselves. That is the verdict of the Jerusalem Council. Today we want to look at how James, our Lord's brother and the leader of the mother church, expresses this message of grace to the Gentile churches.

📖 Read Acts 15:13–18 and summarize how James defends Peter's point from Old Testament prophecy.

Once Peter finishes his defense of grace and Paul and Barnabas illustrate the workings of that grace they have witnessed among the Gentiles, James steps up to speak. It is right and appropriate that he would bring closure to the discussion since it is universally agreed that he is the main leader of the mother church at this time. He quotes from the prophet Amos, his main point demonstrating that God had always intended to reach the Gentiles. This point is made by many other prophets besides Amos, but this passage illustrates the truth effectively. Clearly God never intended to reach only the Jews.

📖 What is James' conclusion in Acts 15:19–21, and why do you think he wants the Gentiles to abstain from the things he mentions?

DOCTRINE
Gentile Believers

The four practices James asks the Gentiles to abstain from were violations of the Law of Moses that would be particularly offensive to the Jews. *"Things contaminated by idols"* refers to food offered to pagan gods and then sold at a discount in temple butcher shops. *"Fornication"* speaks of sexual sin and probably has in mind the temple prostitutes of Gentile worship. Both admonitions call the Gentiles to separate from the pagan worship of their culture. The other two abstentions—*"what is strangled and from blood"* both relate to dietary laws. John MacArthur writes, *"While certainly not imposing those laws on the Gentile believers, James set forth these minimum requirements for fellowship . . . freedom in Christ does not grant the right to sin, or to offend another believer."*

The wording of verse 19 is in the form of a verdict. James brings the doctrinal consideration to a conclusion in an authoritative way, saying, *"Therefore, it is my judgment..."* It is interesting that he speaks of any requirement for Gentiles to be circumcised as "troubling" them. The Greek wording literally means to add additional trouble. In other words, *"The Christian life is challenging enough without adding extra rules to it."* He only mentions four requests and expresses them more as an encouragement than a requirement. The four issues James advises them to abstain from represent the four Jews would find most offensive. His point seems to be that while the Gentiles should not be required to adopt Jewish culture, they should be encouraged to respect it and to not intentionally offend. The message of grace should not be allowed to become an excuse for license.

Interestingly, once the issue is thoroughly discussed, agreement is reached. Two very diverse groups—Jews and Gentiles—had much to disagree about, but in Christ they are able to find common ground. Once a conclusion is reached, everyone sees the wisdom in sending representatives with Paul and Barnabas to communicate this message of grace to the Gentile church at Antioch. It is here in Acts 15:22 that we have our introduction to Silas, a man who would become a close companion and co-laborer with the Apostle Paul.

Look over Acts 15:23–29 and make note of what stands out to you from the letter the mother church sent to Antioch.

The first point the letter makes, after the customary formalities of a greeting, is that those who began this controversy were not operating with the authority and blessing of the mother church leadership. Then the letter makes a most interesting point. It says in verse 25, *"having become of one mind."* This tells us two realities. First, that they weren't originally of one mind, and second, that they came to agreement. The main point of this discussion is not personal opinion but the will of God. Though they disagreed at one point, God has brought them to a place of agreement. When leaders become of one mind, it is clear that God has spoken. Clearly the leadership does not view their conclusion as mere human opinion, for in verse 28 they list the Holy Spirit first as the source of their conclusion. People will always have different opinions, but when all spiritual people come to a place of agreement, that is evidence that God has been heard and not mere humans.

DAY 4

THE REPORT OF PAUL AND BARNABAS: ACTS 15:30–35

DOCTRINE
Of One Mind

Many churches glean two important principles for decision-making from this passage. When Acts 15:25 speaks of the group as *"having become of one mind,"* this indicates first that the decision was made by a plurality and not just by James. Second, this phrase indicates that the decision was made by unanimity, not a simple majority. While a majority may hold to a wrong opinion, when all the leadership become *"of one mind"* that gives evidence that God has been heard. He never holds two opinions. If all have heard from Him, then all should arrive at the same conclusion.

Proverbs 25:25 reads, *"Like cold water to a weary soul, so is good news from a distant land."* The letter and report of the Jerusalem Council must have been good news indeed for the Gentile Christians at Antioch. We are told in Acts 15:24 that the teaching of the Judaizers in Antioch had *"disturbed"* the believers there, *"unsettling"* their souls. The word *"disturbed"* (Gr. *tarasso*) is a strong word meaning *"to deeply upset, to deeply disturb, to perplex, or to create fear."* It is the same word used in John 14:1 to describe the anguish of the disciples when Jesus told them of His impending death. The teaching of these Jews created worry among the Gentile believers that maybe they weren't saved from their sins after all. Although this is the only place in the New Testament the Greek word translated *"unsettling"* (Gr. *anaskeuazo*) appears, it was used in common Greek to speak of going bankrupt or of a military force plundering a town. The days of the church waiting to hear word are rewarded with tremendous encouragement. The message of Law tends to discourage since none can keep the Law fully. But the message of grace always brings encouragement. Today we want to look at the report Paul and Barnabas bring back to the Gentile believers at Antioch.

📖 Read over Acts 15:30–35 and identify all you can glean of the outcome of the Jerusalem Council.

We already saw in Acts 15:25 that one of the results of the Jerusalem Council was unity. What had been a divisive and volatile issue has now been reconciled, and the body has become *"of one mind."* Once the letter and report are brought to Antioch, the outcome is rejoicing from the letter's encouragement (15:31). We also see that peace is a result (15:33). Finally, and perhaps most important, the resolution of this sticky problem gives an unhindered continuing of the ministry of the word of the Lord.

IN THEIR SHOES
Silas

Although this is the first mention of Silas in the New Testament, it is far from the last. He plays a prominent role in the early church. Also called Silvanus, he accompanies Paul on the second missionary journey and is even arrested with him at Philippi. Later he will serve as scribe to Peter, writing the apostle's words down for his first epistle (see 1 Peter 5:12).

📖 Reflecting on what you read in these verses as well as the previous day's homework, why do you think it is helpful that Barsabbas and Silas were sent to Antioch?

We learn in Acts 15:27 that the purpose of Barsabbas and Silas accompanying Paul and Barnabas to Antioch is that they might *"report the same things by word of mouth."* The issue is so important that the mother church wants official representatives to be on hand to interpret the letter and to answer any questions. They want to leave no room for the Judaizers at Antioch to accuse Paul and Barnabas of giving a biased account of what transpired at the Council. We read in Acts 15:32 that Barsabbas and Silas also minister the Word of God while they are there. Instead of adding requirements to the Gentile believers, the mother church add to their ministry with two of its finest teachers, called "leading men" among the believers at Jerusalem (Acts 15:22).

📖 What does Acts 15:34–35 indicate about what ministry needs to center around in the local church?

It is interesting to realize that once Silas witnesses the working of God among the Gentiles, he wants to be a part of it, choosing to remain in Antioch and minister. Paul and Barnabas, as well, decide to stay on with this church so dear to their hearts. It is clear from verse 35 that the church at Antioch is not a mere social gathering. The centerpiece of ministry is the "teaching and preaching" of the Word of God. It is clear from the context that this message they are teaching is the message of grace.

Hebrews 13:9 instructs us, *"Do not be carried away by varied and strange teachings; for it is good for the heart to be strengthened by grace."* Whatever diverges from the message of grace is called *"varied and strange teachings."* We cannot depart from the central theme of our faith, which is the work of Christ for, in, and through us. The message of Law is focused on us and what we do. The message of grace puts all the emphasis on Jesus where it belongs. Notice what the writer of Hebrews tells us about this message of grace: "it is good for the heart to be strengthened by grace." Grace strengthens our heart. It builds us up instead of tearing us down. The legalists fear that the message of grace will be perverted into a license for sin. There is a legitimate danger of that. But it is equally dangerous to detract from grace by giving the impression that we have the power to live out the righteousness of God in our own strength. The Christian life is not me trying hard to be like Jesus—I never could succeed at that. The Christian life is me yielding control of my life to Christ and letting Him live His life through me. That is what the message of grace is all about—not just forgiving grace, but empowering grace.

Day 5

For Me to Follow God

Is it legalistic to keep the Mosaic Law? This is a far more important question than you may realize. Our focus, and the focus of the Jerusalem Council, is on the message of grace, but what is that message? Is it really saying that the Old Testament Law doesn't matter? Is it purporting that Law is bad? Absolutely not! Titus 2:11–12 communicates, *"For the grace of God has appeared, bringing salvation to all men, instructing us to deny ungodliness and worldly desires and to live sensibly, righteously and godly in the present age."*

You see, grace is the freedom to fail. It is the empowerment of God to succeed where the strength of man cannot. But it is not the freedom to disobey willfully or to live as if righteousness does not matter. Grace instructs us to deny ungodliness and worldly desires. Legalism is not about *what* we do. It is all about *why* we do it and how we do it. Legalism is expressed in trying to earn God's favor through human effort. It is not legalistic to keep the Law. But it is legalistic to take pride in what we do instead of in Christ. Righteous and submissive living is to be the response of a dependent and grateful heart. It can never be seen as the reason for our relationship with God. If it does, it will lead us to pride – the sin of the devil.

> *"Are you so foolish? Having begun by the Spirit, are you now being perfected by the flesh?" (Galatians 3:3)*

The apostle Paul wrote to the Galatian Christians, *"I am amazed that you are so quickly deserting Him who called you by the grace of Christ, for a different gospel"* (Galatians 1:6). These are powerful words. Paul calls the legalism that they were struggling with "a different gospel." It isn't even the same faith as ours. Legalism involves trying to be saved by works instead of the work of Christ. But it is not only an issue of salvation. Paul goes on to say, *"This is the only thing I want to find out from you: did you receive the Spirit by the works of the Law, or by hearing with faith? Are you so foolish? Having begun by the Spirit, are you now being perfected by the flesh?"* (Galatians 3:2–3). Law has no power to save us, nor has it any power to sanctify us either. We are saved by grace through faith (Ephesians 2:8–9), and we must live every day of our Christian lives by this same method. This is the true message of grace.

The Law is not unimportant. Paul calls it a *"tutor to lead us to Christ, so that we may be justified by faith"* (Galatians 3:24). The standards of God show us what His holiness looks like and teach us that we cannot attain such heights on our own. He goes on to say though, *"But now that faith has come, we are no longer under a tutor"* (Galatians 3:25). God wants to take the external Law and make it an internal matter of the heart. When we return to Law as the basis of our faith, we reject the whole point of Christianity and deny by our actions the need for a Savior. *"You have been severed from Christ, you who are seeking to be justified by law,"* Paul writes, *"you have fallen from grace."* (Galatians 5:4).

Understanding this, why then do people return to legalism? In part because it appeals to human pride. We want to be able to say we deserve heaven. But there is another reason as well. Some resort to legalism out of a pure but uninformed heart that thinks highly of the holiness of God. No one who loves God should be able to rejoice in sin—even forgiven sin. One of the things that drives people to legalism is seeing grace used as an excuse for sin. From a right heart, they push the pendulum too far. License is wrong, but so is legalism. What we are called to is love. Paul writes, *"For you were called to freedom, brethren; only do not turn your freedom into an opportunity for the flesh, but through love serve one another"* (Galatians 5:13).

As you consider how to apply this week's lesson, take some time to honestly reflect. Where do you see yourself falling on this spectrum?

Legalism  License

You must recognize that neither reflects a true understanding of the message of grace. What misunderstandings have you found revealed as you studied this passage?

Looking at the list below, check each box that reflects where you are. You may be a closet legalist if...

- You think people can be saved by simply living a good life.

- You tend to judge others by the traditions of your church and upbringing instead of the teaching of Scripture.

- You think that a godly life results from trying real hard.

- You believe the church is too lenient on sinners.

- You conclude that God will love you more if you are moral.

- You are proud of how good your life is and don't see your need for a Savior.

- You are motivated by guilt to do things instead of by gratitude.

It is important to realize that we can be legalistic even if our heart wants to be pleasing to God. Legalism is not so much about what we do as it is about why we do it and how we do it. Do we do what we do to earn God's favor or avoid His wrath, or as outworkings of our faith and gratitude? Do we do what we do by striving and trying hard or by submitting to His power and by trusting Him?

The message of legalism is "Christ plus..." It may be Christ plus trying hard, or Christ plus morality, or Christ plus church attendance, or Christ plus baptism. The problem with "Christ plus..." spirituality is that anything we add to Christ takes away from Him. If God's favor requires anything more than Christ, then He and His importance are lessened. What are some of the "plusses" you are tempted to add to Christ?

> *"For you were called to freedom, brethren; only do not turn your*
> *freedom into an opportunity for the flesh, but through love serve*
> *one another." (Galatians 5:13)*

Near the end of the book of Galatians, Paul writes, *"may it never be that I would boast, except in the cross of our Lord Jesus Christ, through which the world has been crucified to me, and I to the world"* (Galatians 6:14).

There is one final issue of application to consider from this week's lesson. It is important to recognize that while the main theme is law vs. grace, the Jerusalem Council also has much to say about Christian relationships. The real conflict was a clash of cultures. The Jews had been raised to have nothing to do with those who did not respect God's Law. Yet many Jewish Christians did not understand how law would relate in the New Covenant. While grace won out in the debate, it is important also to recognize that both cultures were affirmed. The Jews had to concede that Gentiles need not be circumcised to follow Christ. But the Gentiles also had to be reminded not to flaunt their freedoms and cause their Jewish brethren to stumble. Which of these admonitions do you need to be reminded of?

The good news of the Jerusalem Council is that God's people became *"of one mind"* (15:25). To do so requires submitting our opinions to the revelation of God. We must look to Him and not ourselves. We must remain teachable and never think we have arrived spiritually. We must leave room to be corrected.

As you close out this week's lesson, express your heart and what you have learned in a written prayer...

LESSON 3

WHATEVER THE PROBLEM, GOD HAS A SOLUTION

ACTS 15:36—16:40

There is no such thing as an easy life. No one is immune to challenges and difficulties. The only person with all their troubles behind them is a school bus driver. Even in ministry, we can expect that there will be adversity. Sometimes we think that life in the church ought to be trouble-free, and it probably would be if there weren't any people there. But as long as there are people to relate with, we'll find conflict and challenge. Sometimes we won't get along with each other or see eye to eye. As long as there are tasks to be done, we'll have to face the daunting duty of knowing the right path with certainty. And this means we will probably know times of confusion as we wait for that direction. As long as there are unbelievers, there will be some who oppose our faith and persecute us for it—especially as we try to help others find the Lord. The one whose life is opposed to God will also oppose those who stand with God. Life in the church and in service to the Lord will always have its challenges, and the experiences of Acts are no exception. Life wasn't any different for Paul and Barnabas than it is for us today.

There will be problems as we go through life and seek to serve the Lord, but whatever the problem, He has the solution.

If we stopped there, the message of this week's passage might be a discouraging one. But the thread that weaves each of these narratives together is not a dark one. In the midst of each challenge we see the fingerprints of God. We will have to face relationship problems, but God always has the solution and may even be using the problem to accomplish His greater purposes. There will be times when we don't know which direction to take, but this is the very reality that will keep us looking to Him. We can have confidence that He wants us to know His will even more than we want to find it. He will communicate direction to us in a way we can receive it. God wants us to reach out to others in ministry, and that will sometimes mean opposition. But to avoid the opposition also robs us of seeing God changing lives. There will be problems as we go through life and seek to serve the Lord, but whatever the problem, He has the solution.

Day 1

The Problem of Conflict: Acts 15:36—16:5

The first missionary journey is completed. As a result of the ministry of Barnabas and Paul, many new churches had their birth. God has done a mighty work among the Gentiles. With this first journey finished, they returned to Antioch to give a report. They proclaimed all that God had done and rejoiced at *"how He had opened a door of faith to the Gentiles (14:27)."* Barnabas and Paul settled down and spent *"a long time"* in Antioch. While there, a debate arose about whether a Gentile convert should be circumcised. As a result of the conflict, the two of them took the issue to the mother church in Jerusalem. Incidentally, in Jerusalem we find Barnabas mentioned first again (15:12) indicating that there he still has the greater credibility. When the apostles concluded in their favor, they returned to Antioch to give a report and to continue their teaching and preaching ministry (15:35). It is at this point that we see a conflict arise between Paul and Barnabas. What can we glean from this seemingly negative situation? Lots. Let's look closer. Who is right and who is wrong?

> *Paul's burden is to visit the churches, while Barnabas' sense of call*
> *is to continue mentoring Mark as he had done with Paul.*
> *Only by separating can they both be faithful to God's unique call*
> *on each life.*

📖 Look at Acts 15:36–37 and answer the questions that follow.

What is Paul burdened for here (15:36)?

What is Barnabas' burden (15:37)?

Why is Paul opposed to John (also known as "Mark") joining them (see also Acts 13:13)?

It is important to notice that the notion of a second trip is Paul's burden. He brings the idea up. He wants to visit the believers in every place they ministered to see how their faith is progressing. Barnabas, on the other hand, has a burden to take John Mark along. Paul is concerned about the "ministry," while Barnabas is concerned about the "minister." He wants to continue his mentoring work with Mark. In Acts 13:13 Luke tells us simply, *"Now Paul and his companions put out to sea from Paphos and came to Perga in Pamphylia; but John left them and returned to Jerusalem."* We are not given an explanation of why John (Mark) left, but we do know that the journey from Perga to Pisidian Antioch was probably the most difficult and dangerous part of their trip. We know from Galatians 4:13–15 that apparently Paul contracted an eye disease at some point. It seems likely this happened on the first missionary journey. An eye ailment common to the region of Pamphylia was not only blinding but also repulsive to look at. Since this is where Mark abandoned the missionary journey, Paul's illness may explain the reason why. If so, this may illuminate why Paul had a difficult time forgiving him too. It is clear from Acts 15:38 that Paul feels Mark had not done right by leaving the first missionary journey in the middle of the trip. Implied in the word *"deserted"* is immaturity or a lack of faithfulness on Mark's part. Barnabas is not ready to give up on Mark, but Paul is.

📖 Reread Acts 15:36 up to verse 39 and answer the questions that follow.

What results from the difference of opinion between Paul and Barnabas?

What does the previous information suggest about the core of the conflict?

The differing views on Mark between Paul and Barnabas could not be overcome. The result is such *"sharp disagreement"* that the two men who had been partners in ministry for so long decide to part company. What at first glance appears to be a conflict of personalities is in reality a conflict of burdens. You see, it is not that one is right, and the other is wrong. Both are correct, it would seem, and are being faithful to God's call on their lives. Paul's burden is to visit the churches, while Barnabas' sense of call is to continue mentoring Mark as he had done with Paul. Only by separating can they both be faithful to God's unique call on each life.

DID YOU KNOW?
John Mark

Although John Mark may not have made a good first impression on Paul, it is obvious that Barnabas' commitment to stick with him paid off. He would go on to author one of the four Gospels as well as to be a spiritual apprentice to the apostle Peter (1 Peter 5:13). Even Paul would change his mind about Mark, later calling him a *"fellow worker"* (Philemon 1:24). At the end of his life Paul writes to Timothy, *"Pick up Mark and bring him with you, for he is useful to me for service"* (2 Timothy 4:11).

📖 Compare Acts 15:39–41 with the itinerary of the first missionary journey and write your observations.

Some theologians have suggested that after the split, Paul continued the missionary work and Barnabas didn't. That idea doesn't mesh with the facts. When the two of them separate, it appears they divide between them the itinerary of the first missionary journey. Barnabas takes John Mark and follows the first leg of their journey to Cyprus, while Paul takes Silas and follows the later part of their trip. Since Luke also travels with Paul, we only have a written record of Paul and Silas's ministry.

Although the partnership between Paul and Barnabas ends here, the friendship doesn't. We see in the epistles that Paul speaks of Barnabas fondly. Perhaps this conflict is God's way of kicking Paul out of Barnabas' nest and enabling Barnabas to concentrate on John Mark. Although Mark has shown signs of immaturity, Barnabas obviously sees beyond this to his potential. One could logically argue that, humanly speaking, John Mark might never have his significant ministry apart from the discipling and encouraging work of Barnabas, the minister to ministers.

📖 Look at Acts 16:1–3 and identify what you can learn about Timothy's coming to Christ.

We see that by the time of the second missionary journey, Timothy is identified as a "disciple," and that his mother was a Jewish believer. His father was Greek and apparently not a believer. Although his father allowed Timothy to be taught the Scriptures as a child, apparently, he drew the line at circumcision. Now that Timothy is an adult, Paul addresses this issue, so that in ministry circumcision won't be a hindrance. Had Timothy been a full-blooded Gentile, this action wouldn't have been necessary. Luke's only commentary on Timothy is that he is *"well spoken of by the brethren"* in Lystra and Iconium. Paul takes Timothy along as an apprentice. He is performing in Timothy the same kind of mentoring role that Barnabas played in his life. Later in life Paul will challenge Timothy to keep the chain going through mentoring others as he was mentored (2 Timothy 2:2).

IN THEIR SHOES
Timothy's Circumcision

A logical question to ask is "why was Timothy circumcised after the Jerusalem Council concluded Gentiles didn't need to be?" After all, Paul insisted that the Gentile, Titus, not be circumcised (Gal.2:3). Acts 16:3 gives us Paul's reasoning: *"...because of the Jews who were in those parts, for they all knew that his father was a Greek."* Timothy was an unusual case, since he was half-Jewish. Since his Greek father was common knowledge, Jews would assume that he was not circumcised, and it would be a stumbling block to them. It was Paul's practice in every city he visited to first try and reach Jews. If Timothy were to minister alongside Paul, he needed to remove this obstacle to being heard. It was not a biblical requirement that he should be circumcised, but it was prudent to broaden his opportunities to minister. Like Paul, he became all things to all men that he might save some (1 Corinthians 9:22).

📖 Now read Acts 16:4–5.

What is the first item on the agenda when Paul visits these churches?

How are the churches doing?

As Paul visits the churches he and Barnabas had helped to start, he brings these believers the news of the Jerusalem council. This would have been a great encouragement especially to the Gentiles. It is obvious that the churches continue to prosper and grow. Even in Paul's absence God has been working.

We see that Paul and Barnabas part company because of their disagreement over John Mark. Paul's intense personality may have been too much for Mark to handle. Problems with people have to be dealt with, and sometimes even result in parting ways, but God may have a purpose even in that. The departure of Barnabas and Mark leaves a void for Paul and maybe serves as a reminder of the need to be investing himself in others. It would seem that Timothy replaces the role Mark played on the first journey and Barnabas desired him to play on the second—namely, that of apprentice in ministry. This, not seminary, is Paul's method to raise up new ministers.

DAY 2

THE PROBLEM OF CONFUSION: ACTS 16:6–18

It doesn't matter how sincere or mature we are, there will still be times when as believers we aren't sure what to do. Sometimes we think we know what to do when we really don't. In the Lord's Prayer we are reminded to ask that His will be done on earth "as it is in heaven." God's will is always done in heaven or else you are expelled. But it isn't always done on earth. Sometimes we want so badly for something to be God's will we read our own will into what we think He is saying. Occasionally we get into trouble because we run ahead when He is saying "wait." As I look at the example of Paul and his friends, I take comfort in the knowledge that they, too, seem to struggle with uncertainty and confusion. But I take greater comfort in knowing that God clears things up for them. Let's look at what we learn of His guidance in the midst of confusion.

📖 Look at Acts 16:6–8.

What keeps Paul from preaching in the Phrygian and Galatian region?

Why do they not travel into Bithynia?

Sometimes God speaks through open doors. Other times, as in Paul's efforts to take the gospel to Asia and Bithynia (Acts 16:6–7), He speaks through closed doors. We are not told exactly how the Holy Spirit forbids them to preach in Galatia, nor do we know exactly what is meant that the Spirit of Jesus did not permit them to go into Bithynia.

It could be that providential circumstances prevent their travel—perhaps uncooperative weather or political turmoil. Or maybe they are prevented by a weighty burden on their hearts. In any case, after repeated attempts, they conclude God doesn't want them to succeed in their intended course.

We can understand Paul's difficulty. After all, he knows God has called him to minister. He is simply trying to fulfill his call. But ours is not simply a matter of knowing what God's will is. We must also have His direction on the way and timing of doing His will. We must continually look to Him for His guidance. If God's plan were revealed in one large package, we would no longer need to be dependent on Him once we had the destination in hand. But His will is not a package—it is more like a scroll that unrolls a bit at a time. As we are obedient to what He has revealed, He shows us more.

DID YOU KNOW?
Philippi

The fact that Paul looked for a gathering of prayer in Philippi tells us that there was no synagogue and probably not many practicing Jews in the city. Ten Jewish males were required for a synagogue to form. The text tells us Paul's audience was women who gathered for prayer. This was likely an open-air meeting and was located by the Gangites River about a mile and a half west of town.

📖 Read Acts 16:9–12.

What happens after the door to ministry in Bithynia closes? What redirection takes place?

Where does this redirection lead them?

It is not until Paul has drawn the right conclusion about the closed doors in Bithynia that he is open to redirection. As he seeks the Lord, further revelation is given. They are redirected to Macedonia, which will prove to be one of Paul's most fruitful mission fields. It is interesting that the word *"concluding"* in verse 10 means "to join or knit together." Don't miss the switch in the text from "he" to "we." Once the vision is given to Paul, he and his partners make the connection with the previous closed doors and together conclude that God's plan is taking them in an entirely different direction than they had originally been heading. They change their course and head to the main city of Macedonia which is Philippi. In the Christian life it is not wrong to make plans, but we must always allow God to redirect us, for His ways are not our ways.

📖 Consider Acts 16:13–15.

Where does Paul start as he seeks to minister in Philippi?

What fruit does he find there?

Normally when Paul comes to a town, he first visits the local synagogue. Apparently, there is none in Philippi. Instead, he looks in the next most logical place. He suspects if there are Jewish believers, they will gather on the Sabbath in some public place for prayer. Sure enough, he finds them just outside the city. He discovers his first convert in Europe at this Jewish prayer meeting. A businesswoman named Lydia with a heart for God responds to his message of Jesus. Not only does she provide his first fruit of ministry, but she also becomes God's provision for lodgings.

> *"But if any of you lacks wisdom, let him ask of God, who gives to*
> *all generously and without reproach, and it will be given to him."*
> *(James 1:5)*

Gleaning from the example of the apostle Paul, we can confidently say that there will be times when we are confused concerning God's direction for our lives. Sometimes when we think we know what is next for us, we really don't. But if we find ourselves running into a brick wall as Paul does here, hopefully it will cause us to look up. God is faithful to give us the direction we need. James wrote, *"...if any of you lacks wisdom, let him ask of God, who gives to all generously and without reproach, and it will be given to him."* We have the sure promise of God that if we will seek Him in our confusion, He will give us the guidance we lack.

THE PROBLEM OF PERSECUTION: ACTS 16:16–24

No one likes persecution. We all wish we could be liked by everyone, but that is not possible in a world where some do not believe in God. Just as faith automatically unites us into a family of brothers and sisters, unbelief automatically divides. Those who oppose God will end up opposing those who align with God, and that is where persecution comes from. If there is one truth we have learned as we have studied the book of Acts, it is that God can stop persecution whenever He wants. He stopped the persecution from Saul by saving him. He stopped the persecution of Herod by killing him. So why does God let persecution exist at all? Persecution exists only because God can take the evil intent of unbelievers and turn it around to accomplish His purposes. He used the first wave of persecution to scatter believers out of Jerusalem into the other areas that needed Christ. As we will see today, God allows persecution because He can use it in His plan for others.

📖 Look over Acts 16:16–18 and summarize what you can glean from Paul's encounter with the servant girl.

In the process of ministry, Paul crosses paths with a demon-possessed servant girl who works at fortune-telling or divination. Her powers are no farce. She is able to super-naturally reveal information, but God is not the source of her activity. Apparently, Paul's encounters with her are repeated *"for many days."* While what she says of Paul is true, it quickly becomes annoying. Paul goes directly to the source of aggravation and casts the evil spirit out of her. As we will see, getting rid of this problem is going to lead to other ones.

📖 Read Acts 16:19–21.

What is the motive behind this opposition to Paul and Silas?

What does the servant girl's masters do to them?

What Paul's opponents really care about is not the message Paul is preaching, but the fact that his faith gets in the way of their selfish pursuits and profit. As a result, they oppose Paul and his friends and even try to trump up charges against them with the local government. The Jewish faith is not forbidden in Roman provinces, and their actions aren't breaking any law, but that becomes a convenient excuse for Paul's opponents.

📖 Take a look at Acts 16:22–24 and summarize the actions against Paul.

DOCTRINE
Bigger Picture

While it seems unfair that God would allow such harsh treatment to be directed toward those whose only "crime" is proclaiming Christ, God sees the bigger picture. He knows that when believers are treated harshly, their faith shines and is validated by their trust in Him. He allows it because He can use it for good.

We are given no explanation for why the crowd rises up against Paul. They are not directly involved in the case, but probably are carried away because someone they know is against a stranger in town. Remember, these men have been making a profit from the servant girl's divination, so many in the crowd may be former customers. The local leaders side with their townsmen and have Paul and Silas beaten and thrown into prison. To hold them securely, their feet are fastened inside of wooden stocks to make escape virtually impossible.

While we tend to expect that persecution is going to be motivated by philosophical differences, that probably is more seldom the issue than we think. The person who truly has an intellectual struggle with belief is most likely searching and is closer to faith than they want to acknowledge. However, at the core of most unbelief is simply selfishness. It is not that a person has trouble believing in God, but that they want to live their own way and look for excuses to defend their choice. While it seems unfair that God would allow such harsh treatment to be directed toward those whose only sin is proclaiming Christ, God sees the bigger picture. He knows that when believers are treated harshly, their faith shines and is validated by their trust in Him. He allows it because He can use it for good.

DAY 4

THE PRODUCT OF GOD'S WORK: ACTS 16:25–40

Humanity always considers it heroic when someone sets self aside for the sake of other people. A firefighter risking his life to save another is rightly viewed as something noble. A policeman or soldier who puts himself in harm's way to protect or liberate others is deemed worthy of honor. At the core, this high view of their actions is all about the selflessness of their behavior—seeking another's good at cost to themselves. Most of us look at life from the vantage point of self. I guess you could say that it is human nature to look out for "number one." We evaluate events as positive and negative based primarily on how they impact us, not others. When weighed on these scales, being beaten and imprisoned would definitely be a negative. We would avoid it at all costs. But how would our view of this change if we knew that by doing so we could bring eternal salvation to someone? Would we choose the noble route or the selfish one? It does tend to change your perspective if you know that good will come from something bad. For the apostle Paul, that choice was already made in advance. He was so convinced of salvation as the greatest good he could give another, that he was willing to accept any measure of lesser evils to pursue it. In Philippians 1:21–25 we catch a glimpse of his heart:

> *"For to me, to live is Christ and to die is gain. But if I am to live on in the flesh, this will mean fruitful labor for me; and I do not know which to choose. But I am hard-pressed from both directions, having the desire to depart and be with Christ, for that is very much better; yet to remain on in the flesh is more necessary for your sake. Convinced of this, I know that I will remain and continue with you all for your progress and joy in the faith."*

By dying to self, he is free to put the good of others first, even if it means pain or prison. Today we see that these are not idle words but lived-out actions.

📖 Read Acts 16:25–26 and answer the questions below.

What stands out to you from the attitude and actions of Paul and Silas in jail?

What details do you consider most significant from verse 26?

Can you imagine what the other prisoners and guards are thinking when they hear these men who had been brutally beaten rejoicing and singing hymns of praise to God? What a sight that must have been! When believers go through trials, God showcases the difference our faith makes in how we handle such adversity. Rather than bemoaning their plight and the injustice of it, Paul and Silas are focused on God and rejoicing in Him. Luke makes it clear that this does not go unnoticed. God chooses to intervene in a dramatic way. Unlike with Peter, this is no deliverance by stealth. Everyone feels the earthquake and the doors and the chains of all are miraculously opened.

"For to me, to live is Christ and to die is gain." Philippians 1:21

📖 Look over Acts 16:27–34.

Why do you suppose the jailer wants to kill himself?

How do you think Paul's response prepares him for salvation?

Do you believe the jailer's choice guarantees the salvation of the rest of his family?

When the Philippian jailer discovers the open prison doors, he immediately believes the worst. He supposes that all of his charges have escaped. Had that been true, he would be facing the death penalty anyway, so prepares to take matters into his own hands. The fact that Paul and Silas don't run away says something about their trust in God with the situation, and we can suppose that this further impresses the jailer as he considers what kind of men they are. Our message is always made more powerful by lives that demonstrate its validity. Some have taken the offer Paul makes here to mean that when we get saved it brings all our family into a covenant of belief with God. This is not what Paul is saying though, for that would contradict the clear teaching of Scripture elsewhere. The offer should be taken to mean that any of his household who chose to trust Christ would also be saved. This is made clear by the fact that all are baptized, and not just the jailer, and verse 34 indicates the whole household joins in belief. A whole family is changed for eternity as a direct result of Paul's imprisonment.

📖 Reflect on Acts 16:35–39 and summarize what happens next with Paul.

DOCTRINE
Children of God

God has no grandchildren, nieces or nephews—only children. We cannot come into the family of God by virtue of the faith of others. John 1:12 makes it clear, *"But as many as received Him, to them He gave the right to become children of God, even to those who believe in His name."*

The next day the mob mentality that led to Paul's arrest and beating has died down. The city authorities apparently think differently about the situation and seek to release Paul and Silas, dropping the charges. Imagine their surprise when they learn that it is not Paul and Silas who have broken the law but them by arresting and beating Roman citizens without a trial. Had Paul not trusted God's sovereignty in the situation, he could have easily exacted revenge, but ministry is his real goal. He knows that the gospel will gain a greater audience in Philippi with a godly response from him rather than a fleshly one. He guarantees an audience with them by requiring them to appear for his release, and we can assume that Paul uses this opportunity to share the gospel with them. Their own error makes them eager to see Paul out of town.

📖 According to Acts 16:40 what is Paul's last activity before leaving Philippi?

Once Paul and Silas are released from prison, they pay a visit to Lydia's house to meet one last time with the new church that they have birthed in Philippi. As the letter to the Philippians attests, this small beginning will become a significant church in the area and in Paul's life. Before leaving town, he takes time to encourage them in the Lord.

Giving birth is not an easy process so I am told. I have witnessed it four times with my own children, but of course as a spectator rather than participant. I don't remember much of my own birth, so I have to take the word of others on how difficult it is. There is much pain and labor, it seems, before the new child enters the world. But all that difficulty is quickly forgotten in the joy of new life. In the same way, Paul has gone through a lot in the birthing of this first church in Macedonia. But all of that is quickly forgotten in the joy of changed lives he witnesses at Philippi. The nucleus of this infant church will grow and mature into a beautiful body of believers. God never promises an absence of difficulty as we seek to do His will, but whatever problems we encounter along the way, we can be certain He has the solution.

DAY 5

FOR ME TO FOLLOW GOD

We saw clearly this week that the road to ministry can sometimes be a rocky one. There will be some challenges along the way. There may be conflict with people, and we will even part company with some. But if Paul had not separated from Barnabas, he probably would not have connected with his lifelong friend, Timothy. Sometimes we will encounter confusion, but if we seek the Lord, He will clearly show us the way to His will. On the other side of confusion, we often find our most fruitful ministry. Sometimes we will have to face opposition, but God is sovereign even in that. Those problems and challenges and even conflicts may place people in our paths that we would never have met otherwise. Paul likely would not have had a conversation with the Philippian jailer had he not been arrested. God knows how to get us where He wants us. If we will trust Him as we travel the rocky roads, we may be surprised at how they lead us to beautiful places!

God never promises an absence of difficulty as we seek to do His will, but whatever problems we encounter along the way, we can be certain He has the solution.

As you look to apply the principles from this week's study to your own life, let's begin with our relationships. If you have ever encountered a disagreement like that of Paul and Barnabas that ended in a broken partnership, take some time to consider which of the circumstances listed below are relevant to your experience.

- strong disagreement on direction

- differing opinions about people involved

- godly people on both sides of the issue

- lengthy debate

- inability to reach agreement

- other similarities:_____

In your conflict, did you feel the need to determine who was right and who was wrong, or were you able to recognize that perhaps both were right in what they sensed they needed to do?

Are there any aspects of the split or disagreement that still need to be resolved, and if so, how?

We often seek to avoid conflict because we think disagreement is sinful in itself, but in fact, it is sometimes both right and necessary. The key is to disagree agreeably and to not allow the conflict to move into sin. If it does, we need to make sure we make it right with the others involved.

As we saw this week, even the apostle Paul had to seek God for direction, and sometimes the path was unclear. Have you ever experienced thinking you knew the right way to go but the doors remained closed?

When we think we know the right way to go but the doors are closed, we must go back to the Lord for direction, and be sensitive to His redirecting us. If you sense a need for confirmation with direction in your life, recognize that God speaks in many ways. Review the list below and see if there are any avenues you need to pursue as you seek God's guidance.

___ surrender of your will

___ prayer

___ searching the Scriptures

___ seeking wise counsel

___ counting the cost

___ evaluating circumstances

___ checking your heart for peace or the lack of it

___ listening to the still, small voice of the Spirit

___ considering the best stewardship

___ evaluating steps of faith

___ waiting on God

___ making use of the sound mind He gave you

Remember, confusion in our direction may mean redirection or it may mean patience, but it always means we keep seeking God.

> When Paul wrote to Timothy years later, "Indeed, all who desire
> to live godly in Christ Jesus will be persecuted" (2 Timothy 3:12) he
> spoke from personal experience. But he could also give this tes-
> timony: "and out of them all the Lord rescued me!"
> (2 Timothy 3:11)

Another problem we sometimes encounter is persecution—opposition from the ungodly because of our faith. When Paul writes to Timothy years later, "Indeed, all who desire to live godly in Christ Jesus will be persecuted" (2 Timothy 3:12), he speaks from personal experience. But he could also give this testimony: "and out of them all the Lord rescued me!" (2 Timothy 3:11).

Are there any places of persecution you are facing now or have faced?

Have you chosen to trust God with the persecution and look in it for opportunities to minister?

Express your heart to the Lord in a written prayer to close out this week's study.

NOTES

LESSON 4

THE BASIS OF BELIEF

ACTS 17:1–34

As one reads Acts chapter 17, what stands out as obvious is the continuing account of the second missionary journey of the apostle Paul. Like a travelogue, we are invited into his voyage as he takes truth to the untouched regions of Macedonia and Achaia. We will see him reach out with the gospel message to Thessalonica, Berea, and on into ancient Athens. But beneath the surface of Luke's narrative, these glimpses into each city visited also reveal for us the ongoing battle for truth. We are caught up in the clash of world views as what people believe is held up against what God has revealed. We witness the sparks fly, as vain imaginations come crashing down. We see the dividing work of the cross, as some align with the penitent criminal on one side, crying, *"Jesus, remember me…"* (Luke 23:42). Others take the second side and align themselves with the mocking thief, who even in death refused to humble himself. We see responses of rebellion and repentant belief stemming from the same message. But in addition to the historical aspects of how churches are born in these regions, Luke reveals the differing world views and approaches to truth Paul encounters in the ancient world.

In each of the cities visited here in Acts 17 we are exposed to a different world view—a different approach to finding truth and deciding how to live one's life.

This week, as we study the responses to Paul as he perseveres in taking the gospel town to town, we will also look closely at what the text reveals of those world views he encounters. We will discover that the human heart hasn't changed very much in two thousand years. We will see in these long-removed locales the same ideas that dominate the modern world—the same world views and approaches to truth. Hopefully we will learn a thing or two in the process about how others think and how the presentation of the message changes with cultures and contexts, even as the content of the message remains the same. We will also be forced to look to our own beliefs and ask the hard question, "What is the real authority in my life?" We will understand more of why we believe what we believe. We will come to realize that even if we believe the right things, we may be building that belief on the wrong foundation.

We may still be caught in a human-centered world view even as we believe in the One who made humans. Facing the same threat as those saved in Thessalonica, we may still lean on the view that elevates earthly reason above all else. We may believe in Christ, but only because our minds think it's reasonable. Or like the danger facing those Paul leads to Christ in Athens, we may continue to be caught in the clutches of relativistic thinking that rejects the idea of absolute truth. While passionately holding to our Christian beliefs we may wrongly believe them no more valuable or authoritative than the next person's perspective. Hopefully, we will not stay there, however. It is my prayer that we will learn a thing or two from how the Bereans manage their beliefs—not rejecting reason, nor deifying it either; willing to place God's revelation as the cornerstone of an absolute world view.

DAY 1

THE REASONINGS OF THE THESSALONIANS: ACTS 17:1–9

Thessalonica, the second city Paul visits in Macedonia, was originally known in ancient times by the name Thermae (meaning "hot baths"). When Cassander, one of the generals of Alexander the Great, rebuilt the city he also changed its name. He called it after his wife, Thessaloniki, who was the sister of Alexander the Great. In Paul's day, it is a free city of the Romans and the most populous city in Macedonia. It also serves as capital of one of the four Roman divisions of Macedonia which extends from the river Strymon on the east to the Axius on the west. It is about A.D. 58, when Paul and Silas make the hundred-mile journey on the *Via Egnatia* and come from Philippi to Thessalonica. Though violent persecution cuts his journey short, a church will be born through his labors. He likely visits them on several other occasions, and representatives from the church accompany him on some of his ministry journeys (Acts 20:4; 27:2). When he stayed in Corinth, Paul writes two epistles to the Thessalonian Church that are found in the New Testament. Let's look at what we can learn from his visit there.

Read Acts 17:1–3.

Where does Paul seek to minister first in Thessalonica, and why?

What stands out to you from Paul's approach to reaching this group of people?

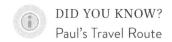
When Paul and company leave Philippi, they travel southwest along the important Roman highway known as the Egnatian Way (*Via Egnatia*). The cities of Amphipolis and Apollonia are most likely mentioned because they would be logical stopping points to spend the night on the way to Thessalonica if the party travels by horseback.

As soon as the group arrives in Thessalonica, the first stop is at the local synagogue *"according to Paul's custom."* We have seen in the missionary journeys this pattern that if the town has a synagogue, he goes there first, and it makes sense. Paul starts with those who already have exposure to the teachings about Messiah and who ought to be the most open to the message of Jesus. It is interesting to note that Paul doesn't focus on all the prophecies concerning the Messiah, but rather, he zeroes in on those foretellings that relate to His death and resurrection—seldom taught and understood among the Jews. Paul then shows how Jesus fulfilled those prophecies. There is much implied in Paul's process. He *"reasoned"* with them (Gr. *dialegomai*), appealing to their logic. In verse 3, two additional terms in this vein are added that speak of his process—he is *"explaining"* and *"giving evidence."* While Scripture is Paul's basis of authority, these words suggest that for the Thessalonians, reason is supreme. They are most interested to see if the message makes sense to them.

📖 Look at Acts 17:4–5. What catches your attention from the contrasting responses?

As we see illustrated so often in the book of Acts, the gospel message leaves no middle ground. People either embrace the message of Christ, or they attack it. Apparently, there are many who come to faith in Jesus. In addition to the unnamed number of Jewish men, *"a large number"* of the God-fearing Greeks (those who had already embraced Judaism) and a number of the leading women believe. The wording used to express the number of women of prominence in the community who believe literally reads "not a small number." We see some evidence of the world view of those who respond positively in the fact that they are *"persuaded."* Even in those who respond negatively, we see that the clear explanation of Scriptures does not convince them out of their traditions and expectations about the Messiah. The real authority in their lives is not the Word of God, but their own reasonings. Because this message does not fit their grid of thinking, they oppose it violently.

📖 Consider Acts 17:6–9 and write what you learn of the arguments Paul's opponents bring up against him and his companions.

From reading what they say in opposition to Paul and his companions, we learn much about the mindset of those who do not believe. First, they refer to them as *"These men who have upset the world."* They don't want the change Paul's gospel is bringing. It implies they have heard of the responses in other cities. Next, the opponents argue that Paul's message of Jesus as king (clearly a messianic concept that Jews should embrace) is in opposition to Roman government. It is ironic that Jews make such a point. To me it suggests that even before Paul arrives, they are more rationalists and nationalists than practicing Jews. God and His Word are not the real authority in their thinking.

> *God created us with brains, and we are supposed to use them. We are not to divorce ourselves from our intellect, but we must guard against a world view that enthrones reason above revelation.*

As in Paul's day, there are many today, even among those who identify themselves as Christians, whose real-world view—their real basis for what they believe and why—is not what God has revealed in the Scriptures, but rather, what makes sense to them. The real authority in their lives is that they deify their own minds and place human reason as supreme. I am not suggesting that to follow God means we divorce ourselves from our intellect, but we must guard against a world view which enthrones reason above revelation.

DAY 2

THE NOBLE-MINDED BEREANS: ACTS 17:10–15

When it becomes apparent that Paul's presence in Thessalonica not only puts him in danger, but also the lives of the local believers, it seems prudent to head on to another town. The next stop on this missionary journey is Berea, another city of Macedonia in the district called Emathia. This location is on the eastern side of the Olympian Mountains in modern Greece, at the base of Mount Bermius. It is an old and prosperous town, whose natural advantages in a well-watered and fertile farming district give it considerable population and importance. A fair-sized city still exists there today. The journey for Paul and his friends from Thessalonica to Berea is about fifty miles traveling southwest. Later on, we don't hear as much about this church as we do about others, since there are no lasting letters from Paul to them. There is one interesting note though. Tradition holds that Onesimus was the first bishop of the Berean church. He is remembered as the slave Paul led to Christ in his first imprisonment who is the subject of the book of Philemon. As we consider the Acts record on Berea, let's see what we can learn from them.

📖 Reflect on Acts 17:10–11 and answer the questions that follow.

Where does Paul begin his ministry in Berea?

> "Now these were more noble-minded than those in Thessalonica,
> for they received the word with great eagerness, examining the
> Scriptures daily to see whether these things were so." (Acts 17:11)

What do you think it means that Bereans are *"more noble-minded"* than those from Thessalonica?

What does verse 11 tell us about why Bereans are more noble-minded?

When the apostle Paul arrives at Berea, he once again makes his way first to the local synagogue. We are told the congregation of Jews there are of higher caliber than those he dealt with at Thessalonica. Luke calls them *"more noble-minded."* The Greek term, eugenes, literally means "from good genes" or "of a good family." They are a cut above. Luke gives us two attributes that set them apart from others. First, they receive the word *"with great eagerness."* They are teachable and openhearted to truth. Second, though teachable, they are not gullible. They hold everything Paul says up against God's Word. They are *"examining the Scriptures daily"* to see if these things are so. They are careful to investigate for themselves. This statement reveals that unlike the Thessalonians, their basis of belief is not dictated by mere human reason. They place their trust in revelation —what God has already revealed of truth.

📖 What do you learn from the Berean responses to Paul in Acts 17:12–13?

Much in the same way as in Thessalonica, we find that many embrace the message of Jesus. In this case, in addition to many Jews, Luke tells us that the Greeks who believe are *"prominent"* in the town. Again, the number of those who believe is literally "not a small number." At the same time, we find that trouble arises again. Antagonism seems to come more from those who follow after Paul from Thessalonica than from the actual citizens of Berea.

📖 What details do you learn of Paul's departure in Acts 17:14–15?

It is interesting to note that only Paul leaves town at this point. Silas and Timothy remain on to continue the fruitful ministry and to ground these new believers. It says something of the character of those who believe that they apparently arrange an "escort" to insure his safe travel. Paul has become a lightning rod, attracting the ire of unbelievers, and he can do more for the Bereans by leaving than by staying. While the text doesn't mention it, God's providence is allowing persecution to give Silas and Timothy greater responsibility and growth as ministry leaders. The last phrase of verse 15 suggests that once Paul gets to Athens, he sees another fruitful harvest field for ministry and sends word for Silas and Timothy to join him as soon as they can.

Though we are not told much more of the Berean church, and the New Testament affords us no correspondence as we have with the Thessalonians, Paul must be taking fond memories with him of these noble-minded believers. We know from Acts 20:4 that, later on, a man named Sopater, from Berea will become a traveling companion. Paul can appreciate their heart for truth and the fact that revelation is the basis of their belief.

Day 3

The Relativistic Melting-Pot of Athens: Acts 17:16–21

"Now while Paul was waiting for them at Athens, his spirit was being provoked within him as he was observing the city full of idols." (Acts 17:16)

The next stop in Paul's travels is the metropolitan city of Athens. It is quite a prominent city. After the Roman conquest, it becomes almost a country to itself. It operates entirely independent of the governor of Achaia (Greece). They pay no taxes to Rome and have internal judicial autonomy. The city was named for Athena, the Greek goddess of wisdom, arts, industries, and prudent warfare. The Athenians are said to possess the keenest minds among the Greeks, and the University of Athens is the most important school, even ahead of those at Tarsus and Alexandria. The Athenians are nominally religious but not truly spiritual and indulge in greatly lascivious behavior at the festival of Dionysus, the god of wine—something akin to Mardi Gras. They also are quite fond of the human slaughter that serves as a spectator sport in the gladiator games. As we will see today, the people of Athens show us yet another way of viewing the world and truth; one which we still see practiced today.

📖 Take a look at Acts 17:16.

What do you think it means that Paul's spirit is being *"provoked within him"*?

Why do you think he is so moved by seeing all the idols?

It is all too easy to see something without really seeing it. When Jesus looked out into crowds of people, He saw their need (e.g. Matthew 9:36). So too does the apostle Paul. As he looks around Athens, his heart is moved. His spirit is provoked within him. The Greek word translated in English as *provoked* means to be moved to action—in a bad sense by anger, or, in a good sense by compassion. For Paul it may be a mixture of both. Everywhere Paul looks he sees idols and their shrines. Instead of believing nothing, Athens believes in everything. It doesn't matter if one belief contradicts another, they accept them all. Through their idolatry, Paul recognizes hearts searching for truth and meaning, and yet, he also sees people who view truth as a relative concept rather than an absolute.

DID YOU KNOW?
The Epicureans

Epicureans were followers of the Athenian philosopher Epicurus. Central to this belief system was a purely mechanical and material view of the world. They taught that pleasure and the avoidance of pain were the chief end of man. At death they thought that the body and soul disintegrated and there was no afterlife. The Stoic philosophers were quite the opposite. They saw self-control as the greatest virtue. They taught indifference to both pleasure and pain, and their goal was to reach a place where one felt nothing. Unlike the Epicureans, the Stoics were pantheists. That such divergent views co-existed together speaks of the diversity and tolerance in Athenian thought.

📖 Read Acts 17:17 and write what changes you observe in Paul's evangelistic strategy.

Just as in every other place, Paul begins his ministry in Athens by targeting the synagogue and speaking of Christ to the Jewish and Gentile proselytes (Gentile converts to Judaism). But we also observe a strategy that we haven't heard specifically mentioned before. Paul practices evangelism with random passersby in the marketplace, witnessing to anyone who just happens to be there at that time. Certainly, Paul may have taken this approach in other places before now, but Luke's mention of it here appears to reflect an intentional plan. It may be that Paul recognizes that this particular population requires a different strategy.

📖 Look over Acts 17:18–21 and answer the questions below.

What differences do you see in the responses of verse 18?

What does the explanation of verses 19–21 say to you of the thinking of these people?

Even among philosophers Paul's message seems to divide. Some call him an idle babbler, while others are intrigued by the prospect of a new god being proclaimed. We learn something of their mindset that those who don't embrace Paul's message are not antagonistic or hostile even if they do mock it. It speaks of the interest of some that they invite him to the Areopagus to hear more. The Areopagus is also called "Mars Hill" after the Greek god of war. In Athens, it is the site of meeting for the Senate which functions somewhere between a congress and a supreme court. It does not appear that Paul is brought here for any charges or trial, but rather, much like one would appear before a Senate committee today to testify on a matter of interest. It is obvious from Luke's commentary in verse 21 that this type of conversation is exactly what these Athenians enjoy. Their beliefs always have room for one more deity, and a *"new teaching"* is always welcomed.

Consider what this passage reveals about how these people think. First, we are told that theirs is a *"city filled with idols."* They make room in their culture for everyone's beliefs. "Tolerance" is the religious watchword. We witness their interest in a "new teaching," and their desire to know more about this deity not yet represented among the many they worship. Like many today, they seem to affirm any belief held in sincerity. Some of the values of these many different idols in Athens are in opposition to each other, but that doesn't seem to matter. Theirs is a world view without absolute truth. "We all find meaning in our own way" would accurately reflect their relativistic way of thinking and the basis of their belief system. Something is true if it is true to you. It might be easy to see Jesus added into their beliefs, but it will be a challenge for Him to be recognized as the only way to God.

DAY 4

BUILDING A BRIDGE TO BELIEF: ACTS 17:22–34

Imagine that you are traveling to a distant metropolis in another culture and are called to testify before governmental leaders about what you believe. You would probably be intimidated but also excited. Which of these emotions reigns stronger might vary from person to person. Being convinced of the validity of Christianity, there would naturally be a desire on your part to persuade them to your way of thinking. But this is no small task, especially if you have been raised as a Christian. For such a person, faith is a natural progression that is consistent with a world view that is compatible. But for those raised with a different world view, there are challenges. For them to change their grid of belief requires a journey, much like going to a different country with obstacles to cross along the way. For those of us who present the gospel message, we must navigate across differing rivers of thought, and to do so, we must start not with where *we* are but with where *they* are. Paul's sermon on Mars Hill is a great model of building bridges to belief. He takes the Athenians where they are and guides them to where he is.

When Paul speaks of the Athenians worshipping in ignorance, this is not necessarily a cutting remark. The Greek word (*agnoeo*) simply means "without knowledge." In other words, he was pointing out that they worship that which they do not know. He is about to give them the knowledge they lack. This Greek word is the root of the term "agnostic"—one who is unsure of God's existence, but not willing to take a stand against it as an atheist would be.

📖 Reflect on Acts 17:22–23 and record what you observe of how Paul begins his conversation with the Athenians.

Before Paul ever tries to explain his beliefs, he addresses the beliefs of his audience. He articulates what he observes of their beliefs without trying to attack them. There is nothing threatening in his opening statement, nor does he start by telling them they are wrong. He simply acknowledges that they have a religious inclination. It seems as if he is affirming them for this. But what he does next is brilliant. Paul's second statement indicates some serious reflection on their culture and way of thinking. He takes something they embrace and uses it to build a bridge to faith. Their altar *"to an unknown god"* shows that they acknowledge there are still other gods than those they know about. This gives Paul a culturally relevant opening to present Christ.

📖 Read Acts 17:24–29.

What points does Paul make about the Creator that force them to rethink their view of gods (17:24–26)?

What do you see in 17:27 that encourages one to seek God?

How does Paul connect with their culture in verse 28?

How does he confront their culture in verse 29?

The core of Paul's message begins by enlarging their view of what constitutes a god. Any god worthy of worship would have to be greater than man, but notice, Paul starts with creation, not Christ. He forces them to think about where they came from. Look at the progression of his argument. The God who could create the world, Paul points out, is bigger than these gods you worship. He doesn't need you to make Him a house. He gave life to you (and ought to be able to take care of Himself just fine). All humankind comes from the first persons He created, and He is the one who decides when and how long they will live. Next, Paul addresses himself to God's desire—that people would seek out their Creator. Paul makes it clear that God is near enough to us to be found. Paul connects with their culture by quoting their poets but confronts their wrong thinking about what a true God would be like. Notice the contrast between the last point of verse 29 and the first point of verse 24. Paul starts by talking about the creator of the world and ends with pointing out that they are worshiping *what they had created* (*"an image formed by the art and thought of man"*) instead of the One who created them.

DID YOU KNOW?
Chronological Approach to Evangelism

The mission agency, Ethnos360, recognized early on a problem with presenting Christ to tribal peoples with radically different views on truth. As Christ was preached, He would often be accepted and then added in as one more god to worship, but not given supremacy in their lives. To address this problem, Ethnos360 developed an evangelistic approach for pioneering with unexposed tribes called the "Chronological Approach." It begins by teaching the story of Creation and moves forward with a biblical timeline. It has proven to be far more successful because by the time they hear the message of Christ, they understand why He needed to die and what makes Him unique.

📖 Look over Acts 17:30–31 and write what stands out to you as Paul speaks of our accountability to our Creator.

Hidden beneath the words Paul uses here are some significant truths about God. First, Paul points to grace as he speaks of God *"overlooking"* humanity's ignorance. Second, Paul reminds them of revelation. This is such an important truth to grasp! God is too superior to humanity for anyone to find Him without assistance. God is knowable by us because He chooses to make Himself known. Paul is lifting high the concept of revelation and the repentance it requires. In verse 31, Paul begins closing his persuasive address. He speaks of the coming Day of Judgment and makes it clear that we are accountable to what God has revealed to us. Through His resurrection, Christ has *"furnished proof to all men"* of His uniqueness.

The central question which must be answered in a relativistic world is "How is Christianity different from other religions?" The answer is in Paul's point: of all the so-called religious figures, only Jesus is still alive. Buddha is dead. Confucius may have been wise, but he is not still with us. Mohammed is no longer among the living. Of all religious figures, only Jesus' grave is empty. The resurrection sets Him apart from the rest. That is why it is such an integral part of the gospel.

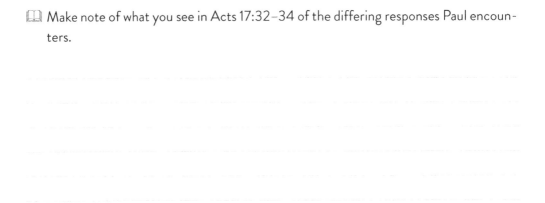 Make note of what you see in Acts 17:32–34 of the differing responses Paul encounters.

While we are beginning to see a recurring pattern in the reactions to Paul's outreach, it is worthwhile to notice that here Luke mentions three responses instead of two. Some begin to "sneer" at the mention of the resurrection. Negative responses like this are common in Paul's ministry. In verse 34 we are told that some *"joined him and believed."* This too has been a pattern. But sandwiched between the unbelievers and the believers is the response of those who are seekers. They are not ready to commit yet, but they are willing to continue considering. Often, we place so much emphasis on making a decision right now that we neglect to cultivate the interest of those who are open but need time to process a new way of thinking. It is impressive that among those who believe right away was a man named *"Dionysius the Areopagite."* Apparently, he is one of the governmental leaders in Athens.

IN THEIR SHOES
The Athenians

As we reach out to others, we can expect to encounter the same responses the apostle Paul saw in Athens...

- some will be sneerers

- some will be seekers

- some will be saved

We can learn much from Paul's ministry in Athens concerning how to reach unbelievers in our own culture. We need to recognize that an increasing number among those who are not Christians operate from a world view of relativism. This presents unique challenges as we bring the gospel, but as we see in Acts 17, there are people ready to believe in every place and from every world view. What an exciting thing it is to be part of seeing others come to Christ!

DAY 5

FOR ME TO FOLLOW GOD

As we study the missionary journeys of Paul, one value that comes forward strongly is that we need to put feet to the gospel. We need to take the message of Christ to others instead of waiting for them to ask or look for it. But this presents challenges. While Christians are unified on core beliefs, pagans are not. All unbelievers (or perhaps we should say, "pre-believers") are not created equal. We see in these three cities Paul visits three separate approaches to truth and world view. We cannot communicate effectively with others if we do not take the time to understand where they are coming from. The more we understand where they are, the easier it is to build bridges to where they ought to be. If we can put on their glasses and look at the world from their point of view, we may actually begin to understand why they live the way they do and how to respond to concerns they have about the Christian faith. For example, to many Christians, a lifestyle of constant partying and drug abuse makes no sense at all. But look at it from the point of view of a non-Christian. I can, because at one point such belief characterized my life. I believed this life is all there is, with no heaven or hell awaiting anyone. I thought morality to be arbitrary instead of absolute, and of human invention rather than the boundaries of God. If that is true, then it makes no sense to be moral. It makes sense to just have as much fun as you can, because you only go around once. My starting point was wrong, but the logic was sound. Now I see the moral boundaries of God as good instead of bad. I see that they serve to protect us from that which ultimately isn't good and to provide for us the best life possible. My world view had to change for me to look at morality differently. I believe as Christians we need to evaluate our own world view, to deal with inconsistencies. And we need to understand how others look at life to be able to help them come to faith.

An Evaluation

As you consider the differing world views Paul encounters in Acts chapter 17, you can summarize them with three terms: Rationalism, Relativism, and Revelation. These are not the only ways to view the world, but they represent three significant and different world views that remain prevalent today.

> *We cannot communicate effectively with others if we do not take*
> *the time to understand where they are coming from.*

Rationalism taken to an extreme says that everything should have a natural, rational explanation—it should make sense to the mind. There are several key problems in reconciling this with the Christian world view. First, it doesn't leave room for the supernatural. This is why some Christians embrace the moral teachings of the Bible but struggle with believing the miracles we see there. This world view deifies human reasoning and logic. It asks the question, "Does this make sense to me?"

The second way of thinking, Relativism, is a world view that does not believe in absolutes. Everything is relative. Even morality is not seen in absolute terms. Ethics are determined by the situation rather than a standard. The basis of belief is *subjective* and internal instead of *objective*. What matters most is sincerity, not truth. This world view deifies human feelings and emotions. It asks the question, "Does this feel right to me?"

The Revelation world view differs from both of these because it begins with God rather than us. It assumes God as the source of life and therefore, the absolute authority on how it should be lived. It presupposes absolute values that are determined by what God has revealed. It expects that God reveals to us what we need to know. It sees Scripture as the final authority on a matter. What God says always trumps what I think or feel. It asks the question, "How does this line up with what God says?" It is important to realize that just because we are Christians that does not necessarily mean that we operate with revelation as the ultimate basis of belief.

Consider these three views and honestly rate yourself.

The dominant world view I was raised with growing up was...

- Rationalism

- Relativism

- Revelation

The world view I tend toward the most now is...

- Rationalism

- Relativism

- Revelation

Based on this week's lesson, are there areas of my world view that I need to reconsider?

It is important to recognize that all three views may be present in our thinking in varying degrees. It is also important to understand what is behind what we believe. The question is not whether or not we will make use of our minds or follow our emotions. God created us with both. The real question revolves around whether or not we will subject both of those to what God has revealed in the Bible. When what we think or what we feel conflicts with what God says, which wins out? Spiritual growth is a process, and as we mature, hopefully we are growing in letting God's word serve as the basis of our beliefs.

As you reflect on the differing ways of looking at the world and the contrasts in the basis of beliefs that different people operate from, try to connect these ideas with people you know. Looking at each of the three world views, write down the names of people in your life who come to mind with each.

Rationalism –

Relativism –

Revelation –

Whether or not we will make use of our minds or follow our emotions is irrelevant. God created us with both physical and emotional qualities. The real question revolves around whether or not we will subject both of these qualities to what God has revealed in the Bible.

Remember the example Paul sets for us in his sermon on Mars Hill. He starts with where they are—their frame of reference. He connects with their way of thinking before inviting them into his. He calls them to think about God in new ways. He starts with Creation instead of Christ. He introduces the concept of revelation before trying to deal with the contents of it. But he is also willing to bring the conversation to closure. He reminds them of our accountability to our Creator and calls them to action. As you reflect on the names you wrote above and Paul's example in Athens, what are some ways you can build bridges with some of these people?

As you close out this week's lesson, communicate your thoughts, decisions and applications in a written prayer to the Lord in the space below...

LESSON 5

JOINING GOD WHERE HE IS WORKING

ACTS 18:1–22

There are two approaches to ministry: achieved and received. Achieved ministry is that which we initiate—trying to do good things for God. What is initiated by us must be accomplished by us. Received ministry is initiated by God, and what He initiates, He anoints. Achieved ministry is us coming up with an idea and asking God to bless it. Received ministry is us hearing from God and following His lead—letting God work through us. The apostle Paul saw his share of both. He had been there. He tried hard to work for God and sometimes even found himself working against the one he was seeking to serve. That was his life as a Pharisee. He actually persecuted the followers of Christ while sincerely trying to serve God as he thought best. But when he met Christ on the Damascus Road, he was introduced to a whole new approach to serving God. He began to learn about hearing from God and waiting on God. After a brief foray into ministry at Damascus and Jerusalem, he spent at least three years in Arabia and elsewhere (see Galatians 1:17–18) studying the Scriptures and listening to God. When Paul writes his epistle to the churches of Galatia he explains, *"For I would have you know, brethren, that the gospel which was preached by me is not according to man. For I neither received it from man, nor was I taught it, but I received it through a revelation of Jesus Christ"* (Galatians 1:11–12). Paul's message did not originate with him, and neither did his methods.

WORD STUDY
Stop Trying!

In Acts 16 we see Paul one minute sensitive to the Lord and the next minute striving. He follows the Holy Spirit's lead in not speaking the gospel in Phrygia and the Galatian region (Acts 16:6). This is clear from the Greek word for *"by"* (*hupo*, meaning beneath or from under) as in *"by the Holy Spirit."* But then he keeps trying to go into Bithynia even as the Spirit of Jesus is blocking him (Acts 16:7). This is clear because *"trying"* is in the "imperfect tense" meaning continuous or repeated action in the past. In other words, he kept trying.

I do not mean to paint a perfect portrait of the apostle Paul, airbrushing out all the imperfections and humanity. I am not saying that before Paul's conversion was his season of achieved ministry and after was a perfect pursuit of received ministry. It is clear already from what we have learned in Acts that Paul has his share of striving even after Damascus. In Acts 16 we see him sensitive to the Lord one minute—and striving the next. He follows the Holy Spirit's lead in not speaking the gospel in Phrygia and the Galatian region (Acts 16:6). But then he keeps trying to go into Bithynia even as the Spirit of Jesus is blocking him (Acts 16:7). I love this example, because I can relate to it so well. Sometimes it is challenging to find the balance between being too passive and taking the initiative too much. Even though our heart wants to do the right thing, we can lag behind in unbelief or run ahead of God and do our own thing instead of following Him. The reason for this is that even when we know <u>what</u> God wants us to do, we still have to let Him lead us in the <u>when</u> and <u>where</u>.

It is not a sin to take initiative when we know what God wants us to do. But we still need to be sensitive to His leading or we may try to make His will happen instead of letting Him work. Paul knows he is to preach the gospel. That is his assigned task (see Acts 9:15). It probably doesn't make much sense not to evangelize Phrygia and Galatia—they need the Lord like everyone else. But God knows better than Paul the right time to do that. God knows when their hearts will be ready to hear, and He protects Paul from wasting time. The gospel will get to Galatia; we know it does, as evidenced by Paul's epistle to them. But now is not the time. God wants Paul to join Him where He is working, in Macedonia.

You see, God is always at work around us. Effective ministry is not simply when we work hard for God. The fruit comes when we look to Him for where He is working and join Him there. Paul expresses that well in Acts 20:24 when he says, *"But I do not consider my life of any account as dear to myself, so that I may finish my course and the ministry which I RECEIVED from the Lord Jesus, to testify solemnly of the gospel of the grace of God"* (emphasis mine). The Lord of the Harvest (Matthew 9:38) knows which fields are ripe and when they need to be picked. This week we want to look more closely at this principle of joining God where He is working as we see it illustrated in the life and ministry of Paul.

DAY 1

THE HARVEST FIELDS OF CORINTH: ACTS 18:1–4

Paul is having fruitful ministry everywhere he goes. That fact makes it obvious that he is walking in "received" ministry. God is working, not just Paul. People are responding and turning to the Lord. Churches form in every city in which he labors. But it is important to realize that Paul does not stop and try to minister in every sizable city he enters as he travels. We read in Acts 17:1 that he and his companions travel *"through Amphipolis and Apollonia."* These are not insignificant cities. In fact, Amphipolis is a larger and more prominent city than Philippi, being the capitol of one of the four merides (mini-republics) the Romans created in this region. Yet it appears Paul may only have used Amphipolis as a one-night stopover. There is no indication that he and his companions preach the gospel there. But he spends weeks in other places where God is working. At the same time, Paul doesn't lag behind in these places even though God is working greatly. He leaves Philippi, Thessalonica, Berea, and Athens behind. Sometimes God helps him along with persecution nipping at his heels, while other times it is simply a settled conviction of God leading him on. But however God leads, he keeps Paul moving. It is harvest time, and the Lord of the Harvest is moving His laborers from field to field. Let's look at this next field we find at Corinth.

📖 Why do you suppose Acts 18:1 indicates Paul goes on to Corinth instead of waiting on Timothy and Silas as he had planned (Acts 17:15–16)?

> ⓘ **DID YOU KNOW?**
> Corinth
>
> The ancient city of Corinth was located on the narrow isthmus that connected the two land masses of Greece. As such, it was the gateway for both land and sea travel and a very prosperous city. It had a population in Paul's day of some 200,000. It was such a decadent and immoral city that the Greek term, *Korinthiazomai* (meaning "to act the Corinthian") came to mean "to practice fornication."

Paul leaves Berea when the Jews from Thessalonica come there to stir up trouble. He leaves Silas and Timothy behind to ground the new believers and continue the work. We are told in Acts 17:15 that he requests they join him as soon as they can, and in 17:16 we find him waiting for them in Athens. Yet here we see that apparently he goes on to Corinth alone (see Acts 18:5). While it is possible that encounters some trouble in Athens, we would expect Luke to mention it if that is the case. It seems more likely that God prompts him to continue to yet another harvest field.

📖 Acts 18:2 introduces us to Aquila and Pricilla. Read this verse and the references below and, write what you learn about them. Then consider the question, "Do you think they are already Christians when Paul meets them?"

Romans 16:3–4

1 Corinthians 16:19

2 Timothy 4:19

Do you think Aquila and Priscilla are already Christians? _____ Why?

DID YOU KNOW?
Corinth and The Epistle of Romans

The apostle Paul most likely came to Corinth about March of AD 51. Silas and Timothy joined him about two months later. The edict of Claudius that evicted Priscilla and Aquila from Rome occurred in AD 49 or 50. Paul wrote the book of Romans from Corinth on his third missionary journey about AD 57, and the church was well-known by then. He did not start the Roman church and did not in fact visit Rome until about AD 59 with his first imprisonment. Most likely the Roman church was started by Jews from Rome who came to faith in Christ through Peter's preaching at Pentecost and took their new faith back with them to Rome. Priscilla and Aquila were probably converted in Rome through the ministry of these believers.

It is in Corinth that Paul first meets Priscilla (called Prisca by Paul) and Aquila who will become among his closest friends. In his letter to the Romans he speaks of them as "fellow workers" who risked their lives for his (Romans 16:3–4). Priscilla and Aquila have come to Corinth from Rome because of Claudius' eviction of the Jews. The fact that they are known by the church in Rome suggests that they may have become Christians there before leaving. Paul mentions them in 1 Corinthians 16:19 as sending greetings to the church there, so obviously they are believers while at Corinth. From what we know of Luke, we would expect him to mention if Paul led them to the Lord. It cannot be said for certain, but, I believe they are already Christians when Paul meets them. Paul's letter to the Corinthians is written from Ephesus, so when he speaks of "the church that is in their house," it is obvious that they become leaders there. They are still there when Paul writes his last letter to Timothy at Ephesus, as he asks Timothy to greet them for him (2 Timothy 4:19).

Look over Acts 18:3–4 and write down your observations on how Paul spends his time in Corinth before Silas and Timothy meet him.

We learn in Acts that Aquila and Priscilla share the same trade of tentmaking as they and Paul work together for a time. It was customary for Jewish fathers to teach their sons a trade, and since tentmaking was an important industry in Tarsus where Paul hails from, it is no surprise to find him doing this. Apparently, his funds run out, making work a necessity. In the time remaining after work, he begins to reach out in ministry. As usual, he starts at the local synagogue trying to persuade its members to put their trust in Jesus as the Messiah. The verb translated *"trying to persuade"* is in the imperfect tense in the Greek, meaning continuous or repeated action in the past.

DID YOU KNOW?
Tentmaker

The term, "tentmaker missionary" comes from this passage and has the idea of those who support themselves with a trade while serving the Lord. Sometimes this is necessary because of political restrictions in closed countries but is not to be seen as a spiritual requirement or somehow a more noble way to serve. In fact, it may be less strategic because of the time it takes from the task of ministry. This is only a temporary practice for Paul, for when Silas and Timothy arrive with funds from the Macedonian churches (see 2 Corinthians 11:7) he devotes himself to full-time ministry.

There is no mention of any positive response to the gospel message in the early days of Paul's work in Corinth. The silence, along with the context we will see in the verses to follow, points us to the conclusion that he doesn't meet with the same successes he saw in the other synagogues he visited on this journey. He keeps persisting though. Joining God where He is working means we must keep our eyes on Him, not on the results. Just because people don't appear to be responding doesn't necessarily mean God isn't working. This is why we need to keep our eyes on God rather than on the results. We will see more in Day Two's study on the conclusions Paul draws about where God is working, but it is too early for such conclusions at this point.

DAY 2

MOVING ON TO RIPER FIELDS: ACTS 18:5–11

What would you do if what had always succeeded for you suddenly doesn't work? The missionary pattern of Paul has always made the synagogue the centerpiece of his outreach to a town. So far that has worked well. Sincere Jews who respond to the gospel become the core group of the churches he plants. Many Greeks believe as well, and so the churches aren't made up completely of Jews. But in Corinth Paul encounters something he hasn't had to deal with before. His attempts to win Jews to the gospel strike out. To be sure, he hasn't been able to give outreach the full attention it deserves. He is working full time and trying to minister on the side. But we have no record of any fruit among the Jews in these first months of ministry before Silas and Timothy join him. If he hopes that is going to change when he begins ministering full-time, he is about to be disappointed.

📖 Read Acts 18:5–6 and answer the questions that follow.

What happens to Paul's tentmaking when Silas and Timothy join him?

What response does he see among the Jews at the synagogue?

How does he respond to that?

When Silas and Timothy finally catch up with Paul, he set his tents aside and becomes a full-time missionary once again. Undeterred by their lack of positive response, he continuously preaches Jesus as Messiah to those he encounters at the synagogue. But when they set themselves against him and actually blaspheme the Lord, he has had enough. These people may be Jews by birth, but they are not so by faith. They have no heart for God, so Paul gives up on them.

Paul makes three statements here in Acts 18:6 that are each significant in their own right. First, he states, *"Your blood be on your own heads!"* This powerful statement draws on the words of the prophet Ezekiel. In the prophecy of Ezekiel 33, God reveals that the job of the prophet is like that of a watchman of a city. When he sees judgment coming, his job is to warn. If he does not warn the city, their blood is on his hands. If he does, and they do not respond, their blood is on their own hands—they are responsible for whatever happens to them. By invoking these words, Paul is pronouncing judgment on these Jews. Second, he says, *"I am clean."* His meaning in this context is clear. He is saying he is free from any guilt. Third, and most striking, Paul pronounces, "From now on I will go to the Gentiles." It says something of the spiritual bankruptcy of these so-called Jews that even these strong words do not produce repentance.

📖 From Acts 18:7–8 write what you learn of those who respond positively.

WORD STUDY
"Were Believing"

As we saw earlier, here is another occurrence of the "imperfect tense" which in Greek use refers to continuous or repeated action in the past. In this case, it is the verb translated *"were believing."* The verb phrase translated *"heard"* is a "present active participle" and could be translated *"hearing."* The Greek present tense, like the imperfect, carries the idea of continuous or repeated action. Both of these grammatical observations point to an ongoing process of people coming to Christ.

Once Paul says his last, he leaves the synagogue. The fact that he goes directly to the house of this man, *"Titius Justus,"* and that Luke calls him *"a worshiper of God"* makes it clear that he has already responded positively to Paul's message. The wording indicates that the conversion of *"Crispus, the leader of the synagogue"* and his household occurs after Paul's strong words, and perhaps because of them. Even though so few of Paul's countrymen respond to the message of their Messiah, these are quality converts. They are joined by a great number of Gentile converts from the Corinthians. The grammatical construction here indicates that both the preaching to the Gentiles and their response are not individual events, but rather, an ongoing process. Paul has found where God is working and joins in that work.

📖 Reflect on Acts 18:9–11.

What are the main points of Paul's vision?

Why do you think a vision is needed by Paul?

What does Paul do with this direction from the Lord?

Most of us aren't awakened in the night by a vision from the Lord, but if we were, we'd certainly pay attention. The Lord first tells Paul, *"Do not be afraid any longer."* This is significant. Apparently, he has been battling fear, and with good reason. In every city since entering Macedonia, he has encountered persecution, including threats, beatings, and imprisonment. There is no reason to expect Corinth to be any different. The Lord tells him to *"go on speaking and do not be silent,"* and gives him two assurances: *"I am with you,"* a promise of His presence, and *"no man will attack you in order to harm you,"* a promise of Paul's safety. There is also a promise of fruit. The Lord informs Paul, *"I have many people in this city."* When we join God where He is working, we can expect that He will make the most of our time and effort. As a result of God's leading, Paul makes a second change in strategy. His first switch from his normal approach comes when he begins to focus exclusively on reaching Gentiles. He settles in Corinth "a year and six months, teaching the word of God among them." Up until this point he usually only stays in one place for a period of weeks.

Corinth turns out to be a significant church in Paul's ministry. They will have their problems, many of which we see addressed in 1 Corinthians, but they will grow through them and follow the Lord as we see reflected in Second Corinthians. While Corinth is a significant city on the one hand and seems large enough to warrant being targeted by missionaries, it is also excessively wicked, and from a human perspective would seem a less likely place for fruitful ministry. It is important to recognize the role of God's leading in Paul's ministry here. First, it is because of a vision that he even heads in the direction of Macedonia and Achaia. But as we see today, it is because of a second vision that he settles down in Corinth and spends so much time there. Received ministry hinges on seeking God. Achieved ministry is usually founded on man's reason and logic. While we would be unwise to check our brains at the door, reason is no substitute for revelation not only in embracing the truth but in ministering it as well.

You may be thinking, "How does this apply to me?" Most of us don't receive direction from the Lord by way of visions. But even if we don't, the principles still apply. The point is not "how" we hear from God, but "that" we hear from Him. Received ministry is joining God where He is working, and this hinges on a continual seeking of Him. It is not enough to gain a direction and then to take off. We must stay sensitive to His leading every step of the way. Most often, God's will and leading are not given in one big package. If they were, we would be tempted to take matters into our own hands from there. God's leading is more like a scroll that unrolls a bit at a time. Received ministry always looks to Him to follow His lead. What we want to be a part of is God's works, not just good works.

Day 3

The Striving of Paul's Opponents: Acts 18:12–17

" . . . the anger of man does not achieve the righteousness of God."
(James 1:20)

In the Epistle of James, we are instructed to be *"quick to hear, slow to speak and slow to anger"* (1:19). While this is good advice for any human relationship, the context of that verse, speaking of *"receiving the Word,"* points to the fact that the primary application is to be in our relationship with God. We need to be quick to hear Him, slow to speak (or draw conclusions about what He is saying), and slow to anger or to act in a response of passion. The very next verse advises, *"for the anger of man does not achieve the righteousness of God."* The Greek word for anger in this verse (*orgē*) was originally applied to any human emotion and came to be associated with anger as the strongest of human emotions. The point is clear. When we follow our feelings instead of following God's lead, it doesn't result in righteousness. This principle explains how a Christian could do something as horrible as bombing an abortion clinic. By letting his anger at the horror of abortion lead him instead of looking to the Lord, he commits a crime equally wrong. This ought to be a warning to us. If we desire to walk in received ministry, we must follow the Lord and not our own passions. Letting our human emotions lead us, instead of looking to the Lord, is a shortcut to striving and achieved ministry. Ironically, in context of these lessons from Paul's life on joining God where He is working, we find an equally potent example of the opposite in the Jews of Corinth—people who claimed to be followers of God. Today we want to study their striving and see what we can learn for our own lives.

DID YOU KNOW?
Gallio

Gallio, the Roman proconsul of Achaia mentioned here was the brother of Seneca, the famous Roman philosopher and tutor of Nero. Seneca describes him as a man of great mildness and simplicity. It is evidence of God's providential protection that Paul is brought before his tribunal at Corinth. Gallio dismissed the case as one not worthy to be recognized by a Roman court, deeming the offense at best a trivial one. Like his brother Seneca, Gallio ended up being executed at the command of Nero.

📖 Look at Acts 18:12–13 and find out who is opposing Paul, how, and on what basis.

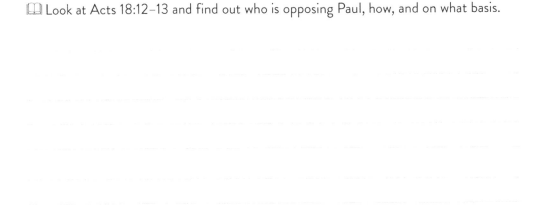

It is no small source of amazement that the people of God could become the opponents of God and His work. Yet we see examples of it throughout the Word and today's world as well. At some point in Paul's lengthy ministry at Corinth, the entire Jewish community—the so-called "chosen people" of God rise up against this messenger of God. This, of course, is not the first time this has happened. Throughout history we see examples of God's people persecuting His prophets, as Stephen points out in his sermon (see Acts 7:51–52). The basis of the Corinthian Jews' argument is that Paul's teaching contradicts their tradition and interpretation of the law.

An important cultural point must be made here. What Jews here are trying to do in bringing Paul to the Roman court is to establish a legal precedent of distinguishing Christianity as a completely separate religion outside the favored status of Judaism, a religion officially tolerated by Rome. If successful, Christianity could be banned not only here in Corinth, but the case could be used as a precedent wherever the gospel goes throughout the Roman Empire.

📖 Read Acts 18:14–16 and write what you learn about how Paul's case is resolved.

God's promise of protection (Acts 18:10) is realized, as we see His working to protect Paul through the governing authorities. Paul doesn't even have to say a word in defense. Instead of giving the Jews the precedent they are looking for, Gallio, the judge presiding over the case, rules in the opposite direction. In throwing the case out, he clearly defines any questions about the teaching of Christianity as an internal matter between Jews, which violates no Roman law. This gives the Jews no legal leverage at all in their opposition to Christianity. The fact that they have to be driven away from the judgment seat makes it clear they don't want to give up the argument.

 Determine from Acts 18:17 how the Jews respond to the verdict, and write your thoughts on why they react as they do.

DOCTRINE
Judgment Seat

The "judgment seat," also called the "Bema" from the Greek term, was a raised platform that stood in the marketplace out in front of the proconsul's residence. It served as a public court where the proconsul could resolve disputes. Being elevated, it gave the leader a position of prominence and superiority. Such a seat could be found in every major town. Paul uses this same term in 2 Corinthians 5:10 when he states, *"for we must all appear before the judgment seat of Christ, so that each one may be recompensed for his deeds in the body, according to what he has done, whether good or bad."* The Corinthian believers would have connected Paul's imagery of Christ's judgment to the platform in their own town.

It is an interesting study in human nature to reflect on the actions of these Jews upon losing their case. It appears they take their frustrations out on their spokesman and violently beat him. Apparently, Crispus, the former leader who converted to Christianity (Acts 18:8) has been replaced by Sosthenes. It is unclear why he is selected for a beating. Some have suggested that his view of Paul and of Christ was changed by the process, and this aggression against him is evidence of him switching sides. This idea is not completely without merit, for when Paul writes his first letter to Corinth, he includes greetings from Sosthenes and calls him *"our brother"* (1 Corinthians 1:1). At some point, yet another leader of the Corinthian synagogue comes to Christ. But if he believes at this point, one would expect Luke to make mention of it. More likely he is attacked because he fails to gain the assistance of the Romans in silencing Paul and becomes the easiest place to vent their anger.

The religiously motivated but misguided actions of these Jews stand in stark contrast to Paul's pursuit of God. Paul keeps his eyes on the Lord. When the Jews of Corinth reject his message and blaspheme the Lord (Acts 18:6), he recognizes that they are not where God is working. Through observation and revelation, he concludes that in Corinth, God is moving among the Gentiles, and they become his focus. He is not working *for* God but rather, working *with* God, and he will see much fruit from his labors. The Jews however, who claimed God as their Father, are really following their own passions. As a result, they find themselves on the wrong side of God's kingdom work. With what they believe to be righteous anger, they commit great unrighteousness as they brutalize their leader in front of the judgment seat of Gallio. They illustrate for us how important it is to keep sensitive to the Lord's leading and to not allow ourselves to slip into an "achieved" ministry. Not only can we end up missing out on what God is doing, we can actually work against Him.

DAY 4

"IF GOD WILLS": ACTS 18:18–22

I am sure it is frustrating for Paul to encounter such opposition from some of his fellow Jews as he sees in Corinth and to see them opposing God instead of embracing Him. Yet that is what he finds in town after town. There might be a temptation toward anger and frustration, but he of all people can feel compassion as well. He had been there. He reacted the same way to messengers of Christ initially. He can understand their spiritual blindness as few can. Writing to the Romans, he says of his heart for the Jews, *"I have great sorrow and unceasing grief in my heart...for the sake of my brethren, my kinsmen according to the flesh"* (Romans 9:2–3). Not only can he understand their opposition, but he can view it with hope. He has only to look at his own life to recognize that God can still change them. Perhaps that explains his patience with them as well as his lack of striving. He knows that God can change their hearts, but he also recognizes that only God can do the real work in their hearts. That is why he is unwilling to go it alone in ministry. He wants to work where God is working. In Corinth, this means staying a year and a half reaching the Gentiles. But it also means leaving when God says leave. The key phrase in explaining how Paul tries to continue in received ministry is found in today's study: *"...if God wills..."* (Acts 18:21).

📖 Review Acts 18:18 and summarize what you learn here about Paul's departure from Corinth.

At the end of Paul's time in Corinth, we are told he takes leave of the *"brethren,"* reminding us that this has been a fruitful stay. This untouched city now has a thriving church, and each of the brethren here can trace their spiritual heritage to the apostle Paul. It is obvious from the fact that Priscilla and Aquila accompany Paul, that they are now part of his ministry team. We are told in passing that while in Cenchrea, Paul has his hair cut, and this gives us reason to believe that he had been keeping a vow for some time prior to the haircut. Though we don't know how long he had been keeping the vow, there is the suggestion that it is at least for the duration of his time in Corinth and maybe for the entirety of this second missionary journey up till the time he arrives in Cenchrea.

 DID YOU KNOW?
Nazarite Vow

Most likely the vow spoken of in Acts 18:18 is a Nazarite vow. The most thorough explanation of this vow is found in Numbers 6:1–21 where in the Septuagint (Greek translation of the Old Testament) the same Greek word is used. Some notable persons who took such vows in addition to Paul are Samson (Judges 13:7), Samuel (1 Samuel 1:11), the Rechabites (Jeremiah 35:6–11), and John the Baptist (Luke 1:15, 7:33). Although normally the vow is taken for one month, in the case of Samson, Samuel, and John the Baptist, it is lifelong. In Paul's day, allowance was made for those away from Jerusalem to shave their heads at the end of the vow as Paul did and then to present the hair as an offering at the Temple in Jerusalem within thirty days (see Josephus, *The Wars of the Jews*, 2.15.1).

How do we join God where He is working? Paul gives us one clue. He is doing everything he can to keep his focus on the Lord and keep attuned to Him. In Judaism, such vows are usually associated with service and devotion. Most likely, Paul is keeping a "Nazarite vow." Such a vow involves abstaining for a season from all wine and fruit of the vine, keeping oneself ceremonially clean—especially from touching something unclean as a corpse of a person or animal, and it involves not cutting one's hair for the duration of the vow. The three parts of the vow picture a life of surrender. It has been suggested that abstaining from wine points to the mouth and pictures surrendering our words to God. Not touching things that are unclean is a surrender of the hands, pointing to giving our service over to God. Not cutting one's hair indicates giving the head over to the Lord, surrendering to Him our thoughts as well as our vanities. Paul wants to join God where He is working instead of just trying to do good for God. The key to such a life of received ministry is not commitment, but surrender—letting God have His will and His way in our life.

📖 Look over Acts 18:19–21 and answer the questions below.

Who all would be included in those Paul leaves behind in Ephesus?

What do you see as the link between Paul leaving some behind and the rest of Acts 18:19–21?

How do you interpret the statement of verse 21 in light of what we have studied this week?

We know for certain that Priscilla and Aquila accompany Paul as far as Ephesus, but that does not mean they are the only ones with him. We do not hear of Silas again in the book of Acts. He most likely stays in Corinth or Ephesus. Timothy is next mentioned in Acts 19:22 where we find him in Ephesus, and again in Acts 20:4 where he is sent by Paul back to Macedonia. He may be left behind in Ephesus with Priscilla and Aquila. During his brief stay in Ephesus, Paul reaches out to Jews, and the context seems to suggest that their eagerness for him to stay longer is why he leaves some of the company behind. The phrase, "if God wills" is the key to understanding why Paul leaves in spite of their openness. It is also the key to understanding the whole chapter.

It is obvious that Paul is following what he believes to be God's will when he leaves Corinth and even when he leaves Ephesus. He stayed a year and a half in Corinth even though his early ministry there didn't appear to be very fruitful. He leaves Ephesus after only a brief stay, even though Jews there ask him to minister longer. He is not being led by circumstances. He is being led by the Savior.

📖 Look up the places of Acts 18:22 on your Bible map to get a sense of the rest of Paul's journey, and write your thoughts on how this relates to the previous verses.

"It seems fitting that Luke would finish his record of Paul's second missionary journey with a reference to 'God's will.' That term characterizes the entire expedition."

Acts 18:22 signals the end of the second missionary journey. Paul lands at Caesarea, goes up and greets the church (probably speaking of the mother church at Jerusalem) and then completes his circuit back to Antioch from which his first two missionary journeys began. The return to Antioch, the unwillingness to tarry in Ephesus, and the ending of his vow, all point to God leading him to wrap up this missionary journey. Antioch is still his home base, and he is eager to report on all he has seen the Lord do.

It seems fitting that Luke finishes his record of Paul's second missionary journey with this reference to God's will. That term characterizes the entire expedition. Paul begins with having to adjust to God's will being different than his. He sees the end of his partnership with his long-time mentor, Barnabas. Yet he also sees that God still has partners for him to labor with. God provides Silas at Antioch before he leaves, and Timothy at his first stop in Lystra. Paul experienceds God closing doors at Phrygia and Galatia and Bithynia, but also has God's clear leading to go to Macedonia where he starts many churches. Every step of the way, Paul is being led. He even has a vision that tells him to settle down for a while in Corinth. In the end it seems, God's will is compelling him home. But he leaves open the possibility that at some point in the future, God will return him to Ephesus. That is in fact be the case, and more fruitful ministry will be the result. Paul has been around long enough to taste the dry straw of trying to drum up ministry through his own efforts. His heart passion is to join God in whatever He wants to do. What a good model Paul is for us!

Day 5

For Me to Follow God

I have a buddy who loves to fish, and I have gone out with him a few times on his bass boat. Of course fishing is not a new pastime. It was practiced in Paul's day and long before that. But the methods have changed over the years. I am amazed at how much technology is available to fishermen today. My friend's bass boat has all the latest bells and whistles. It has a powerful outboard motor to get you to your favorite fishing spot quickly, and then a trolling motor to slowly and quietly move the boat around that favorite spot. He even has a GPS locater that uses satellite information to precisely identify spots that have been successful before. The boat is stocked with several different rods baited with scientifically developed lures, so he can quickly switch to another method if one isn't working. He has aerated live wells to keep the fish alive after they are caught. To me though, one of the most impressive pieces of technology is what he calls the "fish finder." It is a high-tech sonar device that not only tells him how deep the water is but can actually spot fish. Such equipment certainly makes it easier than in Paul's day. In addition to the technology though, my friend reads the newspaper reports and talks with his buddies to know what the fish are biting on and where. The point is, he has a lot more success because he uses all that information and technology to help him be strategic and make the most of his time. He's learned how to go where the action is.

"My Father is working until now, and I Myself am working."
(John 5:17)

There is a clear parallel between fishing and ministry. After all, Jesus even drew the link when He invited His disciples to become "fishers of men." Like fishing, ministry takes work, but spiritual fruit is not just a result of working hard. To really be successful, we need to be working in the right place with the right people. This may integrate strategy, and there is certainly nothing wrong with planning and being strategic, but we have to be diligent to stay Spirit-filled and sensitive to the Lord in the process. God in His sovereignty knows the who and the where far better than we do. He knows who is open and seeking, and who isn't, and He is always working in people's lives. In John 5:17 Jesus says, *"My Father is working until now, and I Myself am working."* The key to making a difference in people's lives is looking for where God is working and joining Him in what He is up to. That is why received ministry is not only more successful but also more satisfying. If we let God initiate, He will lead us to the right places and people. If we are simply trying to work hard for God, we may be working where He isn't, and the end result will be frustration. If we will join God where He is working, He will lead us to people who are ready to respond. What is the key? The key to received ministry is seeking God's will, and that is Paul's aim.

As you look around at your friends and acquaintances and classmates or coworkers, what are some evidences of where God is working?

How can you join God where He is working?

To join God where He is working may mean taking some risks and stepping out in faith. But you will never be able to join God where He is working without trust. Without faith, it is impossible to please Him (Hebrews 11:6). What are some steps of faith you need to take to be part of His work?

What are some evidences that you see in your life or in the actions of others around you of striving and trying to make something happen?

"apart from Me you can do nothing" John 15:5

On the night before Jesus is crucified, He tells His disciples, *"apart from Me you can do nothing"* (John 15:5). I'm not sure most of us really believe that. If we really did, then we would be unwilling to do anything apart from Him. Yet people still try. And to be honest, they do carry out some plans and activities apart from Him. They do what appear to be good works and make sacrifices and accomplish goals. But the problem is, unless these are initiated by God, none of these will last, for He only anoints what He initiates. Nothing done by human initiative apart from God is eternal. And if it isn't eternal, it is eternally insignificant. It really does amount to nothing. Paul writes to the Corinthians later on and reminds them of this.

In 1 Corinthians 3:10–15 Paul writes,

> *"According to the grace of God which was given to me, like a wise master builder I laid a foundation, and another is building on it. But each man must be careful how he builds on it. For no man can lay a foundation other than the one which is laid, which is Jesus Christ.*

Now if any man builds on the foundation with gold, silver, precious stones, wood, hay, straw, each man's work will become evident; for the day will show it because it is to be revealed with fire, and the fire itself will test the quality of each man's work. If any man's work which he has built on it remains, he will receive a reward. If any man's work is burned up, he will suffer loss; but he himself will be saved, yet so as through fire."

What Paul teaches is the difference between received ministry and achieved ministry. He tries to show that when we let God initiate, and follow His lead, He actually begins to work through us. He builds with gold, silver, and precious stones. But when we strive and try to do good things for God in our own strength, it builds with wood, hay, and straw. When we stand before the greatest Bema of all, the judgment seat of Christ, all our works will be evaluated.

This judgment Paul speaks of isn't for the sake of salvation, but reward. Even the believer who loses all his works is still saved. Fire will reveal the quality of those works. Sparks will separate the straw from the silver. Only what God has built through us will matter or last. That is why Paul writes to the Philippians concerning his days as a Pharisee, saying, *"I ...count them but rubbish so that I may gain Christ, and may be found in Him, not having a righteousness of my own derived from the Law, but that which is through faith in Christ"* (Philippians 3:8–9).

If we want to join God where He is working, it will involve several key steps. Look at the list below and check the ones you need to deal with.

___ Surrender ourselves to His purposes

___ Let Him be in control of our hearts

___ Seek Him and His will daily

___ Stay sensitive to any signs that we are going the wrong way or doing the wrong thing

___ Trust Him with challenging situations surrender may lead us

As you close out this lesson, deal with any of these that spoke to you, and ask God for His wisdom and direction. If He convicts you of any striving or self-effort, be willing to repent. Express your heart desires in a written prayer to the Lord in the space below...

NOTES

LESSON 6

CHANGING THE WORLD
ACTS 18:23—19:41

I n the Lord's Prayer we are taught to pray, *"Thy kingdom come."* We utter those words as a supplication, but do we really think it will be answered? Oh sure, we know that someday Jesus will come back and set up His kingdom. But do we really expect the world to be reached in our lifetime? I don't know if you have ever thought about what it would take to reach the world. It is a little hard to visualize to put it mildly. The task is so large, and we are so small. We try to make a contribution but rarely ever feel like we have really made a difference. One of the reasons for this, I am convinced, is because we tend to focus on the entire world instead of one part of it. Imagine if you shared Christ with twenty people this year, an ambitious goal for many of us. Yet, when thinking globally, it is hard to fathom twenty people would make a difference at all in reaching the world. After all, statistically speaking in a world of billions of people, twenty doesn't even rate as a statistic. But what if you shared Christ with twenty people in your neighborhood? That would be a different story. What if your church was able to give everyone in your neighborhood the opportunity to trust Christ? What if a dozen families started walking with God who didn't before? How would that affect your neighborhood?

IN THEIR SHOES
Walk Worthy

It is on the second missionary journey that Paul first visits Ephesus briefly about AD 53 (Acts 18:19–21). About two years later, while on his third journey, Paul stays in Ephesus for at least two years and preaches the gospel throughout the whole area (Acts 19:1–20). During this time, he founds the Ephesian church with the core being the fruit from Apollos' ministry here. It is about nine years later, or AD 62, when Paul writes to his children in the faith at Ephesus. Paul is in prison in Rome (Ephesians 3:1; 4:1; 6:20), and he wants to exhort these believers to "walk in a manner worthy" of the Lord (Ephesians 4:1).

I spent four years directing the Campus Crusade for Christ ministry (now called Cru) at the University of Tennessee. The ministry there was quite small when we started—thirty students on a campus of twenty-five thousand. It seemed an impossible task for us to reach the campus for Christ. But we knew we could reach some of it. We began targeting a few key areas to see where God was working.

One of the first outreaches I did was at the largest fraternity. I had contacted many such organizations on campus to see if they would be open to a lecture on a relevant topic. I was hoping to speak to the whole group, but the president only offered to let me address the freshmen pledges. I later found out he did this as part of their hazing. It was a start though. At the end of my program I gave an opportunity to trust Christ and passed out comment cards to get their feedback and interest. Only two students expressed any interest at all in talking further. Doesn't sound like much of a start for changing the campus, let alone the world. We got back together with these two young men and found one was already a Christian, but the other said he wanted to trust Christ. The two of them were willing to meet for a weekly Bible study, and thus began our Greek Life ministry at UT. I was not very encouraged when a month later I ran into the new Christian on campus as I was heading to a prayer meeting. When I asked where he was headed, he replied cheerfully, "I'm going down to the Strip to get drunk." It didn't look like we were making much progress.

Four years later, the scene was quite different. Those two young men had grown into faithful disciples. One was now president of the fraternity, and the other was chaplain. Through our ministry, over three hundred and fifty UT students were in weekly Bible studies, and forty-five of them were from that one fraternity. That year, what was once known as the wildest fraternity on campus had the first ever "dry" retreat (no alcohol) in their history at UT.

Years later, I look back fondly on the small part I played in those guys' lives, and I think warmly of their faithfulness. Even today, I marvel at how the gospel could so radically change an entire community on campus from such small beginnings. As I reflect on Acts 18 and 19, I notice Luke devotes an awful lot of space to the ministry in this one location. I can't help but wonder if the reason is because of his own amazement at witnessing how the gospel so radically changes an entire community. The message of Christ has that power.

DAY 1

THE TEACHING CLARIFIED: ACTS 18:23–28

In 1 Corinthians 3:6 we read, *"I planted, Apollos watered, but God was causing the growth."* Although Paul speaks of the ministry in Corinth, he could just as easily be saying this about Ephesus. Acts 18:19 records Paul's brief ministry in Ephesus at the end of his second missionary journey, reasoning with the Jews in the synagogue. He helps sow the first seeds of the gospel there. But it is Apollos that God brings along behind him to water those seeds. Acts 18:23 marks the beginning of Paul's third missionary journey, but Luke takes a detour a verse later to introduce us to a young man who will become Paul's friend and co-laborer in the mission effort. Apollos bursts onto the scene with more zeal than knowledge, but God uses him, nonetheless. He models for us the fact that God can *work through* us even while He is still *working in* us. As we will see today, we don't need to have arrived spiritually to be able to minister to others. The flip side of that coin, though, is that just because God works through us doesn't mean He is finished with His work in us. As we will also see today, Apollos needs his teaching and doctrine clarified.

📖 Summarize from Acts 18:23 the first stage of Paul's third missionary journey and what that looks like.

We were first introduced to the Galatian region and Phrygia in Acts 16:6. For whatever sovereign reason, Paul was *"forbidden by the Holy Spirit"* to preach the gospel there. But here on his third missionary journey, we find him not only ministering freely, but we also discover that there are already disciples in this area he has yet to touch. Most likely these believers can be traced directly to Pentecost, for in Acts 2:10 we find Phrygia and Pamphylia among the nations represented of people who heard the gospel preached in Jerusalem on the Day of Pentecost. Maybe the reason Paul has been restricted from ministry here in the past is so that he could not take credit for all the churches in the region. He has enough reason to struggle with pride without adding this to his accomplishments.

> *"I planted, Apollos watered, but God was causing the growth."*
> (1 Corinthians 3:6)

📖 Read Acts 18:24–26a and record all that you learn about Apollos and his ministry in Ephesus.

Like Paul, Apollos is apparently a devout Jew, but unlike Paul, he had responded to the ministry of John the Baptist at some point. We don't know much about his early spiritual growth, except that he is *"mighty in the Scriptures"* and has been *"instructed in the way of the Lord."* These paint a portrait of him as a pure-hearted Jew who has long studied the Word of God and looked for Messiah. He has obviously been exposed to Jesus through John, and may even have been among His early followers though not one of the twelve. Being an *"Alexandrian,"* he may only have visited Jerusalem for high holy days though. Alexandria is one of the great cities of the day, being the major seaport of Egypt. In any case, he apparently was not in Jerusalem at the time of the crucifixion and resurrection. This seems obvious from the fact that he is acquainted only with the baptism of John. We also learn here that Apollos is an eloquent spokesman and like Paul, begins his ministry in the local synagogue.

📖 Why do you think Priscilla and Aquila have to take him aside and explain the way of God more accurately (18:26) if he is already *"teaching accurately the things concerning Jesus"* (18:25)?

We know that John the Baptist *"preached the gospel"* (Luke 3:18), although his preaching looked forward to Messiah instead of looking back on His work. John's baptism was a baptism of repentance in preparation for the Messiah. Through John, Apollos would know that Jesus is *"the Son of God"* (John 1:34) and *"the Lamb of God who takes away the sin of the world"* (John 1:29). From John he would learn that Jesus *"is the One who baptizes in the Holy Spirit"* (John 1:33). Obviously, everything Apollos preaches of Jesus is accurate, but his message is incomplete. The whole gospel message is not just that Jesus is God's Son who forgives sin. The message of the gospel is the death, burial, and resurrection of Christ (see 1 Corinthians 15:1–6). In taking him aside, Priscilla and Aquila obviously explain this to him. There is a hint as well that he has been overemphasizing "law" at first, for in verse 27, Luke mentions *"those who had believed through grace."*

📖 Look over Acts 18:27–28 and write the details of Apollos' ministry to Corinth.

> *"After me One is coming who is mightier than I, and I am not fit to stoop down and untie the thong of His sandals. I baptized you with water; but He will baptize you with the Holy Spirit."*

—John the Baptist (Mark 1:7–8)

We are not told when Apollos is called by God to go to Corinth, but it is apparently affirmed by the Ephesian church and endorsed by them. He travels to Corinth with the credential of a good reference from the brethren in Ephesus and is a great blessing to the Corinthian church. The phrase, *"greatly helped,"* is not hyperbole. He is a strong voice for the faith in the face of Jewish opposition. We learn from Acts 18:24 that he is *"mighty in the Scriptures,"* and he uses this biblical knowledge to debate and refute arguments of the Jews and to prove Jesus as Messiah.

You might wonder how God can use a man who doesn't have his doctrinal ducks in a row. But we see in Apollos that God can do a work through us, even as He continues completing what He wants to accomplish in us. Each of us is a work in progress. In 2004 the successful actor, Mel Gibson, was the subject of a good deal of controversy over his film, *The Passion of the Christ.* Unfortunately, not all the controversy came from unbelievers. Though most Christians embraced the film, some Protestants argued that it was too Catholic in elevating excessively the suffering of Christ, while not emphasizing enough the victory of the resurrection. Others of faith see the cinematic work as tainted by anti-Semitic statements attributed to Gibson. Whatever your opinion of the actor and his religious beliefs, I suspect if Christ Himself could be asked His opinion it would be very similar to his response when the disciple John said, *"Teacher, we saw someone casting out demons in Your name, and we tried to prevent him because he was not following us"* (Mark 9:38).

It is easy to throw stones at those who don't see Christ and the truths of Scripture exactly as we do. While there are essential beliefs that cannot be compromised, none of us has a corner on the market of truth this side of glory. Jesus replies to John, *"Do not hinder him, for there is no one who will perform a miracle in My name, and be able soon afterward to speak evil of Me. For he who is not against us is for us"* (Mark 9:39–40). Mel Gibson may not have all of his faith perfectly figured out yet. That is okay, for neither do you or I. But clearly with his film—the most successful independent movie yet, grossing over $600 million—he has used the platform of Hollywood to cause a great many unbelievers to consider Christ.

> *"...he who is not against us is for us"*

— Jesus (Mark 9:40)

Apollos, obviously, is a work in progress. We know from other passages he will go on to become a faithful laborer in the kingdom work of the gospel. Some believe him to be the author of the book of Hebrews. The apostle Paul attests to the fact that he has a fruitful ministry in Corinth. But it is important to remember the link between the ministry

God performs through him and the growth within him that happens at Ephesus. In the days ahead we will see what a mighty work God does in changing that city. As we see in Apollos, He is also using it to send out laborers to other places. Very quickly, what starts as a mission field is becoming a mission sending agent.

DAY 2

THE FRUIT PURIFIED: ACTS 19:1–10

The apostle Paul writes in his letter to the believers at Philippi, *"For I am confident of this very thing, that He who began a good work in you will perfect it until the day of Christ Jesus"* (Philippians 1:6). His confidence is not mere theory. Paul has witnessed over and over that God takes responsibility to complete our spiritual growth. He does work through people—as we quoted Paul earlier in 1 Corinthians 3:6, *"I planted, Apollos watered, but God was causing the growth."* Paul understands from first-hand experience in Ephesus that God will see to it that real fruit is cared for and furthered in its spiritual journey for He is the true source of all growth. Apollos ministers in Ephesus from a pure heart with a zeal for God. He may not yet understand everything about the Christian life, but God still uses him to get some spiritual activity going in Ephesus. But as we will see today, God leads Paul there to continue that work and to add what is lacking in what these believers have been taught by Apollos. They understand the message of John the Baptist and have a heart to respond in repentance. God honors that heart and makes sure they hear the rest of the story.

📖 Read Acts 19:1–3 and answer the questions that follow.

How does Luke reference the people Paul encounters at Ephesus?

What do you see implied in Paul's statement in verse 2 and their response?

Looking at the context of Acts 18:23–28, what is the likely source of these disciples' beliefs?

DOCTRINE
Tongues in Acts

Here in Acts 19 we find the final reference in the book to the act of speaking in tongues. There appear to be some noteworthy patterns to observe from this historical record in Acts. First, each time tongues are mentioned (Acts 2:4; 10:46; 19:6), it is apparent that everyone participates. Second, there is no indication that the practice continues with these groups beyond the first instance. Third, each occurrence is with a different group as regards the gospel. The first instance is with those first Jews who follow Christ. The second instance is with the first converts among the Gentiles. The third instance is with these Old Testament believers. Although not specifically mentioned, there is evidence to suggest a similar occurrence in Acts 8 with the first believers from among the Samaritans. Each group seems to experience their own "Pentecost" as proof of their acceptance into the body of Christ. In each of these cases an apostle is present to verify and validate the genuineness of their faith.

It should catch your eye that Luke refers to this group of people Paul encounters as *"disciples."* The Greek term and the context make it clear that these are followers of Jesus. The question Paul asks about when they received the Holy Spirit is an important one with theological ramifications. First, his line of inquiry makes it clear he perceives they have believed what message they have heard. Second, implied in the question is Paul's theological expectation that to receive the Holy Spirit is what would normally happen when one responds to the gospel.

Though their faith in what they have heard of Jesus is genuine, their response makes it clear that they have not yet heard all the message of the gospel. They have been taught of John's baptism of repentance and probably understand as much as we see revealed of Jesus in the Gospels before His death. It is not mere coincidence that at the end of the previous chapter, Luke has just recorded Apollos' ministry to Ephesus before Paul gets here. We know from chapter 18 that he was acquainted only with the baptism of John at that point, and had need of instruction and clarification from Priscilla and Aquila. Most likely these are people who heard Apollos before Priscilla and Aquila clarified his understanding of the gospel message, and they responded in faith to his partial explanation of Jesus.

How does Paul handle the incomplete faith of these he meets in Ephesus (19:4–7)?

When Paul recognizes that these have a sincere heart for the Lord, but an incomplete understanding of the gospel, he takes them from where they are to where they need to be. He emphasizes the fact that repentance is a two-sided coin. It is a turning away from one thing and then a turning to another. These people have turned from their sins and are ready to turn to Jesus. When their belief is complete, they experience their own version of Pentecost. While this crowd is small—only a dozen men—from this beginning will come a significant church.

 Briefly summarize what you see of Paul's ministry approach in Acts 19:8–10.

We have already learned that Paul's custom is to give Jews the first opportunity to respond to the gospel message, and, as usual, we find Paul starting out at the local synagogue. The fact that he spends three months there indicates there are many who respond favorably. But there are some who reject the message as well. After harvesting the fruit there, he continues by making the school of Tyrannus his base of operation. It is possible, if not likely, that Tyrannus becomes one of his converts. In verse 10, Luke gives us a summary statement and tells us that *"all who lived in Asia heard the word of the Lord, both Jews and Greeks."* In the New Testament, this does not refer to the whole continent of Asia, which would include China, but rather, to the western portion—what we normally reference as Asia Minor. The term is also sometimes used in an even narrower way to denote specifically the region of Ionia, of which Ephesus is the capital. Most likely that is the area Luke is indicating here.

DID YOU KNOW?
The School of Tyrannus

Tyrannus was a Greek rhetorician in Ephesus who apparently owned the meeting hall in Ephesus used by Paul. His name means "the tyrant" and may have been a nickname given him by his students. The best historical information seems to indicate that Paul began using the hall each day at 11:00 AM, as soon as Tyrannus stopped his lectures for the day, and then used the hall during the early afternoons when many were observing mid-day siesta. While some suggest that Tyrannus was a convert, we cannot say that for certain.

The spiritual climate of Ephesus is beginning to change. Many people move from unexposed to undecided and then make their decision. Though some ultimately reject Christ, many believe. This change is a process, and Luke emphasizes that it takes time, but verse 10 makes it clear that Paul is successful. He saturates the area with the gospel message. It cannot be emphasized enough the importance of what Luke mentions here and what it says to us. Our job is not to make people believe, but to give them the opportunity to do so. What Luke considers as success is that everyone hears the word of the Lord. The

Great Commission may not have been fulfilled worldwide at this point, but it has been fulfilled in this area. Though the gospel has been shared freely in many places, this is the first place Luke identifies as being saturated with the gospel. Maybe that is another reason he devotes so much time and space to Paul's ministry here. If we are faithful to give people opportunity and to saturate a particular area with the gospel, we will see God change people and communities.

DAY 3

THE MESSAGE MAGNIFIED: ACTS 19:11–22

The apostle Paul writes to the Roman church, *"I am not ashamed of the gospel, for it is the power of God for salvation to everyone who believes, to the Jew first and also to the Greek"* (Romans 1:16). Paul believes that. This explains why he always begins his ministry in a town at the local synagogue—to give Jews the first chance to respond. But it also explains the focus of his trust. He doesn't see himself as having to convince anyone to respond through emotional appeals or arm-twisting. That would be trusting in himself to change people. He recognizes that the message itself has power—the *"power of God."* All he has to do is to trust that life-changing power and unleash it by sharing the message. He certainly does that. As we will see today, God demonstrates His power in many ways at Ephesus, but none greater than by changing the lives of these who respond to the gospel. The message is being validated by the difference it makes in individual lives.

📖 Look at Acts 19:11–12.

What sort of activity is God doing through Paul?

How does that relate to reaching this particular community for Christ?

Luke is a very precise writer. He chooses his words carefully. When he states that God is *"performing extraordinary miracles"* through Paul, he is giving an added emphasis. Without careful scrutiny we might misread *"extraordinary"* and *"miracles"* as saying the same thing. Actually, what Luke is saying is that, even among miracles, what God is doing at Ephesus is unusual. The example he gives of the *"handkerchiefs"* serves to show the extremes of God's working here. We know from the bonfire mentioned later in the chapter that magic and occultism was widespread in Ephesus. It is noteworthy that the only other time Acts mentions miracles happening to a greater degree is in Samaria in the context of Simon the magician (Acts 8:9–13) who astonished people with his magic. There seems to be a principle here. When supernatural occult practices abound, God manifests His power to a greater degree.

DOCTRINE
Handkerchiefs

How do we handle examples of ministry such as we see mentioned here in Acts 19, of God working through handkerchiefs carried from Paul? It is important to hold such unique ministry up against Scripture as a whole. That this happens is evidence of what God is able to do. That this is the only time Scripture records it happening tells us that it is not normal ministry. We must use great caution in trying to repeat this today. Luke tells us that this is out of the ordinary. We must not dismiss the power of God because it is uncommon, but we must not demand it either. Such events are at God's discretion, not ours.

One might ask, "Why doesn't God always show His power in overwhelming displays of signs and wonders?" It is a valid question. Certainly, the Scriptures show that He is able. Yet the biblical record clearly reflects that this is more the exception than the rule. We must remember that what pleases God is faith (Hebrews 11:6). If people only believe because of overwhelming proof, then their belief is based on sight instead of faith. But where people are exposed to a lot of supernatural activity that is demonic in origin, God demonstrates that His power is greatest.

Read Acts 19:13–17 and write your observations on these events and how they serve to authenticate the message of Christ.

It is interesting that these people identified as *"Jewish exorcists"* are even trying to use the name of Jesus. They aren't submitting themselves to Christ, but they are, by their actions, acknowledging the power of His name as well as of Paul's ministry. The wording of verse 13 seems to indicate that the sons of Sceva are not the only ones employing this tactic in their ministry. What the demon says to them though is significant. He acknowledges Jesus which we would expect, but also that he knows Paul. Even the demonic realm is lending credibility to Paul's message. The scene is both humorous and terrifying. The demon-possessed man overpowers the seven exorcists and sends them running wounded, without their clothes, and without finishing the job. God uses the news of this event, which spreads throughout the city, to further authenticate the message of Jesus and the messenger, Paul.

📖 Consider Acts 19:18–20 and record the results you see here of the gospel taking root in people's lives.

_____

_____

_____

"Therefore if anyone is in Christ, he is a new creature;
the old things passed away; behold, new things have come."
(2 Corinthians 5:17)

In 2 Corinthians 5:17 Paul writes, *"if anyone is in Christ, he is a new creature; the old things passed away; behold, new things have come."* One of the surest evidences of genuine salvation is a changed life. When Christ comes into our lives, He changes our desires and gives us the power to say no to habits that controlled us before. We see this principle in action at Ephesus. These who come to Christ are confessing their sinful practices and turning from them. At some point, moved by change in their hearts that Christ has wrought, believers host a public bonfire and destroy their collections of occultist books. Because of the great value of these books, by burning them rather than selling them, the church makes a powerful statement of belief with their actions. The statement of verse twenty provides us with a fitting summary of the workings of God at Ephesus: *"So the word of the Lord was growing mightily and prevailing."* Being in the imperfect tense in Greek, it makes it clear that the gospel makes ongoing progress in Ephesus—making a greater and greater impact on the community.

📖 Look over Acts 19:21–22 and answer the questions that follow.

What do you think are the *"these things"* that Luke speaks of in verse 21?

_____

_____

What does the wording of this verse say about Paul's method of decision-making?

_____

_____

_____

_____

Why do you suppose Paul sends Timothy and Erastus ahead to Macedonia?

_____

_____

_____

_____

The term _"these things"_ Luke mentions in Acts 19:21 seems to speak of the different ministry events he records of Paul's time in Ephesus. Yet there is also a hint in the word _"finished"_ of the fact that the job is done at Ephesus. The city has been saturated with the gospel. Everyone who wants to trust Christ has been given the opportunity. In this one city, the Great Commission has been fulfilled. It is clear from Luke's saying that Paul _"purposed in the spirit"_ that his travel plans are based on the leading of God. Although many translations do not capitalize the word _"spirit"_ here, the most logical conclusion is that it refers to the Holy Spirit, and not simply to Paul's spirit. It appears in the Greek manuscripts with the definite article ("THE spirit") instead of the personal pronoun ("his spirit"). Although he senses the need to stay a while longer in the region of Asia, the area surrounding Ephesus, he wants his co-laborers to go on ahead and check on the churches before he gets there.

We ought to remind ourselves of what we learn from Luke here. God is able to take care of Himself. He is more than capable of causing a respect for the gospel. He causes the message of Christ to be taken seriously in Ephesus. Another way of translating verse 20 is _"according to the power of the Lord the word was growing."_ The way of salvation is made more credible by the miracles God performs in their midst through Paul. The reputation of the gospel is elevated by the fact that even the unbelieving are acknowledging the power of Jesus' name, and by the contrast of others' inability to deal with demons the way Paul does. The good news is authenticated by the change it makes in the lives of those who embrace it. As we are burdened for the place and time in which we live, we need to simply speak the truth of Christ and trust God to cause the seed of this message to take root and bear fruit.

THE FAITH VILIFIED: ACTS 19:23–41

The world doesn't change without a fight. I've seen that proven over and over again in many different places. I remember speaking with a friend of mine a few years ago who was trying to make a difference on a particular college campus. He and his Christian group had taken out ads in the school newspaper that presented the gospel and took a stand on some issues. They had brought in a powerful speaker who was dying of AIDS to give his testimony of faith in Christ at a campus outreach. There were many responding positively, but there was also beginning to be much opposition. He was sharing with me about some of his struggles as the leader of the group and the target of much of the opposition. I was concerned that he might be getting discouraged, but he passed along a Scripture verse that he had taken much comfort from. He said the Lord really ministered to him through Jesus' words in Luke 6:26, *"Woe to you when all men speak well of you, for their fathers used to treat the false prophets in the same way."* In other words, if everyone likes your message then it must be ear-tickling instead of truth. As we will see today, Ephesus is not changed without opposition.

DOCTRINE
Persecution

While none of us wants to be persecuted, the presence of persecution is evidence that we are making a difference and should not discourage us from action. Jesus said that you are *"blessed"* when *"people insult you and persecute you, and say all kinds of evil against you because of Me"* (Matthew 5:11). While we may not feel blessed in such circumstances, Jesus goes on to make two points on why we should not see this as a negative. First, we can know that while ministry may be bringing opposition now, it will bring great reward in heaven. Second, He reminds that we are in good company for such was the response to the prophets of old. We have become identified with God.

Summarize what you learn in Acts 19:23–27 about the basis of the trouble that arises in Ephesus.

About the time Paul begins to expand his work from Ephesus into the whole province of Asia where Ephesus lies (western Asia Minor), Luke tells us that a significant *"disturbance"* arises concerning the Christian faith. At the bottom of the uproar is a man named Demetrius, whose business revolves around the pagan worship of the idol, Artemis. Apparently, he has noticed a significant drop in sales since the gospel began to take hold in Ephesus, for he himself says, *"this Paul has persuaded and turned away a considerable number of people."* While Demetrius appeals to concern for the worship of the goddess Artemis, it is clear that his real motive is money. He mentions in verse 25 that their prosperity depends on this trade, and again in verse 27 that there is a danger of their trade being affected.

 Examine Acts 19:28–34 and record the details of the riot Demetrius is able to start.

DID YOU KNOW?
Artemis

The temple of Artemis (also known as "Diana") in Ephesus, supported on one hundred massive columns, was one of the Seven Wonders of the ancient world. The twin sister of the Greek god Apollo, Artemis was worshiped as the goddess of hunting. Pilgrims would flock to the city, especially each spring during her annual festival, and added much to the local economy. The shrines that Demetrius and his friends made were left at the temple as offerings or taken home as souvenirs.

The words of Demetrius enflame his fellow craftsmen, and the uproar spreads into the whole city. Apparently, a riot breaks out and two of Paul's companions are dragged into the public meeting hall. When Paul desires to go in, the brethren wisely intervene for the sake of his safety. It is clear from the pandemonium that the action is not organized, but rather, a scene of chaos. Most present don't even know the reason they have assembled. But when the Jews put forward Alexander to explain that they have nothing to do with Paul, the crowd rallies around their goddess, Artemis, and cheer for her for about two hours.

 Consider the resolution of the riot in Acts 19:35–41 and write out your observations.

At some point in the melee, a local clerk official steps in and subdues the crowd by calling for calm and for the concerns to be redirected to the judicial system. The term *"town clerk"* is the Greek word used in the Gospels of a "scribe." It refers to a recorder and reader of official documents and is usually in close association with those in authority but carries no official authority of its own. He warns that there is a danger of the whole crowd being accused of a riot from the *"disorderly gathering"* by those with ultimate authority in Ephesus. That all assembled seem to have respect for the man is reflected in the fact that he is able to calm the situation and dismiss the crowd.

Apparently, that is the end of the resistance to the gospel in Ephesus. Acts 20:1 indicates that the uproar ceases and then Paul decides it is time to depart for his planned itinerary. Although it must have been a troublesome scene, there is no real harm done. Luke seems to include this account to balance the many positive things that have happened in this one place. To give an accurate view of ministry, we must acknowledge that there will be opposition. It should be expected and mustn't be interpreted to mean God isn't working. In fact, it is one of the evidences of God being at work in our midst. We have consistently seen throughout the book of Acts that the gospel message polarizes. In most of Luke's accounts while some respond positively, there are also those who don't. We should take comfort in knowing that if not everyone speaks well of us, it is proof that our message is requiring people to make a decision about the Lord. From those who refuse to submit to the Lord we can expect opposition.

Day 5

For Me to Follow God

The apostle Paul ministers in many different places and sees God work mightily. But the city of Ephesus will hold a special place in his heart. The letter he writes to them will become one of the most practical and powerful books of the New Testament. Years later as his life nears an end while imprisoned in Rome and while his favorite disciple Timothy is leading the church in Ephesus, Paul writes two letters of advice to the Ephesians that also become books of the Bible. He is able to look back on his time there with fondness and remember a fruitful ministry with remarkable impact. He is able to see the gospel radically change an entire community. Luke devotes much time and space in the Acts of the Apostles to the ministry in Ephesus—more than just about any other location. It seems the reason is that Ephesus illustrates in graphic fashion the ability for the gospel to change not only individual lives but entire communities as well. We need to see this to help us trust God to do the same thing in our own communities.

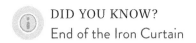
In June of 1989, Poland held free elections for the first time since becoming communist after World War II. They became the first country in the so called "Iron Curtain" countries of the Warsaw Pact to switch to a democracy. One by one, the other countries of Eastern Europe followed suit, and moved toward freedom. Poland was one of the first three countries from this region to be added to NATO, and in May of 2004 were welcomed as full members of the European Union. While the Solidarity Trade Unions provided much of the leverage, many did not realize that it was the Catholic Church in Poland which undergirded much of the resistance to communism.

For me personally, this concept has been so helpful. I used to pray for the Great Commission to be fulfilled in our lifetime but struggled with believing it could be so. But in 1986, I joined with a group of campus ministries in Kentucky and Tennessee to form a partnership with collegiate ministries operating covertly in the major cities of communist Poland. For nearly a decade we supported those ministries with prayer, finances, training, and manpower. I made numerous trips myself. In 1989 when Poland became the first domino in the fall of the "Iron Curtain", these ministries were well-established and poised to take advantage of the new freedom to share the gospel. I witnessed the ministry grow and flourish to the point when the American missionaries could move on to other places, as hundreds of Poles took their places as full-time Christian workers and filled the leadership roles of the movement. One of the most rewarding milestones was when we began to see Poland send some of these workers out to reach neighboring countries like Belarus, Ukraine, and Russia. The mission field had become the missionary sender. It was hard for me to trust God for the world, but it became easier when I started asking him for one country. In the years since that relationship began, I have seen what was originally just a vision become reality, and it has increased my faith to trust God it can happen all over the world.

How would you rate your own personal vision for seeing the world reached for Christ?

UNBELIEF   1   2   3   4   5   6   7   FAITH

What are some practical things you learned this week that can help you progress in this area?

In one of his sermons (#0098) Charles Spurgeon related this story:

> During the troubled times of Scotland, when the Popish court and aristocracy were arming themselves to suppress the Reformation in that land, and the cause of Protestant Christianity was in imminent peril, late on a certain night John Knox was seen to leave his study, and to pass from the house down into an enclosure to the rear of it. He was followed by a friend, when, after a few moments of silence, his voice was heard as if in prayer. In another moment the accents deepened into intelligible words, and the earnest petition went up from his struggling soul to heaven, "O Lord, give me Scotland, or I die!" Then a pause of hushed stillness, when again the petition broke forth, "O Lord, give me Scotland, or I die!" Once more all was voiceless and noiseless, when, with a yet intenser pathos the thrice-repeated intercession struggled forth, "O Lord, give me Scotland, or I die!" And God gave him Scotland, in spite of Mary and her Cardinal Beatoun; a land and a church of noble loyalty to Christ and his crown.

Knox held such zeal for this country that the salvation of the Scots came to be the most important thing to him, and God honored that heart. What is the one particular nation or nations on which your heart for the world can be focused?

Consider the list below and check some application points to help your heart and passion for that nation grow...

___ Set aside a regular time to pray for the work of God in that nation.

___ Research that country and learn more about the beliefs and needs of its people.

___ Find a missionary who serves in that country that you can build a relationship with.

___ Take a short-term trip to that country to see first-hand the work of God there.

___ Support a national Christian worker there.

___ Stay in a relationship with that nation so that you can see the progress of the gospel over time.

___ Other: ___

Is there a local area or community to which you can make a similar commitment?

For me, the partnership with Poland grew into a passion for the whole region of Eastern Europe. As a result of staying in that relationship, I have been blessed to witness the world changing. Through the process I have learned some important principles about ministry. One is the necessity of a target on which to focus. For years my heart for evangelism was focused on the whole world, but the application was random, and I never had any sense of progress. Through that focus becoming more specific, the goal has become more tangible, the results more encouraging, and its fulfillment more attainable. That principle has spilled over into my ministry here at home. I have learned that focusing my service in one area or a few has greater impact than spreading myself too thin.

IN THEIR SHOES
Keys to Successful Ministry

➤ Having a specific, manageable target

➤ Building to "critical mass" before moving on

A related principle I have observed is the power of "critical mass." For me, the term originates from my physics classes in college where I first understood nuclear fission. The atomic activity of uranium or plutonium is an ongoing reality, but it is not until that activity is concentrated together that a physical phenomenon occurs where the reactions become self-sustaining. We call this stage "critical mass." At this point, instead of needing energy added, the process is continued through its own energy and in fact, it begins to have an excess of energy. This is a simplistic explanation of the goal of a nuclear power plant. But this concept also holds true in ministry.

When our ministry is focused in a concentrated area and the job is done well and thoroughly, it will eventually get to the point that it takes on a life of its own. Instead of needing our energy, it will become self-sustaining and will even have power to share with other areas. I have seen this theory become reality in college dorms and local communities, just as I have witnessed it in countries. Sadly, most ministries never see this dynamic because they are so scattered and spread thin that the progress they see is barely noticeable and the job never really seems to be completed anywhere. I have seen this principle hold true in many different areas, but also in issues. For example, how many churches focus on spiritual gifts long enough for the concept to be understood well enough for people to act on it? Or how many teach three or four different things at the same time through the sermon, Sunday school lesson, prayer meeting, and training classes? Think how the impact would change if all of those were centered on the same theme for a season.

How do the principles of targeted ministry and critical mass relate to you and your church or ministry?

Are there any changes that need to be made?

Why not cement what you are learning by closing out this week's lesson with a written prayer to the Lord in the space below...

NOTES

LESSON 7

PASSING THE TORCH
ACTS 20

Have you ever wondered why Jesus' earthly ministry only lasted three years? Humanly speaking, it doesn't really make a lot of sense. If one wants to change the world, shouldn't they work as hard as they can for as long as they can? Yet God's ways are higher than our ways. Jesus operated from a perfectly planned strategy. He always listened to the Father's leading, and He always made the most of His time. Everything He did was intentional—including leaving. You can roughly divide the three years of Jesus' work in the lives of His disciples into three levels of challenge and instruction. It was about the time of the Passover when Jesus began His public ministry.

DID YOU KNOW?
Four Callings

There are four distinct callings Jesus gave His disciples that correspond to four different phases of His ministry in their lives...

"Come and See" – the Observation Phase
"Follow Me" – The Apprentice Phase
"Take up your Cross" – The Enlistment Phase
"Abide in Me" – the Deployment Phase

The first year—and the first level of Jesus' ministry—was what I call the observation phase. His invitation to those disciples of John who would end up following Him was *"come and see"* (John 1:39, 46), and that phrase really captures what that first year was all about. He invited twelve men into His life. They were with Him at the wedding in Cana when He turned water into wine, and they were with Him when He confronted the moneychangers in the Temple. But for that first season, watching was about all they did. He didn't require much of them other than to see what He was about. After about ten months, He sent them back home to consider what they had seen. When Jesus came up to Peter on the beach at Galilee and said, *"Follow Me"* (Mark 1:17, 2:14), it was actually His second invitation and signaled the second phase of His ministry. It occurred *"after John had been taken into custody"* (Mark 1:14) around the second Passover and was roughly a year after He first met these men. This is what I call the apprentice phase. During this second year, Jesus began to give the disciples training and manageable tasks. He never asked them to do something He had not modeled for them, but neither would He let them stay in the comfort of the nest. As their wings grew, He made them put them to use. During that year, He sent the disciples out by twos to witness. He let them face the challenge of the demon possessed. He gave them work to do and feedback on how they did it. He was molding them into leaders.

But as the third Passover approached, Jesus' ministry took a significant change. He began teaching of the cross, and many from the crowds stopped following Him. He challenged His disciples to each *"take up his cross"* (Luke 9:23) and follow Him. I call this the enlistment phase. At this point He shared with them deeper truths that they weren't ready for in the beginning. He warned them of the dangers of the false spirituality of the Pharisees, and He prepared them for the next step. The night before His arrest, as he celebrated that fourth Passover with His men, Jesus gave them conflicting instructions. He said, *"Abide in Me"* (John 15:1) and yet told them He was going away. He was preparing them for something they could not fully grasp yet. It is the last—the unseen phase—of Jesus' ministry. I call it the deployment phase. He recognized that for them to become the leaders they had been selected and trained to be, He needed to get out of the way. For them to bloom, He must step to the side and bring them out of the shadows. It was time to pass the torch. As we will see this week, God has a plan for Paul to step aside as well.

DAY 1

GOODBYE TO EPHESUS, MACEDONIA, AND GREECE: ACTS 20:1–5

It is ironic, but apart from Jesus leaving for heaven, Peter and the other disciples never become the leaders we see in Acts. Their faith cannot keep growing while they walk by sight. The book of Acts could not be what it is without the ascension of Jesus. The apostle Paul also becomes a mighty leader in the early church and like Jesus, has many disciples he trains and prepares for leadership. And like Jesus, he too has to eventually step aside for these men to be all that God wants them to be. Acts 20 records much of Paul's long goodbye. We see him make a quick journey to many of the churches he founded. For most, whether they recognize it or not, this is the last time they will see Paul on earth. He even says as much to the Ephesian elders. In Acts and in other historical accounts, we have no record of Paul returning to any of these places again that he visits in the chapter. It is his swan song—his farewell tour. The chapter is filled with relationship and tears. But even this is a necessary part of the plan of God for the church. And we must remind ourselves that Paul will be reunited with all of them in heaven.

In Acts and in other historical accounts, we have no record
of Paul returning to any of these places again that he visits in
chapter 20.

📖 Read Acts 20:1.

Looking back to chapter 19, what is the uproar verse 1 speaks of?

What disciples would we expect are involved in this goodbye?

How does Paul say goodbye?

> "Any place that does not receive you or listen to you, as you go out
> from there, shake the dust off the soles of your feet for a testimony
> against them" (Mark 6:11)

In chapter 19, we looked at length at an event at the end of Paul's ministry in the area of Ephesus—the boiling over of persecution from those of another religion—the worship of the Roman goddess, Artemis. Of course, we also saw that the real object of worship for those opposing Paul was money, and the loss of business was behind the riot that ensued. Once the dust settles, Paul calls the disciples—presumably not just those now following the Lord in Ephesus, but all who have come to Christ in the region. Luke tells us Paul sends for *"the disciples."* We learned from Acts 19:22 that Paul left the city of Ephesus and began ministering in the region of Asia that surrounds it. We know that he wanted to address the rioters, but for his own safety, the disciples prevented him. It is unclear if Paul is in or out of the city, but Luke's wording makes it sound as if he has the disciples come to him instead of him going back into Ephesus. We are told he exhorts them. He challenges them and encourages them in their faith. The picture is almost that of a coach getting ready to send his players out onto the field or court. Paul has been a player in Ephesus, but now he is coaching others in the contest.

At this point it is worth addressing the fact that Paul leaves town as soon as persecution surfaces. As we have seen in the previous missionary journeys this fits a pattern of leaving before things get out of control.

It would be wrong to conclude that leaving is somehow cowardly. To begin with, we know from Acts 19:21 that Paul senses God's leading to leave before the riot ever breaks out. But an additional point is in order. Jesus instructs in Matthew 10:23, *"But whenever they persecute you in one city, flee to the next; for truly I say to you, you will not finish going through the cities of Israel until the Son of Man comes."* There are several sound reasons for this advice. First, they were not just instructed to leave, but Jesus taught, *"Any place that does not receive you or listen to you, as you go out from there, shake the dust off the soles of your feet for a testimony against them"* (Mark 6:11). Paul and Barnabas did that very thing when they left Pisidian Antioch over persecution (Acts 13:51). To leave was a physical testimony against those who rejected the message.

Second, to leave was a safeguard for those who had accepted the message. Often the persecution becomes focused on the *messenger* more than the *message*. Once a teacher like Paul leaves town, the persecution dies down even though a church has been established. Such was Paul's experience in Berea (see Acts 17:13–14).

In Corinth, God gave a specific vision to Paul, instructing him to stay when the persecution started (Acts 18:9–10). This was necessary because the normal plan would have been for him to leave at that point.

Third, persecution breaking out is a sign that people have made decisions regarding Christ. It gives evidence that the initial job is done and that it is time to move on to another unreached place.

Finally, to leave is inevitable. The question is not "if" but "when." As much as we would like the security and comfort of leaders over us, at some point they become a hindrance to our own maturing and create dependence instead of independence. Paul cannot pastor the church in every one of these towns. Leaders have to be raised up, and then allowed to lead. As Paul departs, he exhorts. He coaches and encourages those who will do the job long after he is gone.

 WORD STUDY
Exhortation

The Greek word translated "exhortation" (*paraklesis*) is derived from two Greek words, para (to the side of) and kaleo (to call). It has the idea of coming alongside someone for comfort, encouragement, instruction and/or challenge. Exhortation is closely related to teaching in that it focuses on truth, yet emphasizes not just information, but the practical application of that knowledge.

📖 What churches are likely represented in the district of Macedonia (20:2), and how does Paul leave them?

Paul planted many churches with Barnabas on the first missionary journey, but the churches of Macedonia must have held a special place in his heart. They were the first he planted by himself, having been directed to them by a vision from the Lord on the second missionary journey. They were also the first Europeans to come to Christ. The likely participants included at least the churches of Phillipi, Thessalonica, and Berea. As with the believers in Ephesus and Asia, Paul gives them *"much exhortation."* We don't use the term *"exhortation"* much today, but the basic idea is the giving of practical advice, and one gets the sense that this is not just general exhortation. Paul knows he is passing the torch of leadership, and most likely is giving instruction to the new leaders for the days ahead.

📖 Look over Acts 20:3–5.

What churches would Paul likely have visited in Greece?

Write down what you learn about the details of Paul's departure from Greece and who accompanies him.

When Luke tells us Paul spends three months in Greece, we can assume that this mainly means Corinth. It makes sense that his goodbye there is long, for so too was his ministry there. It is interesting that God uses a plot formed against him to redirect Paul's travel plans and he actually has the chance to spend a little more time in Macedonia. I especially appreciate the list we find in verse 4 of the people who travel with Paul. In them we see tangible evidence of the impact Paul made in each of these cities. But we also get a sense of the love and affection these men have for their spiritual leader that they want to accompany him. This is yet another evidence that all realize their time with Paul is coming to an end.

Luke is the master of detail, but he doesn't waste words or information. He is making a point when he tells us where Paul's traveling companions are from. Most likely they represent some of the key leadership in these churches Paul labored to raise up. Though

Paul tarries a few places (probably for lingering, tearful goodbyes), the group goes ahead to Troas. Reading between the lines, this appears to be a formal delegation, escorting Paul not so much for safety, but out of love. It may also be seen as a sort of traveling seminary as Paul adds to the faith and character of these emerging leaders. Everything we see in this chapter tells us this isn't just another trip for Paul, the world traveler.

Day 2

The Farewell Service at Troas: Acts 20:6-12

In Romans 13:7 the apostle Paul writes, *"Render to all what is due them…honor to whom honor."* It is worth noting that Paul writes these words during his three months in Greece just before this visit to Troas. As we will see today, this time—and even this whole trip—seems to be a time when the churches are able to reflect on all they owe Paul and to express some of their appreciation. As is the case with Paul, often the labors of leaders are most appreciated after they are done. It is also a time for Paul to give instruction and exhortation one last time to people he values and worries over like a parent. It is interesting that Paul's last message in Troas appears to be his longest of record, but no one seems to mind. Today we want to examine the farewell service of Paul in Troas.

After looking at Paul's trip on your Bible map, write down your observations on the details of Acts 20:6.

When a plot on his life redirects Paul back through Macedonia, he apparently stays in Philippi to observe the Passover. For Christians this celebration has taken on added significance since it is also the anniversary of Jesus' death and resurrection. It is a time to rejoice in the forgiveness of sins Christ bought. The five days it takes to get from Philippi to Troas give us a sense of how much time is spent in travel for Paul to get from one place to another.

As you consider Acts 20:7 make note of what this reveals about the early church gatherings.

WORD STUDY
Gathered Together

When Luke says in Acts 20:7 that the disciples are *"gathered together,"* the Greek word here (*sunago*) is where the term "synagogue" is derived. It means "to assemble as one" and emphasizes the common belief of those gathered. This is not just a social gathering or a group of people who happen to be at the same place at the same time, but the term in the Christian context usually means a church gathering.

While it is easy to miss on first reading, Luke makes a point of the fact that the believers in Troas gather together *"on the first day of the week."* The Jewish Sabbath was Saturday. Since most of the early believers are Jews who see faith in Christ as the completion of Judaism rather than a separate religion, they continue to worship with their Jewish friends on the Sabbath at the Temple in Jerusalem or local synagogue. But early on in church history, Sunday becomes an additional day to gather for those who identify with Christ, since it was on that day of the week that He rose from the dead. They likely gathered in the evening, as Sunday would not be a common day off from work as it is in modern Western culture. Sunday worship consisted of a teaching message, observance of the Lord's Supper ("to break bread"), and probably some singing as well. While there is not a cultural expectation of a twenty or thirty-minute message, Paul's teaching on this occasion seems unusually long. This is fitting, however, in the context of him saying goodbye. Even though he only mentions to the Ephesians that this will be their last time to see him, it seems that all of the churches he visits grasp that reality.

📖 Look over Acts 20:8–10 and summarize the circumstances of the young man's fall from the window.

To fully appreciate Luke's narrative here, we need to place ourselves in their culture. The "many lamps" he mentions would be oil lamps whose flames no doubt, along with the many people in the room, result in a decreased oxygen level in the room. Being after the Passover (see 20:6), it would be late spring and warm weather. In these days before air conditioning, an open window is an attractive place to sit. Add to all these factors a lengthy lecture and a late hour, and it is not surprising that the young man falls asleep. Unfortunately, he also falls three stories to the ground below and is apparently killed by the fall. The implication of Paul falling on him and embracing him is that Paul raises him back to life.

📖 Read Acts 20:11–12 and identify from the details of the text what the rest of the evening looks like.

ⓘ DID YOU KNOW?
   Troas

The seaport town of Troas holds a special place in Paul's heart and in church history. It is here on the second missionary journey that Paul receives the "Macedonian Vision" (Acts 16:8–11), redirecting him from Asia into the region of Macedonia, which proves to be some of the most fruitful ministry of his life. It is this directional change that brings the gospel into Europe, and establishes the churches of Philippi, Thessalonica, Berea and Corinth.

The boy's fall from the window takes place about midnight, according to Acts 20:7. After taking care of him, Paul and the others go back upstairs to observe communion, and then Paul continues his ministry with them the rest of the night. While most of us are not used to a church service that would last that long, we must remember that this is not a normal service but rather, a special time with a man God has used greatly in their lives, and as we have said before, probably their last chance to visit with him. Luke tells us that they are *"greatly comforted."* This is not only because the boy has been raised but is also because of Paul's ministry to each of them.

Think for a moment of the person God has used in your spiritual life more than any other. If there is one particular person who fits that description, imagine if you have an evening to visit with that person, and you know it will be your last occasion together. You would want to make that time last as long as you can. It is easy to identify with these believers as they say goodbye to their beloved Paul.

DAY 3

REMEMBERING THE PAST WITH THE EPHESIAN ELDERS: ACTS 20:13–27

Carl Sandburg in his epic biography of Abraham Lincoln, at the end of it, writes that "a tree is best measured after it has fallen." In a tangible sense it is usually not until the end of a project or work that we can take stock and really assess what all has been accomplished. Although he doesn't know everything that is ahead of him, a season of Paul's life is coming to a close, and he is beginning to realize that. This is the end of his missionary journeys in the structured sense. He still has many travels ahead, and he will eventually get to Rome and minister there for a couple of years—but as a prisoner rather than simply a traveling preacher. Luke's narrative stops with his imprisonment and doesn't answer our questions about what happens after that. Some speculate that between his first and his final imprisonment, he travels onward to Spain, though there is no confirmation of that theory. We do have a sense though that his ministry in this part of the world is coming to a close. He will make spiritual investments from a distance through his letters, but not through visits. He must be nostalgic as he reflects back on the many adventures he has experienced and challenges he has faced. There must be some joy and pride at seeing the churches grow and progress. As we will see today, this is a season of reflection and remembrance.

DID YOU KNOW?
Pentecost

Pentecost is one of the three great Jewish festivals in which all males are required to appear before God. The term means "fiftieth part" and is so called because it is celebrated on the fiftieth day, counting from the second day of the Festival of Unleavened Bread or Passover. It is a festival of thanks for the harvest, which begins directly after the Passover (Deut. 16:9ff.) and hence is also called Day of the Firstfruits (Num. 28:26). Josephus tells us that in his day great numbers of Jews came from every quarter to Jerusalem to keep this festival.

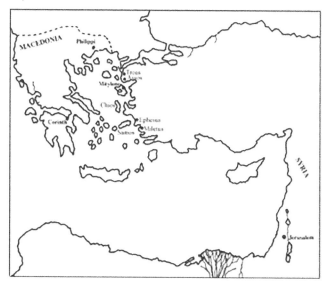

📖 On the map above, trace Paul's journey from Troas making note of each day's travel, so you can have in your mind the places mentioned in Acts 20:13–17.

As you reflect on the geography mentioned here, remember that Paul originally intends to go from Corinth to Syria, but the plot against his life leads to rerouting through Philippi. We know from Acts 20:6 that they leave Philippi after the Passover, and we learn in 20:16 that they hope to be in Jerusalem by Pentecost. Since there are fifty days from Passover to Pentecost, and since they have already spent five days getting to Troas before spending a week there (20:6), we get some idea of the time constraints Paul is facing if he is to accomplish his deadline. This reality is underscored by the fact that it takes at least three days to get to Miletus from Troas and takes another couple of days to get word to the Ephesian elders and for them to journey to meet him.

📖 As you look at the points Paul makes in Acts 20:18–21 about his ministry in Ephesus, write what you think Paul might be saying to these leaders through reminders of his own example.

As we have already seen, Paul's journey in this chapter is a season of passing the torch. Although he has been raising up leaders all along and equipping them for the task of shepherding these flocks, now is the official changing of the guard. Here he reminds them of how he ministers in what appears an intentional instruction to them of what they need to do. He emphasizes being *with* the people (verse 18) and serving with humility (verse 19). He reminds them that with leadership comes tears shed over those who are unfaithful and trials from those who oppose. Through his example he models courage in the face of opponents (verse 20). He defines a ministry leader as one who says what is helpful and needs to be said, and one who teaches even in the context of opposition. On a practical note, he also shows a teaching strategy of both large group ("*teaching you publicly*") and small group ("*from house to house*") instruction (verse 20). Finally, Paul reveals some of the content of his gospel message—"*repentance toward God and faith in our Lord Jesus Christ,*" as well as his audience—"*both Jews and Greeks*" (20:21). Paul says a lot with these few words.

📖 What do you see in Acts 20:22–24 of why Paul is going to Jerusalem and what he expects to find there?

Perhaps the most telling phrase in these verses is that Paul is *"bound in spirit"* to go to Jerusalem (verse 22). It isn't just a strategy or a whim for him. He is compelled forward by God's Spirit, even though he also knows that affliction and even arrest await him (verse 23). What keeps Paul going is a clear sense of purpose for his life and the confidence that comes with it. He knows that his ministry is "received," not achieved. God has laid out a *"course"* for his life to communicate the *"gospel of the grace of God"* (verse 24). That phrasing by Paul seems to emphasize the contrast of the ministry he *"received"* when he met Jesus on the Damascus road, with the ministry he had tried to achieve as a legalistic Pharisee, persecuting the followers of Jesus. Paul is so convinced that this ministry is God's will that it is more important to him than even his own safety or life. Again, Paul is not just mentioning this for his sake, but he is emphasizing the example he wants these leaders to follow as they serve the Lord.

📖 What difficult knowledge does Paul reveal in Acts 20:25–27, and what else of his example does he hold up for the Ephesian elders to imitate?

> *"If I bring a sword upon a land, and the people of the land take one man from among them and make him their watchman, and he sees the sword coming upon the land and blows on the trumpet and warns the people, then he who hears the sound of the trumpet and does not take warning, and a sword comes and takes him away, his blood will be on his own head. He heard the sound of the trumpet but did not take warning; his blood will be on himself. But had he taken warning, he would have delivered his life. But if the watchman sees the sword coming and does not blow the trumpet and the people are not warned, and a sword comes and takes a person from them, he is taken away in his iniquity; but his blood I will require from the watchman's hand." Ezekiel 33:2b-6*

The words of verse 25 must come as a huge blow to these men who love Paul dearly. He will see them no more. This is their last time together this side of eternity. We assume from the context that Paul knows this by revelation of the Spirit. His testimony of verses 26 and 27 is made all the more impactful by the knowledge that his labor here is over. He can say with confidence, "I am innocent of the blood of all men" (20:26). This cultural phrase is drawn from Ezekiel's parable of the *"watchman"* (Ezekiel 33:1–10) where an unfaithful guard of a city has the blood of any who die through his negligence on his own hands, while he is innocent of the blood of those who die after not heeding any warning he gives. These words are usually spiritually applied to evangelism, but here seem also to include discipleship because of the audience and the fact that the message is "the whole purpose of God."

As we reflect on the reminders of Paul's fruitful ministry at Ephesus, perhaps most striking is what he doesn't say here. Absent are the types of metrics preachers normally use to measure success. There are no references to statistics or numerical growth, no reminders of successful building campaigns or pointing to growing budget offerings. Likewise, we also see omitted any past grievances or people who have hurt or misused him. Instead the focus is on faithfulness. Paul speaks volumes through his words here. The real yardstick for measuring successful ministry is not "bodies, bucks, and buildings" but being faithful to God's calling. The results of that faithfulness are at God's discretion.

DAY 4

PREPARING FOR THE FUTURE WITH THE EPHESIAN ELDERS: ACTS 20:28–38

Have you ever noticed that people on their death beds never talk about the weather? Discussion is limited to topics of the greatest importance. When my wife failed to reach remission after intense chemotherapy for her battle with cancer, the prognosis was bleak. We had gone from a forty percent chance of survival to a twenty percent chance to no chance apart from a bone marrow transplant. Over the course of that month my wife began to plan for her own departure. She recorded messages for our children to be listened to later. She recorded what she would want to say to them on their significant birthdays, graduation, and their wedding day. Even though God's gracious intervention spared my wife's life, those are still significant messages because of the context they came from. They were her words when she believed she was ready to die. They were meant to be her last words to her children. Here in Acts 20 we find a similar record. Paul has communicated the reality that he will never see these men again on this side of eternity. That context makes his advice to them all the more compelling.

> *The real yardstick for measuring successful ministry is not 'bodies, bucks and buildings' but being faithful to God's calling. The results of that faithfulness are at God's discretion.*

📖 Look over Acts 20:28–30.

What does Paul tell these men to do and why (20:28)?

What do you think the "savage wolves" are and where will they come from (20:28–9)?

How will they attack (20:29)?

Paul's final admonition to the Ephesian elders is to be good elders. His reminders here follow a logical flow. First, he tells them to guard themselves, and then to guard the flock they oversee. A shepherd who is not guarding his own walk will be of no use to others. Paul goes on to mention some specific dangers they will face, the most prominent of which is the danger of false teaching. Notice he identifies the ones they are to watch out for as "savage wolves" because of the damage they will do. It is interesting that they will arise from inside the church rather than from the outside, and their method of attack is to use false teaching to draw away disciples (followers) to themselves. Paul instructs these elders that they must guard the body from doctrinal error, but to do this, first they must guard their own doctrine. They cannot teach others nor can they recognize error without being students of God's word. They must handle that word accurately. Then, they must also guard what is taught to the body. Elders cannot allow anyone to teach whatever they want. It is the shepherd's job to ensure the feeding of the flock is without poisons or nutrition-less straw. Perhaps most important here is the appearance of yet another reminder that the flock belongs to God, not to the elders.

📖 As Paul tells these men again in Acts 20:31–32 to be on the alert what additional input does he give on how to fulfill this?

If we do not understand Paul's objective here, we might be tempted to wrongly interpret his message. He once again comes back to talking about himself. The point though ought to be clear. He is not self-focused. He is reminding them of specific things he has done which now they will need to be doing. One of the most important aspects of training is modeling, and Paul never asks of others more than he himself has already done. He reminds the Ephesian elders that the job is not a "9 to 5" task, but a "24/7" one. He points out that it requires admonishment and passion. Finally, he emphasizes once again the message of grace, which builds a person up instead of tearing them down as the Law does. Hebrews 13:9, speaking in the context of the preparation of leaders says, *"it is good for the heart to be strengthened by grace,"* and in that same context calls any instruction other than the grace message *"varied and strange teaching."*

> *"...it is good for the heart to be strengthened by grace"*
> (Hebrews 13:9)

📖 In this context of "passing the torch" what do Paul's exhortations of Acts 20:33–35 say to these leaders he addresses?

Paul switches in the middle of these verses from what he has done to what they must do. It is clear from this that he intends for them to follow his example. The first value he reminds them of relates to money. A leader has power and influence, which must be used responsibly rather than selfishly. An additional point he seems to be making is that materialism and ministry don't go together. A second value Paul highlights from his own example is the necessity of working hard and meeting needs. Ministry done right is no life of leisure. It is a life of giving yourself to the needs of others. Yet such a focus is a blessed way to live. Paul reminds them of the words of Jesus, instructing us that blessing comes from giving of ourselves, not from taking from others.

📖 Summarize in your own words the things reflected in this goodbye scene with Paul and the Ephesian elders in Acts 20:36–38.

I've not been in many situations when I have heard grown men weep aloud. Perhaps Greek culture is freer with emotions, but even with that, the scene Luke describes is exceptional. The Greek word for weeping here (*klauthmos*) is unusual. The only other way it is used in the New Testament is to describe the weeping when Herod kills every male child younger than two years old, and to describe the weeping of people in hell. Theirs is an extremely strong expression of grief here. They hug Paul and kiss him repeatedly. To see such actions by a group of grown men shows you the depth of love they have for their spiritual leader, Paul, and the terrible grief they feel with the realization they will never see him alive again. Luke's last phrase, "And they were accompanying him to the ship," gives us a sense of a prolonged goodbye.

DID YOU KNOW?
Men Paul Mentored

Paul apparently mentored Silas (Acts 15:40), Timothy (Acts 16:3), Priscilla and Aquila (Acts 18:18), Erastus (Acts 19:22), Sopater, Aristarchus, Secundus, Gaius, Tychicus, and Trophimus (Acts 20:4), as well as countless others. When he challenges Timothy in 2 Timothy 2:2, *"The things which you have heard from me in the presence of many witnesses, entrust these to faithful men who will be able to teach others also,"* he was only asking Timothy to keep the chain going.

The baton has been passed. These men feel the full weight of responsibility for the leadership of the church. But their sadness has nothing to do with that. They grieve in knowing they will no longer be able to lean on Paul's companionship and leadership. He has been their mentor, and they are indebted to him for everything they know about Christ and ministry. Yet as much as we feel their sadness—as much as we would feel the same way—Paul's departure is a necessary component of their spiritual growth. The secret of church growth we see revealed in the ministry of Paul is that he trains people to lead and then steps out of the way and lets them do what they are capable of. This is how one person can start so many different ministries. It is impossible to say goodbye without sadness, but Paul must also feel a measure of pride and of joy as he realizes his labor has not been in vain. These people will carry on his work after he is gone. The torch has been passed.

DAY 5

FOR ME TO FOLLOW GOD

The church is built on leaders. Its growth is dependent on building more leaders, and its continuance requires new and emerging leaders to take the place of departing leaders. It may be that Paul first began to learn this principle at Antioch. He must have been aware of the hole that was left behind when he and Barnabas set out from there on the first missionary journey. He must have seen both the need for more leaders and the benefits of developing those leaders. Barnabas was instrumental in his becoming a leader in the early church. He sponsored Paul with the mother church when the original twelve apostles would have nothing to do with him (Acts 9:27). It is Barnabas who brings

Paul into the work at Antioch as a co-laborer (Acts 11:25–26). Ironically, it is Barnabas' commitment to developing future leaders (Mark) that leads to he and Paul splitting their partnership (Acts 15:37–39). Paul probably understands better now how he needed the chance to step out on his own. He follows Barnabas' example and continually takes young and emerging leaders under his wing to develop them and assist their growth (Acts 15:40; 16:3; 18:18; 19:22; 20:4). It is for this very reason that Luke accompanies Paul in so much of his ministry and records it for us in Acts. Paul is continually working himself out of a job. This ensures that he has the freedom to move on to other opportunities of ministry, and it also ensures that his work continues after he is gone. This is what passing the torch is all about.

Today however, the passing of the torch of ministry often isn't as successful as we'd like for it to be. New leaders fail. New leaders give up. Sometimes new leaders don't even show up. But much of that is the fault of the church and its leadership. We look for those who are already leaders instead of building those with potential to that point. We fail to bring prospective laborers to the work of ministry from the inside to give vision and a sense of need. Leaders don't allow future workers into their lives so they can see a practical model of what leadership looks like in different situations of ministry. We ask people to serve, but we don't equip them to be successful at it. But perhaps the greatest mistake of all is we fail to get out of the way so budding spiritual leaders can gain necessary experience as workers while we're still there to give them feedback and help them improve. We must step aside from time to time to let them take their first steps in ministry. And of course, at some point we must pass the torch to them, affirming their abilities and exhorting their faithfulness. If we haven't adequately prepared them, the work takes a step backward when we step away.

> *A healthy church doesn't just look for leaders, it makes leaders for its own needs and to share with the world.*

Consider these principles in the context of your church, small group, or other area of ministry and check the ones that are being done well:

- ☐ identifying potential leaders and concentrating on helping them take the next step
- ☐ exposing potential leaders to vision and need
- ☐ modeling healthy ministry principles and values for emerging leaders
- ☐ equipping people to succeed at what we ask them to do
- ☐ providing necessary opportunities for skills to be honed and improved
- ☐ passing the torch in a way that is both challenging and affirming

Now go back through this same list and identify those areas which need to be improved upon.

- [ ] identifying potential leaders and concentrating on helping them take the next step

- [ ] exposing potential leaders to vision and need

- [ ] modeling healthy ministry principles and values for emerging leaders

- [ ] equipping people to succeed at what we ask them to do

- [ ] providing necessary opportunities for skills to be honed and improved

- [ ] passing the torch in a way that is both challenging and affirming

Along with this value is the reality that God has called each of us to be ministers and leaders in some context. We all have gifts that are to be used in service. We all have responsibilities and areas of influence—whether that is in the context of a family, a job, a ministry, or the kingdom as a whole. What steps are you taking to develop personally through ministry? What steps do you need to take?

Another principle we observe from this chapter on passing the torch is the rightness of affirming and appreciating those who have served us and led us. It is sad to acknowledge, but pastors and church leaders are sometimes the least honored people in our culture. Their educational requirements are like those of lawyers and MBA's, yet their income is normally a fraction of other professionals. For many of the pastors I know, each October comes and goes without a single acknowledgement that it was "Pastor Appreciation Month." This is especially true of associate pastors whose hard work is performed in the shadows instead of on stage. Yet a church large enough to have them could not function without them. I am grateful for the affirmations I have received from the people I serve.

While human affirmation should not be the motive of anyone's service, Paul exhorts that we do take time to honor those whose labors are worthy of honor. To Timothy he later writes, *"Those who rule well are to be considered worthy of double-honor, especially those who work hard at preaching and teaching"* (1 Timothy 5:17). He also makes the point to the Corinthians that it is more needful to honor members of the body which seem less important (see 1 Corinthians 12:22–24). This principle certainly applies to pastors but should not be limited to that. It includes disciple makers, teachers, small group leaders, parents, and really anyone who makes significant investments in who we are.

Hebrews 13:7 exhorts, *"Remember those who led you."* What are some things you have done to acknowledge, affirm, and appreciate those who have invested in your life to help you become what God wants you to be?

"Those who rule well are to be considered worthy of double-honor, especially those who work hard at preaching and teaching"
(1 Timothy 5:17)

Name some people whom you have not done that with but need to?

What are some practical ways you can acknowledge, affirm, and appreciate?

As we close out this week's lesson, express your heart and your points of application in a written prayer to the Lord in the space below...

LESSON 8

WHEN GOD'S WILL IS HARD
ACTS 21:1—22:29

Just before beginning his long journey to Jerusalem the apostle Paul writes the book of Romans to prepare this church for his intended visit. In Romans 12:2, Paul uses three different adjectives to describe the will of God. Paul expresses that in each and every situation, God's will for our lives is *"good and acceptable and perfect."* It is qualitatively good, meaning it is beneficial and benevolent—acceptable. The Greek word here has the idea of "well pleasing, agreeable." In other words, when all the cards are on the table, I won't ever look at God's will and disagree. God's will is perfect. Like a tailor-made suit, it fits me and my needs exactly. My will doesn't have nearly so much to offer. Yet we must realize that God defines good from the vantage point of eternity, and He speaks in ultimate terms. This is important to recognize, because that isn't the way we tend to think. We think that if God's will is good, then it must be easy and desirable. That isn't always the case. Sometimes what works for the greatest good in the long run is the least desirable in the short run.

> *Sometimes what works for the greatest good in the long run is the least desirable in the short run.*

We think that to be in the center of God's will means great successes and miraculous deliverances. I believe it always does, but we don't always define success or deliverance the same way God does. We think success means great impact, and of course, we measure that impact by what we see immediately rather than what happens ultimately. Let me illustrate. Which is the greater success—Jesus' ministry to the five thousand He feeds with some loaves and fish or His discussion with the woman at the well? While feeding the five thousand certainly seems more dramatic, the ministry with the woman at the well, so far as Scripture records, has a far greater eternal impact. The Samaritan woman goes back to her village and tells everyone about Jesus and a whole Samaritan town turns to Christ. We have no record of anything more happening with the crowd of five thousand. Sometimes what looks significant in the short run really isn't. And often what appears small ends up being really big. Real success isn't measured by initial results, but rather, by whether or not God's purpose is accomplished.

Not only do we have difficulty determining what is ultimately significant or successful, but we also are equally impaired when it comes to identifying what constitutes deliverance. We think of biblical examples like Daniel in the lion's den or the three Hebrews in the fiery furnace, and we assume that God's deliverance always means the particular happy ending we are looking for. But sometimes God delivers in another way. In 2 Timothy 4:17 Paul promises, *"The Lord will rescue me from every evil deed."* Shortly afterward he is beheaded on the Ostian Way. So what has happened? Why doesn't the Lord deliver him? We look at such circumstances and try to evaluate them based on what we define as good. But that kind of thinking is enthroning the present rather than valuing eternity. God's will is always good, but we don't always know what is good and what is evil. Paul says with certainty that God will deliver him from "every evil deed." What his own experience teaches us is that if it is evil, God delivers. If God doesn't deliver, then it must not be evil. We think for Paul to be martyred is bad, but Paul recognizes that this is his entry into the presence of God. He continues in 2 Timothy 4:17 by saying, "and will bring me safely to His heavenly kingdom." That is ultimate good and permanent rescue. God's will is ultimately the best—always—but we need to recognize that sometimes God's will is hard. Even though Paul knows that prison awaits him, he keeps heading to Jerusalem because he trusts the goodness of God's will. He understands that prison within the will of God is better than paradise outside of it.

DAY 1

THE DIFFERENCE BETWEEN OUR OPINIONS AND GOD'S WILL: ACTS 21:1–14

One of the most challenging lessons I have had to learn in ministry is to be able to distinguish between an intelligent, informed opinion and God's will. You see, in the Christian life, once you get past the basics, the most difficult decisions are not between good and bad. The hardest decisions to make are those between good and best—between good and God's will. I have learned over and over that good and godly leaders can disagree. I have also learned that when they disagree, often both sides can back their points up with Scripture. Yet decision-making is an essential part of spiritual leadership and spiritual life. So, what do you do when you have different opinions? You have to look not just for what is logical, but for what is the Lord's leading.

When Samuel is sent by God to the house of Jesse to find the replacement for King Saul, Jesse brings his sons in one by one. When the oldest son Eliab comes in first, Samuel looks at him and thinks, *"Surely the Lord's anointed is before Him"* (1 Samuel 16:6). It all makes sense to Samuel. He knows he is on the right track because God has sent him to Jesse's house. This is the oldest son, the most mature, the one with the most life experience. He looks like a king to Samuel. But the Lord says, *"Do not look at his appearance or at the height of his stature, because I have rejected him; for God sees not as man sees, for man looks at the outward appearance, but the Lord looks at the heart"* (1 Samuel 16:7). It is not that God's will is illogical. It is just that God sees not as man sees. God can see more than Samuel. The prophet learns his lesson though. With each of the succeeding sons that parade before him, his response is, "The Lord has not chosen" this one or that one. Obviously, he learns to look to the Lord and not just to logic. God's choice makes sense if you know all that God can see (the heart), but with the limited sight of a human vantage point, no one expects the smallest and youngest son to be God's choice for king.

"God sees not as man sees." (1 Samuel 16:7)

As Paul approaches Jerusalem, in every city there were warnings of what he will meet there. Human logic would dictate a change in plans. But as we will see today, sometimes God's will is to go right into the hard circumstance. Paul's confidence in God's leading to Jerusalem is so strong that he keeps going even though he knows hard times are ahead. He has laid logic on the altar of the Lord's leading.

📖 Follow Paul's course in Acts 21:1–4 on your Bible map, and then record what message Paul is hearing from the disciples he meets.

_____

_____

_____

_____

When we look at Paul's itinerary it is hard to not do so through the eyeglasses of modern travel. But he and Luke could not access the Internet and book two seats on the next commercial flight to Jerusalem. Often each leg of the journey would require making separate arrangements after arriving in the city. That would mean delays and detours. There are no passenger boats, so travelers often book passage on cargo ships with space to spare, fending for themselves for food. Apparently, Paul's seven days in Tyre are at the discretion of the ship he is traveling on, as it unloads cargo. The layover is spent fellowshipping with local believers who have the same message for Paul he has been hearing in every city (see Acts 20:23)—that difficult times lay ahead in Jerusalem. Paul and his companions will not be dissuaded however, and when the ship is ready to sail, all the brethren come to the beach and see them off with prayer.

📖 Look over Acts 21:7–11.

Describe the message Agabus shares with Paul and the company?

_____

_____

_____

Why do you think Luke mentions Philip's daughters in this context?

_____

_____

_____

_____

Why do you suppose Luke mentions the details of this particular prophecy in the context of so many saying the same thing?

_____

_____

_____

_____

 WORD STUDY
"Not"

There are two different Greek words which are translated "no" or "not" in the New Testament. The stronger word of the two (*ou*) generally refers to the absolute negative. The other word (*me*) refers to a more relative negative. It is this second word which is used in Acts 21:4 as the believers keep telling Paul through the Spirit "not to set foot in Jerusalem." At a glance it would seem Paul is disregarding God's will by continuing, but the word for "not" helps us interpret. If the text had used *ou*, then the message from the believers would have been "You cannot go!" Instead, *me* tells us their message is "You should not go." In Acts 20:23 Paul tells us the Spirit's message in each town is simply that "bonds and afflictions" await him. Apparently, that is the case here, and the admonition that he shouldn't go is from the people, not the Spirit. In Acts 20:22 Paul has already told us he is bound by that same Spirit to go to Jerusalem. God is leading him there but is also letting him know what to expect on his arrival.

Like a broken record, Agabus becomes yet another telling Paul of the difficulties that await him in Jerusalem. It may be that Luke gives so much detail to Agabus' prophecy because he is already well known. You will remember that this same man prophesies a famine about the time Paul begins in ministry at Antioch (Acts 11:28). It seems likely though that the main reason Luke gives so much of the details on this particular prophecy is because from all that he and Paul hear, this is the most memorable with its visual effect of making use of Paul's belt. This particular vignette puts a human face on the prophecies. While some suggest that Luke mentions Philip's daughters because they too prophesy of Paul, we cannot conclude this with certainty. What we can say is that Paul certainly is in a place to hear from God.

📖 Read Acts 21:12–14 and answer the questions that follow.

What is the impact of Agabus' prophecy on the group with Paul?

What stands out to you from Paul's response to them?

What is the ultimate conclusion of the group?

I can't imagine how hard it is to keep heading to Jerusalem when you know going there will mean prison and suffering. It must make it even harder when everyone in the group begs you with tears not to go. It says much of Paul's confidence that he has heard from God that he is able to resist their passionate appeals. Clearly Paul has counted the cost. He knows that not only prison, but even death could be the outcome, and he is ready to pay whatever price to be obedient to God's leading and to testify of Christ in the Holy City. One cannot help but sense the finality of Luke's remark, *"The will of the Lord be done!"* It seems this is the point when everyone concludes that this is indeed God's will for Paul.

"The will of the Lord be done!" Acts 21:14

Certainly, it is right and biblical to seek the counsel of others in major decisions, but Paul illustrates for us here that the real goal is not to listen to what human counsel has to say. Rather, we must be ever listening to what God might be saying through them. Sometimes we must hear what God is saying in spite of the advice of others. Luke's honesty here, including himself in those who try to talk Paul out of God's will, serves to remind us of the limitations of human opinion. We can use our logic to evaluate what seems prudent, but that logic must always remain surrendered to the will of God. We must be sensitive to the difference between having an opinion and having heard from God.

DAY 2

GOD'S WILL IS NOT ALWAYS WELCOMED BY GOD'S PEOPLE: ACTS 21:15–26

Paul has been prepared for months. Every city he visits on his way back to Jerusalem warns him of the persecution that awaits him there. But he is confident in God's will. He knows with certainty that God has led him to Jerusalem. He must be anxious about when and where the trial will begin. But at least he can expect to be welcomed and safe among the church in Jerusalem. There are many believers here, and Paul must look forward to their support and prayers whenever trouble begins. Little does he know that his first trial will be found among the church. As we will see today, before facing opposition from antagonistic Jews, Paul will first have to navigate choppy waters of strife in dealing with the assumptions of his fellow Christians.

📖 What do you learn in Acts 21:15–17 of Paul's initial reception with his host in Jerusalem?

Escorted by believers from Caesarea, Paul finally arrives at Jerusalem and is welcomed by a mature believer who gives him lodging. The initial response Paul finds among the brethren is a positive one. They receive him gladly. There is nothing in these actions to prepare him for what will transpire next.

📖 Examine Acts 21:18–21 and make note of all the specifics you observe in the response that greets Paul in his audience with the leaders of the mother church.

It is expected and appropriate that Paul would immediately seek to meet with the leadership of the mother church in Jerusalem. As one of Christianity's strongest proponents, Paul has done much to advance the message of the gospel, and since Jerusalem is still the center of the Christian faith, they have a vested interest in hearing a report on his progress. When the leaders hear of God's working among the Gentiles through Paul, they glorify God. The celebration is short-lived however, for almost immediately, the elders share with Paul a rumor that is circulating among Jewish Christians that he has not only abandoned his Jewish roots but is teaching other Jewish believers to do the same. These hurtful rumors are not true, and no one indicates exactly where they get started, but clearly Paul is known in the church at Jerusalem in a negative light.

DOCTRINE
Abstain

Here in Acts 21 the Jerusalem elders affirm once again the four restrictions they agreed upon for the Gentile converts to Christianity. Of those four, only "fornication"—sexual immorality—is affirmed as sinful in New Testament. These are not essentials of salvation, for then the message would be they are still under Law. Instead, these four issues are matters of fellowship deemed important for walking in love with their Jewish brethren. There is freedom in grace, but if we flaunt that freedom to those who don't view matters the same way, then we are no longer walking according to love.

How in Acts 21:22–25 do the Jerusalem elders instruct Paul to counter the slanderous accusations that are being spread about him?

The leaders of the mother church have obviously had more time to think about Paul's reputation than he himself has. They propose a plan to give Paul the opportunity to show through his actions that he has not turned his back on his Jewish heritage. Apparently, there are four men keeping a Nazarite vow who are too poor to complete the full requirements and need someone to act as a benefactor on their behalf. Paul is encouraged to participate in this Mosaic practice to prove he has not abandoned the Old Testament teachings but rather, that he walks *"orderly, keeping the Law."* These men are clearly on Paul's side, and once again affirm the verdict they participated in at the Jerusalem Council (Acts 15) concerning Gentile converts.

What does Acts 21:26 reveal of Paul's response to the advice of the elders?

Paul had every right to protest the false rumors being spread concerning him. In Matthew 18 Jesus gives clear instructions on how Paul, or anyone perceived to be in sin, should be treated. Had these steps been followed, all could be resolved quickly. But instead of going to Paul in private, his accusers air their concerns in public without giving Paul the chance to explain or defend himself. We learn much of the maturity of his character in the fact that rather that becoming defensive or retaliating, Paul follows the elders' advice immediately and fully.

DOCTRINE
Conflict Resolution

What do we do when our brother sins? In Matthew 18 Jesus lays out four steps for resolving conflict among brethren and for restoring one caught in sin. Step one is to go alone to the brother in private. Most often this step alone produces repentance, and the other steps become unnecessary. If going alone does not produce the repentance needed, then step two is to take one or two with you as witnesses to whether or not the person is repentant. Step three, if the sinning brother is still unwilling to turn, is to tell it to the church. If that still does not work, then the final step is to break fellowship.

One of the early heroes of the Christian faith is getting ready to face his greatest trial. The armies of the enemy are about to be unleashed in his direction. He has been faithful to the call on his life to take the gospel to the Gentiles (Acts 20:24) and has the confidence of the leadership of the mother church that his doctrine and ministry practice are correct (Acts 15). Yet there are apparently a great many Jewish Christians who think and speak ill of him for simply being obedient to God's will. At the time when he most needs the prayers, support, and encouragement of fellow believers, he finds instead that he has to dodge bullets being fired at him by his own comrades. It is a sad indictment, but all too often the safe haven of our fellow believers is not what it ought to be. God's will for Paul is already hard enough without being compounded by innuendo and gossip from judgmental and uninformed Christians. One wishes such tragic scenarios are limited to the early church, but unfortunately similar scenes occur with regularity today as well.

DAY 3

DOING GOD'S WILL DOESN'T ALWAYS MAKE LIFE EASIER:
ACTS 21:27–40

There are times when our theology and our experience don't match. As our lives unfold like a drama, there are moments when, if we push the pause button on the movie, justice will seem perverted and righteous living will appear to be punished instead of rewarded. Such is the experience of Asaph in the Old Testament. In Psalm 73:1 he begins with his theology—"Surely God is good to Israel, to those who are pure in heart." But in the verses that follow he begins contrasting what he has been taught to believe with what he is experiencing. He speaks of "the prosperity of the wicked" (Psalm 73:3) and the problems of the righteous. In verse 13 of this painfully honest psalm he exclaims, *"Surely in vain I have kept my heart pure"* and speaks of the reward for his righteousness as being *"stricken all day long and chastened every morning"* (73:14). He had been taught that God rewards righteousness and punishes sin, but at this point his experience isn't matching what is supposed to be true. Like Asaph's dilemma, this excerpt from the life of Paul we will consider today shows us that there will be times like that in our own lives. Paul is obeying God and even showing himself to be a model of submission to the human authorities of the mother church. As we will see, instead of making his life easier, God's will is making it harder.

 Study Acts 21:27–30 and identify who opposes Paul and how they incite others against him.

DID YOU KNOW?
The Dividing Wall

The Jewish Temple was separated into two halves—the outer half (the court of the Gentiles) and the inner half (the court of the Jews). Archaeologists have discovered a plaque which hung on the Dividing Wall, and the inscription warns Gentiles of the death penalty for entering the court of the Jews. Jesus did away with this barrier and made both groups into one body in the church. In Ephesians 2:12 Paul speaks of this division between Jews and Gentiles saying, *"For He Himself is our peace, who made both groups into one and broke down the barrier of the dividing wall."*

Paul probably spends his first days in Jerusalem looking over his shoulder. He meets with the elders on his second day in town, and the day after that acts on their counsel and goes with the men who are completing their Nazarite vows according to the law. Their purification takes seven days, and all is quiet for most of that time. The rituals require Paul to visit the Temple on the third and seventh days, so this is apparently the last of his visits. He is in Jerusalem more than a week before the prophecies of persecution begin to unfold. Remember, Paul pressed to be in Jerusalem by Pentecost, and so a great many Jews from all over have converged at the Temple to observe the feast and festival associated with this holy day.

Undoubtedly it is Jews who opposed Paul in the cities where he planted churches that recognize him in the Temple and begin to stir up trouble. I find it ironic but revealing that the devoutly religious who oppose Paul will violate the teachings of their own faith to attack those they determine are a threat to it. By exaggeration and fabrication, they bear false witness against Paul, stating that he preaches against the Jews, the Law, and the Temple. They add other accusations to what they know to be lies, based only on mistaken suspicions. Having seen Paul with a Gentile companion in the city, and having already a biased view against him, they jump to the false conclusion that Paul has defiled the Temple by bringing his Greek friend into the holy area reserved only for Jews. Convicting Paul without a trial, overreacting to the trumped-up charges of his enemies, the mob drags him out of the Temple and begin to beat him.

📖 Summarize from Acts 21:31–36 what happens when the Roman authorities get involved in the commotion surrounding Paul.

Roman government holds little tolerance for civil unrest in its provinces, and a commander who does not squelch an uprising quickly puts his own life in jeopardy. As soon as news of the disturbance reaches the local leader, he hurriedly brings troops to the Temple and breaks up the mob. Seeing Paul as the object of the violence, he quickly takes him into custody as he seeks to understand the reason for the riot. The injustice of the attack is underscored by the fact that the crowds that have come upon him can't even agree on the reason why. Although the soldiers arrest Paul, their actions probably serve more for his protection than harm. Clearly the swarm of people would kill him if given the opportunity.

📖 Look over the verses of Acts 21:37–40 and make note of how the situation progresses and how Paul handles it.

The Jewish Historian Josephus confirms what Luke mentions here in Acts 21:38 of an Egyptian who led a revolt against Roman occupiers. He proclaimed himself a prophet and gathered a large crowd promising that at his command the walls of Jerusalem would collapse. His force was attacked by Felix, but he and some followers escaped into the wilderness. Josephus mentions a much higher number involved in the revolt than Luke's four thousand. His account may be exaggerated, or it may be that Luke's is the number not of the whole crowd but of those who escaped the Roman crackdown. Both agree that the leader of the revolt was still at large, and of course would have been on the minds of the authorities. The assassins were the terrorists of Jesus' day and developed a tactic of murder by stealth, sneaking up on the target in a crowded public place, stabbing him with a short dagger hidden under their cloak, then vanishing into the crowd or pretending to call for help or sometimes even joining in the mourning for the victim. Such disturbances were more likely around events such as the feast of Pentecost, so the Romans were on high alert.

Luke's detail here makes it clear that he is an eyewitness of the events as they transpire. The coolness under pressure that we see in Paul underscores his maturity, but also must be recognized as the fruit of his confidence at being in the center of God's will. Even though beaten by a mob, his focus is already on using the occasion as an opportunity to testify of Christ. In polite submissiveness he asks of the commander, *"May I say something to you?"* Like the crowd, it seems the commander also has jumped to some conclusions, associating Paul with an Egyptian rebel that is still on the loose. Recognizing Paul's use of Greek reveals him to be a cultured and educated man and helps convince the leader that he is not a local Palestinian troublemaker who would speak only Aramaic. Paul asks for and is given the chance to speak to the crowd. Wanting to build a bridge to those he seeks a chance to witness to, Paul speaks to them in Hebrew which commands the attention of the gathered Jews.

Paul learned from his missionary journeys to let God lead him. He obeyed the Spirit when he was forbidden to preach in certain regions of Asia (Acts16:6–7). Likewise, he followed the Spirit's lead into the fruitful ministry he enjoyed in Macedonia (Acts 16:9–10). His desire to come to Jerusalem has been prompted by the Spirit (Acts 19:21), and that leading has become a sense of compulsion by the Spirit (Acts 20:22). When Paul speaks of being *"bound in spirit,"* the Greek verb is in the perfect tense. It is a settled matter in his heart, and he is being obedient. Even though God's will is proving to be hard, Paul sees his circumstances not as difficulties to be avoided, but as trials that were purchasing for him opportunities to minister Christ in new fields. Rather than bemoaning the injustice of his treatment, he seeks to make the most of the audience his suffering gathers.

SPEAKING GOD'S TRUTH IS NOT ALWAYS APPRECIATED: ACTS 22:1–29

The Bible tells us that the time will come when people *"will not endure sound doctrine; but wanting to have their ears tickled, they will accumulate for themselves teachers in accordance to their own desires, and will turn away their ears from the truth"* (2 Timothy 4:3–4a). Paul is no ear-tickler. Even in the face of persecution he can say, *"I did not shrink from declaring to you anything that was profitable"* (Acts 20:20). He is brave enough to speak truth no matter what the cost. He recognizes sharing the gospel as God's mission for his life—the ministry he *"received from the Lord Jesus, to testify solemnly of the gospel of the grace of God"* (Acts 20:24). So, when Paul speaks out to share the gospel, he knows it is God's will. But just because speaking truth is God's will, that doesn't mean it will always be appreciated. Sometimes when we deliver a message from God to people, it is words that they don't want to hear. We must decide if we want to please people or please God. Paul called himself a *"bondservant"* (Romans 1:1). This means his life is surrendered to doing always and only the will of God. He will speak the truth of the gospel in Jerusalem even if to do so costs him his life. In Acts 22 we find that Luke records word for word this powerful sermon Paul preaches to the Jews who want to kill him.

📖 As you look at how Paul introduces the story of his conversion to Christianity in Acts 22:1–5, write down the words and phrases which his audience can identify with that he employs to describe what he was like before he met Christ.

It is worth noticing that from the very beginning of his speech, Paul seeks to build a bridge to his audience by speaking to them in the common Hebrew dialect (Aramaic) instead of Greek. The effectiveness is seen in the fact that they listen quietly. Paul makes a number of points to build a sense of common ground with his audience. He reminds them that he too is a Jew and was brought up in Jerusalem. He was *"educated under Gamaliel,"* one of the most prominent rabbis of his day. He mentions that he was raised *"strictly according to the law of our fathers"* and grew up *"zealous for God"* in like manner to the way they are behaving presently. To defend this premise, he reminds them of his role in the persecution of Christians with full authority from *"the high priest and all the Council of the elders."* Having scattered the church from Jerusalem, he *"started off for Damascus"* to spread the persecution there. Paul can identify with his audience even more than they realize.

DID YOU KNOW?
Gamaliel

The apostle Paul was a student of Gamaliel (Acts 22:3, 5:34), one of the most noteworthy rabbis in Jewish history. It is Gamaliel who advises caution as the Sanhedrin wants to put Peter and John to death in Acts 5. According to the JewishEncyclopedia.com, Gamaliel was the grandson of the famous conservative rabbi, Hillel and took over his school in Jerusalem. The school established itself with a concern for biblical accuracy and put forward Hillel's "Seven Rules" for the interpretation of Scripture. It was said of Gamaliel, "When he died the honor [outward respect] of the Torah ceased, and purity and piety became extinct" (Sotah xv: 18). Clearly his teaching and ministry impacted Paul.

📖 What words or phrases in Acts 22:6–11 stand out to you as showing that Paul has turned to Christ?

While most of us do not have the same dramatic conversion experience as the apostle Paul, there are principles to observe from what Luke records here. First, at the revelation of the bright light, Paul falls to the ground—an act of submission. When asked, *"Saul, Saul, why are you persecuting Me?"* Paul calls the one speaking *"Lord."* Another act of submission is seen in the question, *"What shall I do, Lord?"* Although Paul is blinded by the brightness of the light, he obeys what is instructed as best he can. Paul intended to take Damascus by storm but ends up being led there by the hand. His humility and brokenness though give evidence of a changed heart toward Jesus.

📖 What evidences do you see in Acts 22:12–21 that indicate Paul's life has been changed after becoming a Christian?

Can you imagine what it would take for a Christian from Damascus to call Saul (Paul) "Brother"? Yet Ananias is convinced Paul has truly given his heart to the Lord. We see obedience in Paul's being baptized. The physical act pictures the spiritual reality that he has indeed called on Jesus' name, and had his sins washed away. While praying in the Temple, Paul sees Jesus who instructs him, *"Make haste, and get out of Jerusalem quickly, because they will not accept your testimony about Me."* The fact that Jesus says this indicates that Paul has a testimony and intends to share it. Another evidence of change is in Paul's repentant attitude about his role in the persecution of Christians. But perhaps the greatest evidence of change is when Saul the Pharisee becomes known as Paul the Christian and devotes his life to reaching out to the Gentiles.

📖 Read Acts 22:22–30.

What is the attitude of the Jews to Paul's testimony?

_____

_____

_____

Why do you think Paul appeals to his citizenship to avoid a beating?

_____

_____

_____

How has God used the Romans to benefit Paul?

_____

_____

_____

_____

 DID YOU KNOW?
Understanding the Authority Structure

The headquarters of the Roman occupation forces in Jerusalem was Fort Antonia, located on a precipice overlooking the Temple grounds. From its towers, sentries had a clear view of the Temple area, where civil unrest in Jerusalem was most likely to break out. During major religious celebrations, such as Pentecost, the Romans were especially watchful (MacArthur, *Acts 13–28*, Moody Press, p.260). A Roman commander oversaw one thousand troops (a cohort) and was the ranking Roman official when the Governor was not in the city. The seriousness of the disturbance is reflected in the fact that the commander himself, Claudius Lysias, attends to it, along with "centurions" (plural). Each centurion commanded one hundred troops, so the suggestion is that at least two hundred troops attend in a massive show of force.

The Jews listen to what Paul has to say until he talks of God calling him to the Gentiles. It says much of their hatred for anyone who isn't a Jew that they want a man dead just because he has compassion on the Gentiles. To them, that is a crime worthy of death. As the crowd begins to get out of control, the commander brings Paul inside and intends to whip him. Perhaps he hopes that by giving Paul some kind of punishment, he can appease the wrath of the crowd and silence them. Even though Paul knows it is God's will for him to be arrested, he certainly isn't in any hurry to die. His citizenship as a Roman gives him rights, and there is nothing wrong with exercising those rights. Paul is ready to suffer and die for the gospel, but it makes no sense to suffer or die needlessly. These same Romans who were about to unlawfully scourge Paul have probably saved his life though.

Paul's ordeal is far from over, but for the moment he is in safe hands being jailed by the Romans. He has come to Jerusalem knowing that it is God's will, but also knowing that God's will, in this case, will be hard. His confidence in God's leading though gives him security and the ability to stand firm in the midst of his trials. He tries to seize the opportunity his arrest gives and turn it into another chance to witness. He does make a point of his own conversion, but he will have to trust God to work through his testimony in the hearts of the Jews. Sadly, speaking God's truth is not always appreciated.

Day 5

For Me to Follow God

I'm no fan of pain, even though I've experienced my share of it. But I have learned to recognize that not all pains are equal. I know the pain of cutting yourself in a foolish accident or senseless altercation. I had stitches four different times as a teenager for such reasons. But I have also felt the cut of a surgeon's knife. Though both may wound as deeply, hurt as much, and take as long to heal, we view it quite differently when the pain has a greater purpose. We endure because we know the pain is balanced by benefit. I believe all who claim the name of Christ ought to embrace the will of God in every situation. But I think it is important for all believers to recognize that sometimes God's will is hard. We sometimes wrongly think that God's will is going to be easy and fun and instantly fruitful. That isn't always the case. Sometimes doing God's will is harder in the short run than disobedience. But like avoiding surgery because we don't want the pain, such a choice robs us of the benefits and rewards that come from doing the right thing. The easy way is harder in the long run. God's will is the better way even if it is hard. His pain is never accidental, and I believe He only leads us to pain or difficulty when the return on the other side far outweighs the cost.

Paul's tribulations in Jerusalem were not easy. But in Acts chapters 22–26 Luke records six different opportunities of which Paul was able to take advantage to defend the Christian faith. These chances to witness were before some of the most influential people of the day, and all were possible only as a result of his arrest. When God's will for our lives is hard, we can trust that like the wounds of a surgeon, the pain has been determined by the Lord to be necessary for the greater good of us, others, or both.

DID YOU KNOW?
Paul's Opportunities in Jerusalem

Luke records that Paul's arrest in Jerusalem leads to at least 6 different opportunities to witness of Christ before some of the most influential people of the day. Paul speaks to...

1) the Roman commander and a Jewish crowd (Acts 22:1–30)
2) the Jewish Sanhedrin – the Pharisees and Sadducees (Acts 23:1–10)
3) Felix, Governor of Judea from AD 52–60 (Acts 24:10–23)
4) Felix again, along with his wife Drusilla (Acts 24:24–27)
5) Porcius Festus, new Governor of Judea in AD 60 (Acts 25:8–12)
6) Festus, King Agrippa II (ruler of Palestine—AD 53–70), Agrippa's sister Bernice, and a large audience (Acts 26:1–32)

We also know that because of his appeal to Caesar (Acts 25:11), Paul will have an audience with the Emperor and perhaps other governmental officials in Rome. We also learn from Philippians 1:13 that this arrest leads to his being able to share Christ with *"the whole Praetorian guard,"* the soldiers of the Governor's Palace in Rome.

What are some examples in your past or present experience of the reality that sometimes God's will is hard?

How do you normally respond when following God's leading becomes hard?

☐ trust God's sovereignty

☐ doubt God's goodness

☐ question if I have missed God's leading

☐ look for an easier solution

☐ look for opportunities to minister

☐ grumble and complain to God and others

☐ Other: _____

As we saw in Day One, there is sometimes a big difference between our logical opinion and God's leading. Can you think of an example when you have seen the two of these be in conflict with each other?

One discouraging reality we witness in Paul's experience with judgmental attitudes is that sometimes other Christians don't support us as we seek to follow God's will in ministry. Instead of embracing God's will for our lives, they criticize and sometimes even slander us. We must remember that Jesus too was criticized for some of the people He sought to minister to and was negatively called a *"friend of tax collectors and sinners"* (Luke 7:34).

Have you ever criticized others for the people they keep company with?

Are there any who have criticized you for such things?

Have you ever not reached out to someone because of what others might think?

One of the ways God's will can sometimes be hard is in the persons He calls us to minister to. The bottom line is that sometimes such opportunities force us to decide between pleasing God and pleasing people. We need courage to be obedient to God's will in such cases, and we need wisdom to not hinder others from doing what they sense God is leading them to do in ministry.

What are some additional practical applications that stand out to you from this week's lesson?

Although application often involves action, we must remember that one facet of application is simply belief in the truth Scripture reveals. Even if we take away nothing else from this lesson, we must see that the central application is to understand that just because we follow God's will, that doesn't mean our path will always be easy or blessed by human measurements. We see this truth graphically illustrated in the life experiences recorded here of the apostle Paul. From him we also learn that when God's will is hard though, it is often when opportunity to minister is the greatest. As you reflect on this week's lesson, why not close out by expressing your heart in a written prayer...

LESSON 9

THE FALSE SOLUTION OF FOLLOWING OUR FLESH
ACTS 23

In Acts 20:24 Paul says, *"I do not consider my life of any account as dear to myself, so that I may finish my course and the ministry which I received from the Lord Jesus, to testify solemnly of the gospel of the grace of God."* We have seen this idea of *received* ministry reflected much in Paul's writings and exploits. By that term he seems to mean ministry that is initiated and empowered by God rather than human initiative. The contrast to *received* ministry is what I would call *achieved* ministry. That is ministry or activity initiated and empowered by people rather than God. If God does not initiate it, He will not anoint it with His blessing, power, and results.

If we want to do our own thing, God will let us. But God's blessing is on His plans, not ours. We see this idea illustrated quite graphically throughout the Scriptures, but perhaps nowhere more so than with Abraham. God promises him and his wife Sarah a son. But after waiting a while for God to work, Sarah comes up with a plan to help God out. She suggests Abraham use her maid as a surrogate mother and Abraham agrees. Of course, the result is not Isaac through whom all the nations will be blessed, but Ishmael, who is *"a wild donkey of a man"* (Genesis 16:12).

> *If God doesn't initiate it, He isn't going to anoint it with His blessing, power, and results. If a person wants to do their own thing, God will let them. But God's blessing is on His plans, not ours.*

On the night of Jesus' arrest, we see another illustration of trying to help out God without His permission. After observing the Passover with His disciples, Jesus goes to Gethsemane to pray and takes Peter, James and John with Him. It is here in the garden that Judas comes with the priests and soldiers to betray Him. In Luke 22:49 we are told, *"When those who were around Him saw what was going to happen, they said, 'Lord, shall we strike with the sword?'"* They ask the right question and inquire of the right person, but one of them doesn't wait for a response. Before Jesus even has a chance to answer, Luke tells us, *"And one of them struck the slave of the high priest and cut off his right ear"* (Luke 22:50). John's account of this incident informs us it is Peter who reacts and tries to defend Jesus. It just doesn't make any sense to Peter to allow Jesus to be arrested, so he does what makes sense and reacts out of his own flesh instead of waiting to see what Jesus has to say. The result is disastrous. Notice what Peter does. In a crowd of heavily armed soldiers he attacks the least threatening person—an unarmed slave. And he doesn't kill the man. He just cuts off his ear with what the Greek identifies as a small dagger, not a long sword. *"But Jesus answered and said, 'Stop! No more of this,' and He touched his ear and healed him"* (Luke 22:51).

In the account we find in Matthew's gospel, we are told that after Jesus instructs Peter to put his sword away, He goes on to explain that all He would have to do is ask the Father and He would immediately put at His disposal *"more than twelve legions of angels"* (Matthew 26:53). Jesus does not need Peter's help. When Peter follows the false solution of his own flesh, all he does is make a mess that Jesus has to clean up. Remember, in the midst of His arrest and betrayal, Jesus stops and heals the man's ear. Jesus could have defended Himself without any assistance from anyone just by speaking the word, or He could have called down legions of angels from heaven. Think of what an army that would be! A legion contained six thousand soldiers, and in 2 Samuel 24 we learn that one angel killed seventy thousand troops and was about to destroy the whole city of Jerusalem until God stopped him.

No, Jesus doesn't need help from Peter's pocketknife. Peter had his moments of "received" ministry. When he makes his famous confession, *"You are the Christ, the Son of the Living God,"* Jesus blesses him and says, *"flesh and blood did not reveal this to you, but My Father who is in heaven"* (Matthew 16:16–17). It isn't something he's thought up on his own. It is revelation he's received from God. But that doesn't mean he always walks in received ministry. After calling Him the Christ, in the next moment Peter is rebuking Jesus for talking about the cross. In the garden of Gethsemane, Peter gives us yet another illustration of following flesh instead of Christ. We also see in Paul's life (and probably our own too), examples of both received and achieved ministry. It is important to recognize that the potential to take matters into our own hands and try to help God out doesn't end when we meet Christ. This week we want to look more at what we can learn from Luke of the false solution of flesh.

Day 1

Flesh against Flesh: Acts 23:1–5

Have you ever noticed that it is easy to be nice to someone who is nice to you? But it is a different story with those who treat you badly. In my opinion, one of the greatest triumphs of faith, one of the greatest evidences of the difference Christ can make, one of the marks of the miraculous, is when a person returns good for evil, blessing for a curse, kindness for hostility. That is something truly divine and supernatural. It is something transcendent and unnatural that only God could accomplish. But when a person gives insult for insult and injury for injury, that is the way of the world—the way of flesh. Paul has been treated unjustly. The charges against him are fabricated and groundless. The trial before him is a mockery of all that is spiritual and of God. So often we see Paul tackle such circumstances with grace and power. Sadly, what we see from Paul in today's study is different though. Instead of Spirit, we see flesh. We see him respond out of himself rather than letting God move and work through him. It is a decidedly human portrait that may disappoint at first glance, but in the end makes Paul someone easier to identify with.

Acts 22 closes out by telling us that the Roman commander arranges for an organized trial for Paul, calling the chief priests and the Council together to meet and hear the case. As we have already seen and will see more in the chapters ahead, Paul's imprisonment purchases opportunities for him to witness of Christ that can be obtained no other way. He will get to testify before kings and emperors just as was prophesied at his conversion in Damascus. But only by the Spirit can he make those chances count.

📖 Read Acts 23:1–2.

What is Paul trying to communicate with his statement in verse 1?

Why is the high priest offended by what he says (23:2)?

WORD STUDY
Brethren

Surprisingly, Paul addresses the Sanhedrin here as *"Brethren"* (the Greek literally reads "men, brethren"). This language communicates Paul viewing them as peers rather than superiors, and stands in contrast to Peter who calls them *"Rulers and elders of the people"* (Acts 4:8) and Stephen who calls them *"brethren and fathers"* (Acts 7:2). Undoubtedly Paul knows many of them personally. He has been a practicing Pharisee with them and was probably a member of the Sanhedrin years before (Acts 26:10). He likely studied with some of them under Gamaliel. It is possible that this greeting is interpreted as a lack of respect and contributes to the offense taken by Ananias.

In a sense, Paul's response to the Sanhedrin is very similar to how Peter and John respond in their meeting with them years earlier when Peter says, *"Whether it is right in the sight of God to give heed to you rather than to God, you be the judge"* (Acts 4:19). In both cases the message is one of a heart that wants God to be pleased rather than just playing to a human audience. Paul is affirming that his conscience is clear before God even if people aren't pleased. This does not mean Paul is sinless, but rather, that there is nothing he has been convicted of as sin in his life that has not been dealt with (see 1 Corinthians 4:4). When Ananias the high priest commands him to be struck, the Greek word (tupto) does not mean a mere slap, but rather "to beat with a stick, club, or fist." He is obviously incensed that Paul would even suggest that there is nothing wrong in his life. Ananias has already judged Paul in his mind and concluded that he is wrong. The problem is Ananias doesn't even realize that his own opinions have become his law instead of the words of God.

Ananias is the son of a man named Nedebaeus and reigned as high priest for eleven or twelve years, beginning in AD 47. He was one of the most cruel, evil and corrupt men to ever hold this office. According to the Jewish historian Josephus, he stole the tithes from the common priests, which were meant for their support and beat any who opposed him in this (*Antiquities* 20.9.2). He was made to appear before the Emperor Claudius in Rome for suspected abuse of the Samaritans but was not convicted (*Antiquities* 20.6.2–3). Flesh seems to be his defining characteristic. He is a tyrant, hated by his own people, and in the end, they kill him when a Jewish revolt breaks out against the Romans in AD 66 (Josephus, Wars 2.17.9).

📖 Examine Paul's response to Ananias in Acts 23:3 and identify what appears to be right and what appears to be wrong.

IN THEIR SHOES
Whitewashed Wall

Paul's name-calling of the high priest is reminiscent of Jesus' words in Matthew 23:27 when He identifies the Pharisees as hypocrites and likens them to *"whitewashed tombs"* because they look beautiful on the outside, but on the inside, are full of death. Perhaps Paul is among those who hear Jesus speak those words. If so, the metaphor of Jesus seems to be lost though, for a *"whitewashed wall"* does not convey as clear an image of being attractive on the outside while masking death inside. An equally valid theory is that Paul is referring to the wall plastered over with *"whitewash"* of Ezekiel 13. Ezekiel confronts the false prophets of his day who predict peace even though judgment is coming. They are compared to those who, instead of building the walls of defense, waste time decorating them with whitewash. God promises to tear down the "wall plastered over with whitewash" (Ez. 13:14–16) and in the same way, remove the false prophets.

There is much truth in Paul's response to the high priest here, but clearly not much in the way of love. Paul is correct in affirming that God will judge this judge one day and makes a valid point that it is not in keeping with the Law to strike a man who has yet to be formally charged, let alone convicted of any violation. Yet Paul is disrespectful and rude to the authorities before which he appears. Although we may be tempted to excuse Paul's frustration and harshness under the circumstances, his response does not compare well with that of Jesus. When He is wrongly struck before being convicted of anything while appearing before the high priest Annas, the Lord simply replies, *"If I have spoken wrongly, testify of the wrong; but if rightly, why do you strike Me?"* (John 18:23). Peter, who witnesses Jesus under trial tells us that *"while being reviled, He did not revile in return; while suffering, He uttered no threats, but kept entrusting Himself to Him who judges righteously"* (1 Peter 2:23). In this particular instance, what squeezes out when Paul is put under pressure is Paul rather than Jesus.

📖 Look at Acts 23:4–5 and answer the questions that follow.

How do the bystanders interpret Paul's words?

Do you consider the explanation Paul gives as a valid reason for his response?

What do you think are the ministry consequences of Paul's fleshly actions here?

> *"...and while being reviled, He did not revile in return; while suffering, He uttered no threats, but kept entrusting Himself to Him who judges righteously;"* (1 Peter 2:23)

It is quite obvious that the *"bystanders"* who witness Paul's response are shocked by his rudeness and offended by his disrespectful manner. They in turn rebuke him, calling into question his audacity to "revile God's high priest." At a glance, Paul's explanation seems plausible for he has not been associated with the Sanhedrin for many years and is supposed by some to have poor eyesight. But here the Greek word used gives clarity. The term translated revile (loidoreō) is usually associated with insult and is the same word Peter uses to describe what the authorities did to Jesus and what He refused to do in return (1 Peter 2:23). Ignorance of the high priest's position, even if true, does not excuse Paul's fleshly outburst. While acknowledging that his own actions violate the law, Paul falls short of humility or a true expression of repentance, trying to dismiss his wrong as oversight instead of sin. Sadly, what is a divinely provided opportunity to bring Christ to a place and persons where He is greatly needed becomes a closed door because of Paul's flesh. Perhaps Ananias is beyond hope of responding to the gospel, but that cannot be said with any confidence of all those present.

In fairness, we can understand Paul's stumbling here. He has been wrongly arrested and abused by an angry mob. He knows many of these who accuse him and had once been a peer with them. People want to kill him. He is probably tired and uncomfortable in his chains and is being accused by a godless high priest who makes it difficult for any to respect, even though he is supposed to be God's representative to the people. Yet while these may explain Paul's response, they do not excuse it. When we encounter a response of flesh from others, it does not make it right for us to retaliate with our own flesh. *"The anger of man does not achieve the righteousness of God"* (James 1:20), for our flesh does not achieve a righteous response; this must be received from the Spirit.

DAY 2

DEFLECTING THE SPOTLIGHT: ACTS 23:6–11

A day before, Paul stands before a huge crowd of his countrymen and is able to turn his own trial into an opportunity to share the hope of the gospel with many. We don't know how those in the crowd were affected, but one hopes that some were touched by the truth of Christ and how He had changed Paul from persecutor to preacher. Unfortunately, the same cannot be said for Paul's management of his trial by the Sanhedrin. His own flesh gets in the way of the gospel. Instead of the spotlight being on the message, it is now on the mess of his own rudeness and rotten attitude. As we will see today, Paul uses his knowledge of his opponents to take the spotlight off him and what he might say. Unfortunately, in so doing, he effectively closes the door of opportunity this trial affords.

📖 Review Acts 23:6–7 and identify how Paul uses the differences between the groups to draw attention away from himself.

DOCTRINE
Sadducees

The theology of the Sadducees is similar to that of liberal Christians today and embraces four principal tenets:

1) A denial of the divinity and consequent authority of the oral law, the body of commentary on the written Law. The Pharisees on the other hand, without any historic evidence, maintained that the oral law was handed down by tradition from the Law-giver Himself.

2) The Sadducees accepted only the teaching of Moses and seem to reject the later books of the OT.

3) The denial of man's resurrection. They maintain that the soul dies with the body (Matt. 22:23). Of course, the doctrine of future rewards and punishments falls with it, likewise the belief in angels or spirits (Acts 23:8).

4) The fourth principal tenet is that humans have absolute moral freedom, for upon this freedom depends the moral quality of their actions. This tenet is, however, so excessive as to almost entirely exclude the divine government of the world.

Paul is well aware of the theological differences existing between the two main divisions of the Sanhedrin. The two major rival parties on the Jewish religious scene are the Pharisees and the Sadducees. Although less numerous than the Pharisees, the Sadducees hold great influence since the High Priests during the time of Jesus and the disciples are all Sadducees. They are for the most part wealthy aristocracy and landowners. Paul, being a Pharisee himself, tries to identify with their side of the theological divide, apparently intentionally working for the dissension mentioned in verse 7 to draw attention away from his own fleshly response to the high priest.

📖 Write what you learn in Acts 23:8–9 of the differing views between the Pharisees and Sadducees and how Paul uses them to his advantage.

The Sadducees are the materialists of their day in more than one sense. Not only are they the wealthy, but they also hold to a belief system that discounts any spiritual realm or afterlife. The Pharisees on the other hand, believe in a life after death, in the angelic realm and the spiritual dimension. By focusing attention on those differences, Paul ignites a debate and momentarily succeeds in drawing some of the Pharisees over to his side in the trial. They have to acknowledge at least the possibility that he has received revelation from an angel or spirit or else deny their own teachings.

📖 Consider the narrative in Acts 23:10 and record the ultimate results of Paul's deflection strategy.

The Sanhedrin is not a homogeneous group. By drawing attention to their differences, Paul actually uses their own flesh against them. As the men passionately jump into the debate, they war with themselves instead of uniting against Paul. The trial with the Sanhedrin effectively comes to an end when the commander, fearing for Paul's safety, has him removed and brought back to the barracks.

📖 Reflect on Paul's vision in Acts 23:11 and write your thoughts on how it relates in this context.

A day later, after everything settles down, the Lord comes to Paul with a vision of encouragement and assurance. Paul must feel a measure of guilt when the Lord compliments him for solemnly witnessing to the cause of Christ at Jerusalem. Although he faithfully did that at the Temple, he blows this chance to witness to the Sanhedrin. The Lord confirms to Paul that he will still get the chance to witness in Rome. This appearance by the Lord, in the context of what has just happened, must be seen as a tremendous expression of grace

> *This appearance by the Lord, in the context of what just happens*
> *must be seen as a tremendous expression of grace.*

One can only imagine the internal turmoil the apostle Paul experiences in the twenty-four hours between his blown opportunity for ministry and the reassuring vision from the

Lord. We must conclude that the delay is intentional. Paul needs time to reflect on what he did and what he should have done. Although Luke does not record the specific details of Paul's repentance, the lack of further rebuke from the Lord coupled with what we know about Paul makes a full and complete turning to the Lord a safe assumption. God gives Paul time to come to grips with his sin and turn from it and then lets him know that the plan for him to go to Rome is still on. We see graphically illustrated that flesh keeps the religious leaders from listening to the Lord as He is moving in their midst. We see a feeble and frail portrait of Paul's own battle with flesh. The point cannot be clearer that following flesh is a failed strategy.

DAY 3

A COMMITMENT TO KILL: ACTS 23:12–22

Is commitment a good thing? We usually believe so. In fact, it is normal to applaud examples of great commitment. Those who exhibit great commitment are described with adjectives like devoted, passionate, and convinced. And yet, just because someone is committed does not mean they are correct. You can be fully committed and completely wrong. As we consider the contrast of achieved ministry verses received ministry, commitment actually falls more naturally on the achieved side, which emphasizes human effort as the supreme agent. The most important word in the Christian life is not commitment, but surrender. Commitment can be a good thing, but it can also quite easily exalt *what I do* instead of *what God does*. Surrender is an acknowledgement that I can't go it alone. I am dependent on what God does. As we continue our look at the false solution of following flesh, we will consider yet another example Luke gives of the principle in this chapter. Today we will see a group of people who exhibit extreme commitment to a religious cause, and yet they fail because the cause is on the wrong side of God.

In Acts 23:12–15, identify as many details as you can of the cause these people take up and how they are committed to it.

WORD STUDY
Oath

When Luke says the men bind themselves under an oath, the literal commitment is that they bind themselves under a curse. The Greek word here is *"anathema."* The men are calling on God to give them over to eternal damnation if they do not fulfill the promise of killing Paul. This same Greek word is translated "accursed" in Galatians 1:8, 9.

More than forty Jews join together and commit themselves to the cause of killing the apostle Paul. He is a hated man. They bind themselves with solemn vows. They promise to *"neither eat nor drink"* until the murder is accomplished. After informing the Jewish leaders of their intent, they offer a plan to help bring it to pass. They request the religious leaders to lie to the commander about wanting another trial, so they can ambush Paul as he is brought to them. It is amazing that when one follows flesh, they can justify all sorts of wrong to accomplish what they see as right.

📖 Record the details you learn in Acts 23:16–18 of how the plot is discovered.

By providence, Paul's nephew is somewhere in the proximity of the plot and brings the information to his uncle. What some might call a lucky coincidence is actually God's providential protection in action. It is interesting that this chapter reveals more about Paul's family than the rest of the New Testament combined. In Acts 23:6 we learn that not only is Paul a Pharisee, but apparently his father and ancestors as well. Here we learn that Paul has both a sister and a nephew. We are not told how the young man learns of the plot. He may be following in Paul's footsteps and studying to be a rabbi. In any case, his family interest prevails, and he moves to protect his uncle by informing him of the plot. Paul obviously takes the plot very seriously and arranges for the information to be passed to the commander.

📖 What do you see in the nephew's meeting with the commander in Acts 23:19–22 that affirms he takes the news seriously?

Everything in the process suggests that the commander is already siding with Paul in his own mind. Perhaps he sees through the motives of the Jewish antagonists. He obviously has given Paul the freedom to receive visitors. That he takes the news of the plot seriously is seen first in the fact that he gives the nephew a private audience and even takes him by the hand. If deemed a small matter, he would not take the time to go to a private place to meet. By instructing the young man to tell no one that he has been informed of the plot, it is obvious he takes it seriously and intends to circumvent it. He doesn't want his knowledge of the plot to reach the assassins, for he doesn't want to give them time to form a different plan. The commander has a natural affinity for Paul in this case because, unlike his accusers, Paul is a Roman citizen, and this is where the commander's allegiance lies. But there seems also to be recognition of the injustice in Paul's treatment at the hands of the Jews.

In the end God does not allow fleshly strategies to prosper.

The Jewish assassins place their hope in secrecy. Their fleshly strategy is sneaking around, but once again Luke shows us that fleshly striving is a false solution. One of the earmarks of striving can be hiding our actions. Righteous deeds initiated by God do not usually need to be kept out of view. It ought to be a warning to us that perhaps our actions are not right if we don't want them to be known. In the end, God does not allow fleshly strategies to prosper. We will see that point driven home in tomorrow's study.

DAY 4

THE MANPOWER OF MISSIONS: ACTS 23:23–35

I don't recall exactly what the circumstance was, but a conversation with a fellow believer shortly after I became a Christian taught me an important truth I have never forgotten. I found myself in a favorable circumstance, and I commented to my Christian friend about how lucky I felt. She lovingly but firmly rebuked me, saying, "There is no such thing as luck." After a moment of reflection, I concluded she was right. It was not luck. It was blessing, and it was the Lord whom I should have thanked and not my lucky stars. In that moment I experienced a huge paradigm shift. I realized that to believe in luck was to view life as random and to ignore the sovereignty of God. We do not live in a random universe, for God has not abdicated His throne. From that point forward, I quickly lost the habit of talking about luck. The word dropped out of my vocabulary. What we see in this vignette from the life of Paul attests not to luck but to the providential protection of God. It is not random chance that allows Paul's nephew to learn of a secret plot. It is not coincidence that Paul's citizenship is so important to his protection and wins him favor in the eyes of the Roman commander. As we will see today, this man goes to great lengths to protect Paul, but the real protection over him is the sovereignty of God.

📖 Examine Acts 23:23–24 and make note of all the commander does to protect Paul and provide for him.

The Roman commander quickly forms a plot of his own. His plan is to slip Paul out of the city by night before anyone knows he is gone. He commits a great amount of resources to ensure his plan's success. In all, some 470 troops are guarding Paul as he goes. The forty plus assassins are outnumbered ten to one. This significant army represents one third of the forces at the garrison in Jerusalem. To ensure stealth, the commander makes plans to leave at three hours after dark. To ensure haste, he also provides horses for quick travel to Caesarea and the governor.

📖 What does the commander's letter to Felix in Acts 23:25–30 tell you about how the commander views Paul's case?

When a Roman commander sends a prisoner to a superior officer, he is required to write a letter of explanation. In his letter, Claudius Lysias gives Felix the basic details of the riot, his rescue of Paul, and the trial before the Council. He informs Felix that Paul is a Roman citizen and also passes on news of the plot against him. In addition to the facts, the Roman commander adds his own opinion, making it clear that he considers Paul innocent of any charge worthy of death or even imprisonment. Lysias passes the case on and lets Felix know that he will have the Jewish accusers come to Caesarea to make their case. It is clear that this man is on Paul's side.

📖 Read Acts 23:31–33 and make note of the details you observe of Paul's trip to Caesarea.

A Roman Centurion is a leader of one hundred troops. One can hear in the Latin term a similarity to the word "cent" (one hundredth of a dollar) or "century" (one hundred years) since they share a common root. The title itself means a ruler of one hundred. Claudius Lysias calls two centurions in order to dispatch two hundred Roman Legionnaires. These are the greatest fighting men of the ancient world. They are the main protection for Paul, though the additional horsemen and spearmen add to the appearance of intimidation.

This rather large contingent makes the thirty-five to forty-mile trip to Antipatris, which serves as a rest stop between Jerusalem and Caesarea. Traveling that distance in so short a time must be a great hardship, especially for the foot soldiers. Because the greatest danger is in the early portion of the trip, and because the absence of so many soldiers weakens the security force in Jerusalem, all but the seventy horsemen take their leave at this point and return to the fort. The smaller group successfully delivers their charge to the governor in Caesarea.

📖 Wrap up your study of this chapter by summarizing the end of the journey as recorded in Acts 23:34–35.

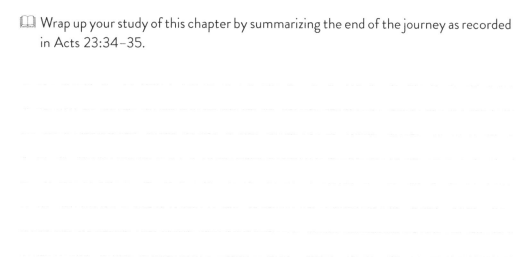

Once Felix reads the explanation from Claudius Lysias, he inquires of Paul as to where he is from. It is likely Felix is hoping to find a reason to avoid the case. But since Cilicia at this time is under the authority of the Legate of Syria to whom Felix is responsible, he has no choice but to handle the trial. He communicates to Paul that he will indeed hear the case as soon as the accusers can get there for a trial. In the meantime, Paul will be kept under guard at the governor's palace.

It is quite ironic that Paul actually finds better treatment from these foreigners than he receives from the religious Jews who are supposed to be following God. But religious flesh is far worse to deal with than unrighteous ignorance. Paul may not be comfortable in chains or having his freedom restricted, but he is safe here, and for a prisoner, he is treated quite well.

DAY 5

FOR ME TO FOLLOW GOD

You are faced with a sticky problem, and God hasn't provided a solution on your time-table. Something needs to be done, so you take matters into your own hands and do what you think is best. But your solution ends up being worse than the problem. We've all been there. We've all done that. The solution of following our own flesh is always flawed. It never brings about the good result we intend. In Acts 23 we see flesh coming out from every direction. We witness it in the Jewish mob. We see it in the high priest. We are given a remarkably human portrait of the apostle Paul as his flesh comes out before the Sanhedrin. In honest fashion Luke underscores his mentor's own imperfections. We observe the fleshly zeal of a band of assassins who are willing to be accursed themselves rather than let Paul live. But beyond all that, we must make sure not to miss the main point. Flesh happens, but the more important lesson is that God does not let any of that flesh prosper. The mob is unsuccessful in killing Paul. The high priest is not allowed to complete his trial. Paul's flesh slams the door on a potentially significant opportunity to share the gospel. The forty assassins either die of hunger and thirst or eventually give up their sworn task. In every single instance God thwarts the false solution of flesh. We can learn this lesson from this chapter, or we can learn it through our own experience but sooner or later we will have to learn it.

> *In Acts 23 we see flesh coming out from every direction... but the more important lesson is that God does not let any of that flesh prosper.*

Flesh always causes problems, and it always has consequences. For Paul, flesh causes a lost opportunity to witness, and helps instigate a murder plot against him. For the men dedicated to his death, their conniving produces a failed plot, and a lot of lost credibility. What are some examples you see in your life or those you know of flesh causing problems and bringing negative consequences?

Proverbs 15:1 says, *"A gentle answer turns away wrath. But a harsh word stirs up anger."* One of the problems with flesh is its remarkable ability to reproduce itself. One fleshly action tends to lead to a fleshly reaction. Often, we want to blame a negative or frustrating circumstance, but really, that is merely the pressure which squeezes out of us what is already going on inside. If we are walking in the Spirit, then pressure squeezes out spirituality. If we are walking in the flesh, then pressure squeezes out flesh. We want to blame the pressure instead of seeing our own hearts as the real problem. As you reflect on your personal experience, in which of these areas do you have the most struggles with "squeezed-out" flesh?

☐ at work

☐ in my marriage

☐ my children

☐ driving in traffic

☐ with my relatives

☐ in my neighborhood

☐ during recreation activities

☐ at church meetings

☐ other:_____

What is usually the catalyst which brings your flesh to the surface?

What do you need to do differently to cut down on these flesh eruptions?

"A gentle answer turns away wrath. But a harsh word stirs up anger." (Proverbs 15:1)

The "squeezed-out" variety of flesh is what I would call "bad flesh." It is the more obvious kind of flesh, and when it surfaces everyone usually recognizes it immediately. But there is another kind of flesh I refer to as "good flesh." Now, I realize that is an oxymoron, for there is no such thing as fleshly behavior that is good, but what I mean by this is "good-looking flesh." It is not ugly as outbursts of anger and may not be recognized as flesh at all until later on. But it is flesh just the same. Instead of the "squeezed-out" variety, this is usually manifested in the "help-out" strategy. It is when we get impatient and try to help God out by doing what we think is best. But it is done at our initiation rather than His. It is our idea instead of His instruction. And since it started with us instead of Him, its only power is our strength and what we can make happen by trying hard. This "help-out" flesh is usually drowning in good intentions, but it will have no more of the blessing of God than its ugly stepsister, "squeezed-out" flesh.

What kind of situations can you think of where "help-out" flesh shows up?

As you consider these two kinds of flesh, perhaps another way of identifying them would be that the "squeeze-out" variety of bad flesh could be termed "rebellious flesh." The "help-out" efforts of good flesh may rightly be called "religious flesh." It usually arrives dressed up in its Sunday best. It may not look as bad, but in the end, it may be even worse than its more obvious counterpart. Of these two, which would you say you struggle with more?

We may not always recognize our own flesh right away. Often others see it in us before we notice it ourselves. We may be better at seeing it in others. But we do have God's Spirit living in us, and the first defense against flesh is to be sensitive to His conviction. When we become aware of flesh rearing its ugly head in our lives, we must deal with it, and the sooner the better. The longer flesh is allowed to reign the more damage it does. We deal with flesh in two simple steps (notice I said "simple." I didn't say "easy"). **Step One** is to confess. We must acknowledge our sin to God, and perhaps to those on the receiving end of it as well. **Step Two** is to yield. Invite God to again take His rightful place on the throne of our heart and ask for His power and help.

Before we end, there is a final lesson we must not miss from Acts 23. Humans have lots of fleshly efforts and activities. We see that. God doesn't allow flesh to prosper. We acknowledge that. But we must also recognize that God has grace for our flesh. Even though the door of ministry slams shut when Paul's flesh goes on parade, God promises other chances. Luke will give them to us in great detail in the chapters to come. And just as God protects Paul from the angry mob, He also protects him from the plot on his life by using his nephew and the Roman commander. God knows we are imperfect. Psalm 103:14 states, *"He is mindful that we are but dust."* He has an abundant supply of grace for our fleshly failings. But to draw on that grace we must turn from self and back to Him.

As our lesson comes to an end, write a prayer to the Lord expressing what you are learning...

NOTES

LESSON 10

THE FRUIT OF PATIENCE
ACTS 24

Patience is a virtue. You probably heard this quip many times growing up. Most of us know we need patience, but few of us want to enroll in the schools where it is taught. Often the very situations which require patience are the tools God chooses to use in our lives to produce it. We pray for patience and then are surprised when God brings across our path the people and circumstances which demand it of us. God certainly wants to work patience into our character, but it is important to realize that patience is not simply the result of lessons learned. In Galatians 5:22–23 the apostle Paul identifies what he calls the *"fruit of the Spirit."* He is expressing the character qualities that are produced in us when the Spirit of God is in control of our lives instead of the flesh. He begins, *"But the fruit of the Spirit is love, joy, peace, patience,"* and continues his list from there. The Greek word he uses for patience (*macrothumia*) literally conveys the message of being *"long to anger"* and specifically has the idea of patience with people. We see from this that patience is not just a skill, it is a character quality that is produced in us by God Himself. When His Spirit is in control, we are able to manifest patience which is part of His own character. But notice what Paul places before patience on the list. First and foremost, he mentions love. Love may not be the same thing as patience, but it is definitely related to it. We are patient with people we love. In fact, in defining love in 1 Corinthians 13:8 Paul states, *"Love is patient."* The next fruit of the Spirit is joy, and this too relates to patience. Have you ever noticed how much more patient you are in traffic or in the supermarket line when you are in a good mood? A joyful heart finds it easier to be patient. Likewise, peace, next on Paul's list, contributes as well. When our heart is at peace, we can be patient even when we recognize that others are wrong. God is patient (2 Peter 3:9) and wants us to be as well.

> In 1 Corinthians 13:8 Paul states, "Love is patient." To be impatient,
> therefore, is to be unloving.

Acts chapter 23 is not a high point for Paul, spiritually. We see Paul's weaknesses come to the surface as he reacts in the flesh to his accusers. What could have been another opportunity to speak the message of Christ as Messiah to the leaders of the Jewish nation comes to a quick end because of his stumbling. Though there may very well have been persecution anyway, Paul's flesh adds fuel to the fire of Jewish animosity, and a death plot is formed against him. If one aspect of the fruit of the Spirit is *"patience,"* then it makes sense that one of the ways the fruit of the flesh is reflected is in impatience. But it is clear from Acts 24 that Paul has learned an important lesson through all of this. As we will see in our study this week, the chapter is marked by patience in Paul's response as well as patience regarding his release. It is encouraging to recognize through Paul that not only does God desire patience in us, but He also exercises patience with us in how He deals with our flesh. He gives Paul time to reflect and repent. And then He affirms that He is still going to accomplish what He has promised in taking Paul to Rome. In this week's lesson we will see a marked difference, as Paul seems far more patient with people and with his circumstances.

DAY 1

PAU'S ACCUSERS MAKE THEIR CASE TO FELIX: ACTS 24:1–9

What are you tempted to do when you hear someone passing information to one of your authorities that you know is not true? As a parent of four children, I have sat through countless conversations where one of my children was bringing an accusation against another. While such incidents occur less frequently than they used to, in most of them the kid making the accusation is invariably interrupted by outcries of "That's not true!" While adults may not rant and rave about it as children do, they are equally adept at jumping into the fray and impatiently moving to defend themselves. While we may be tempted to chalk it up to human nature, a more accurate assessment is that it is a result of *fallen* human nature. In other words, it comes from the impatience of flesh. In Acts 24:1–9 we will see Paul exhibit patience as his accusers make their false charges against him.

📖 Make note in Acts 24:1 of the time factor in Paul's case coming to trial and give your thoughts on the potential impact to Paul.

WORD STUDY
Patience

There are two different Greek words for wrath in the Bible. The word *orge* is a consistent, abiding state of anger. It is not losing one's temper, but rather, anger resulting from contemplation. It stands in contrast to the word *thumos*, which is woven into the word for patience (*macrothumia*). *Thumos* (from which we get our term "thermal") has the idea of a sudden boiling over of anger. The prefix *macro* (meaning "large" or "long") makes the word mean "long to anger" or in other words, to not have a short fuse; to be slow to lose your temper. Patience can still have anger over the right things but does not lose self-control because of anger.

As an author, Luke is ever attentive to detail, but at the same time, he is not excessive. He always has purpose in the information he gives us. He wants the reader to know that it takes five days for Paul's next trial to happen. We know it is only a two-day journey, but perhaps delayed by preparations, it is five days before the high priest Ananias arrives with an attorney and some of the elders. I'm sure that the guilty are never in a hurry to see their case come to trial, but I would think the opposite to be true for those who are innocent. I would expect that they would want their name cleared as soon as possible, especially when they have to wait in jail for their trial. Luke doesn't tell us anything specific to indicate special patience from Paul during this time, but once he speaks, we will see no evidence of a surge of impatience. God is making Paul wait, but He is also shaping his character to be better at waiting, and that will be helpful in the days ahead.

📖 Write down all that stands out to you in Acts 24:2–4 of the Jewish attorney's attempts at flattery to win Felix to his way of thinking.

The Jewish attorney begins his case, not by arguing its merits but by going overboard in flattery of Felix. Look at all Tertullus gives the governor credit for. First, he credits Felix for giving much peace. Even if true, it probably should be the Roman commander who is being applauded. Next, he links reforms for the nation to Felix's foresight. The flattery drips off his tongue as he speaks of acknowledging these things *"in every way and everywhere...with all thankfulness,"* and calls the governor, *"most excellent Felix."* The flowery speech of this attorney continues as he feigns concern over the possibility of "wearying" the governor, or taking too much of his time, so he *"begs"* for a brief hearing. Such wasted words are the norm when appearing before a prominent leader but seem to be taken to the extreme here.

📖 What is the gist of the accusations Tertullus brings against Paul in Acts 24:5–6a?

Tertullus briefly lays out four charges against Paul, only one of which has any element of truth. Paul is accused of being "a real pest," which, though annoying, probably violates no Roman law. The second charge is a little more serious. Paul is identified as one who *"stirs up dissension among all the Jews throughout the world."* The Romans constantly are worried about civil uprisings and always take this threat seriously. Third, Paul is blamed as being a "ringleader of the sect of the Nazarenes." While this is the only accusation that comes close to being true, it violates no Roman law, so the accusation is of little consequence. Finally, Paul is charged with trying to "desecrate the temple." It is interesting that originally in Acts 21:28 Paul is accused of being the man who "preaches to all men everywhere against our people and the Law and this place" (i.e., the Temple), as well as trying to "desecrate the temple." The first charge would have offended Jews only, but is changed to "dissension," something the Romans would consider a threat.

DID YOU KNOW?
Dissension

Israel at the time of the book of Acts is not a self-governing nation. It is a conquered country under Roman occupation. Rome is the dominant world power of the day, and controls most of Europe and the Middle East. Spread out over such a vast territory, the Romans constantly worry of uprisings in one of their provinces. To cause dissension or to lead a revolt is quite a serious charge and were it true of Paul, he would most likely be put to death

 Look at Acts 24:6b–9 and write the details of how Tertullus closes his introductory remarks and explains how the case comes to Felix.

The Jewish attorney Tertullus tries to paint the Roman commander Lysias as interrupting with violence an orderly pursuit of Jewish law and forcing Felix to deal with the case unnecessarily. Of course, that is a gross misrepresentation of the facts. Lysias actually quells a riot and protects a Roman citizen. But with passionate zeal, the Jews begin shouting their agreement with the charges raised by Tertullus.

Conspicuously absent from these first nine verses are any words from Paul. He knows that the accusations are groundless and that the Jews are distorting and misrepresenting their own actions. But unlike the last trial, Paul has learned from the mistakes of his own flesh. This time the fact that he is walking in the Spirit is seen in the fruit of his patience.

Day 2

Paul's Defense: Acts 24:10–15

One aspect that stands out from the trials of Jesus leading up to His crucifixion is His silence. He knew what the outcome would be, and though He knew the charges against Him were groundless, He felt no need to jump to His own defense. He remained quiet, though he was battered by relentless questioning. He saw no need to defend Himself. You see, a mark of flesh is the need to be proven right. As a result, flesh foments arguing and strife. Paul mentions *"strife, jealousy, outbursts of anger, disputes, dissensions"* and all other sorts of things as the fruit of the flesh (Galatians 5:19–21). He also mentions strife as a defining evidence of the fleshly Christian who doesn't live as a spiritual man (1 Corinthians 3:3). In Acts 23 we see Paul causing strife and adding to it. But here in Acts 24 we see a different man—one controlled by the Spirit rather than flesh, and as a result, one who is able to be cool and patient under trial. We see a man who is more like Jesus.

📖 Identify from Acts 24:10 when Paul speaks and how.

Instead of interrupting impatiently as flesh is prone to do, Paul waits until governor Felix invites him to speak. Paul is polite and respectful in his greeting to the governor but uses none of the vain flattery like that of the Jewish attorney. Perhaps the most important word Paul uses in verse 10 is the word *"defense."* It is translated from the Greek word apologia, from which we get the term, "apologetics." Paul intends to build an intellectual case for his views as well as his innocence.

📖 Make a thorough scrutiny of Acts 24:11–13, and list all the ways Paul defends his innocence in these verses.

"...for you are still fleshly. For since there is jealousy and strife among you, are you not fleshly, and are you not walking like mere men?" (1 Corinthians 3:3)

Paul systematically lays down the details of his innocence in a way that is quite logical. First, he makes note of the fact that according to his Jewish accusers, he is supposed to have made a pest of himself and stirred up dissension. Yet since the trial has taken five days and he first went to the Temple twelve days ago, all this trouble-making they are claiming is supposed to have been accomplished in seven days. Even if he were so inclined, there has not been time for him to stir up a rebellion. Second, though they accuse him of dissension, Paul basically challenges them to prove he even talks with anyone. It is pretty hard to stir up dissension without having a discussion.

📖 Read Acts 24:14–15, and identify what Paul admits to and how he redefines their characterization of Christianity as a sect.

Paul freely admits being part of "the Way," knowing that he is violating no law in doing so, but he takes issue with their calling it a sect. The Greek word here (*hairesis*) is where we get the term "heresy" and pictures the Christian faith as a departure from Judaism. Paul makes clear that rather than departing from his Jewish faith, he sees himself as completely in line with it and with the Scriptures. When one recognizes Jesus as the Messiah, then everything associated with worshiping Him is fulfillment of the Jewish faith rather than deviation from it.

It appears with his words here, Paul exhibits not only patience with his trial, but seems to regain his patience with his accusers. He now is trying once again to win them to Christ. He wants even them to understand that Jesus is "the Way," and that to follow Him is not a sect or a departure from all the Jews hope in. He appeals to the values these men believe in—the Old Testament with its major divisions of Law and Prophets, and the hope of future resurrection.

DAY 3

A SECOND CHANCE TO WITNESS TO ANANIAS: ACTS 24:16–21

Ours is the God of second chances, and what an encouragement it is to know that. Failure doesn't have to be final. When Abraham blows it with Sarah's plan to help God out, unintended results follow (Genesis 16:12). But even though Abraham's striving is failure, Isaac still comes *"at the appointed time"* (Genesis 18:4). Not only does God give Abraham a second chance, but this term, "appointed time," when coupled with God's omniscience, makes it clear that God's plan takes into account his failure. God knows every time we will blow it, so our mistakes can't mess up His plan. And He also knows when we will repent. God gives Paul another opportunity to testify before the high priest, and this time he makes the most of it.

DID YOU KNOW?
The Law and the Prophets

The phrase, "the Law and the Prophets," is Jewish terminology to refer to the major divisions of the Old Testament. The Law (or Pentateuch) represents the first five books written by Moses. The Prophets of course, represent the whole of prophetic writings. There is a third division called "the Writings" which represents all the wisdom literature such as Psalms, Proverbs, Ecclesiastes, etc. It is most common, however, to refer to see people reference two major divisions of Law and Prophets (see Mt.7:12, Jn.1:45). These do not contradict the work of Christ, but rather, support it (Jn.5:39).

📖 Compare Acts 24:16 with Acts 23:1 and write your thoughts on the difference.

The difference in Paul's opening statement before the Sanhedrin and his words here are subtle but significant. Instead of asserting that he has kept a clear conscience all his life, he adds two qualifiers to the equation. First, instead of saying *"I live with,"* implying perfection and consistency, he says, *"I do my best."* Do you notice he drops the word *"perfectly"* from the previous statement? He links the consistency with effort rather than performance. Second, he makes no claim of always having a blameless conscience, but rather that he *"maintains"* a blameless conscience. Maintenance speaks of correcting the things which deviate. James 3:2 makes it clear that *"we all stumble."* The right heart before God without ever sinning is not possible for us to attain in this life, but it is possible to deal with every offense of conscience so as to maintain a clear conscience before God. Paul clarifies that though he is not perfect, there is nothing in his life that has not been dealt with before God.

📖 What do the statements of Acts 24:17–18a say about how Paul's actions align with the Law?

Paul communicates that it has been a lapse of several years since he has been able to come to the Temple. Of course, this is because of his missionary travels in Asia and Europe. His actions while at the Temple express devotion to the Law rather than violation of it. He brought alms (charitable gifts to the poor) and offerings to God. He also was *"purified"* according to the requirements of the Law. Finally, Paul asserts that all his actions were done *"without any crowd or uproar."* This is a truthful and accurate account of Paul's time at the Temple, and there is nothing anyone can find fault with in this.

📖 Who does Paul credit in Acts 24:18b–19 as the source of the trouble?

DID YOU KNOW?
Accusers

The case against Paul by the Sanhedrin is greatly undermined by the fact that his original accusers— Jews from Asia—are not present at the trial to testify. "Roman law was very strong against accusers who abandoned their charges. The Jews from Asia are the ones to bring the charges; the present accusers are disqualified" (Rogers and Rogers, *Linguistic and Exegetical Key to the Greek New Testament*, Zondervan, p.298). Technically the case could be dismissed on this alone.

Paul rightly lays the blame for the Temple disturbance at the feet of the *"Jews from Asia."* These are men who opposed Paul and his ministry in the synagogues of Asia—probably at Ephesus or somewhere similar. Since they are the ones who started the whole mess, Paul rightly points out that they *"ought to have been present before* [Felix] *and to make accusation, if they should have anything against* [Paul]." How can there be a fair trial without the original accusers giving testimony? The point would not be lost on the governor.

📖 Since Paul's original accusers are not present, what does he invite his present accusers to do in Acts 24:20–21?

Paul opens his life up for examination. He invites the men to build a case against him of any *"misdeed"* they see in him. He makes careful choice of his words here though. The Greek term for "misdeed" (*adikema*) speaks of criminal activity. The root word literally means "without justice." Paul could not claim he was totally in the right during his last trial, but he can with good conscience maintain his innocence of any crime. Paul places his claim of belief in the resurrection of the dead as central to the case.

In Paul's previous trial, he was a hothead who reacted out of his flesh. This time, he is yielded to the Lord and exhibits patience and calm. He brings the attention of those present back to what is the central issue. If they are going to convict him of anything, he wants to make sure it is the right thing. He is willing to suffer and die for the cause of the resurrection of Christ. As we see in all of Paul's writings, he places that as the centerpiece of Christianity.

DAY 4

THE VERDICT OF FELIX: ACTS 24:22–27

When a believer responds in the flesh in the midst of conflict with one who does not know Christ, then the unbeliever has an excuse for his own flesh. Proverbs 15:18 says, *"A hot-tempered man stirs up strife, but the slow to anger calms a dispute."* Paul has personal experience with both sides of this proverb. When we yield ourselves to the Spirit's control and in His strength respond to conflict rather than react to it, then the unbeliever has nothing to blame for his own fleshly response except himself. Anyone who witnesses such a conflict with an objective eye is able to see quickly who is right and who is wrong. Paul's first trial was clouded by his own fleshly response, but that is not the case now. As we see in Day Four of this lesson, Felix doesn't buy into the Jewish accusations. Though he may not handle the case with ethics and righteousness, it seems clear he is no enemy of Paul.

What do you see revealed in Acts 24:22 of Felix's view of the case?

"A hot-tempered man stirs up strife, but the slow to anger calms a dispute." - Proverbs 15:18

It is interesting to read between the lines in this particular trial. Paul invites the Jews to prove their case, but Felix sees no need for that. First of all, he is apparently somewhat familiar with Christianity. Though Felix is certainly not a believer, his actions belie a sympathy for Paul. Felix doesn't give the Jews a chance to take their case any further. Instead, he puts off deciding the case until *"Lysias the commander comes down."* It is important to remember that Felix already knows that Lysias thinks Paul is innocent. All this delay will do is strengthen Paul's defense and weaken the case against him.

What does Acts 24:23 say about Paul's treatment and Felix's view of him?

Everything about verse 23 speaks of leniency. Clearly Paul is not seen as a threat, and the treatment suggests Felix probably sees him as not guilty. The case cannot be dismissed without a proper trial, but Paul's confinement can be characterized as "minimum security." There is mention of "custody" but no mention of chains. He is to be given "some freedom," and by allowing visitors Paul is afforded quite a comfortable incarceration. In fact, although technically a prisoner, he is really in "protective custody," as all this serves to keep him inaccessible to those who vowed his death.

 Read Acts 24:24–26.

What do you see reflected here of the spiritual interest of Felix?

DID YOU KNOW?
Felix and Drusilla

Felix marries three times, once to the granddaughter of Cleopatra and Anthony, and Drusilla is his second wife. She is the daughter of Agrippa I and is fourteen when Felix assumes office. Shortly thereafter, she is married to Azizus king of Emensa, but Felix, enchanted by her beauty, gets a magician from Cyprus to persuade her to leave her husband and marry him. She is probably about sixteen years old (see Josephus, *Antiquities*, 12:23, 19:354, 20:141–144).

Why do you suppose Felix is frightened by the discussion with Paul?

What motive is revealed in verse 26 for Felix's treatment of Paul?

It is probably not fair to call Felix a "seeker," for although he inquires of Paul about the Christian faith, the interest seems to be more from curiosity than from conviction. He seems mildly interested until Paul begins to speak of *"righteousness, self-control and the judgment to come."* Felix's godless lifestyle is something he is unwilling to give up, so he doesn't want to think about judgment. Yet he cannot leave Paul alone either. The phrase, *"At the same time too,"* in verse 26 reveals divided motives. Although clearly, he hopes for a bribe from Paul, and gives him every opportunity to do so, the term "too" makes it clear that this is only one of his motives. There is the suggestion that, through Paul, God is working on Felix, but there is not a clear indication of a positive response to that working. Regardless, Paul is given many opportunities to talk about Christ with one of the most prominent people in the region.

📖 What details stand out to you from Acts 24:27?

It takes a moment of reflection for the reality of verse 27 to sink in. Paul's predicament goes on for two whole years. Although his confinement is more like "house arrest," still this innocent man finds his freedom restricted on false charges for quite a long time. Even though Felix eventually is replaced as governor, for the sake of appeasement of the Jews, Paul remains in prison under the new administration.

As we think about Paul's circumstances, the word "patience" is an appropriate identification of the time. There is no resolution to the flimsy case against him. But there is also no indication of grumbling or complaining from Paul. He has turned a corner in his attitude about the situation. The spiritual fruit of patience is clearly seen. One of the truths that must undergird Paul in this patience is the recognition that God is giving him strategic opportunities to witness. His trust in God's sovereignty drives him to the conclusion that none of this is wasted time.

Day 5

For Me to Follow God

In America convenience is king. When we want instant breakfast, we just add milk. Dinner goes from the freezer to the microwave to the table in less than ten minutes. When we need instant cash, we have automated teller machines available twenty-four hours a day. If we want a letter to go overnight, we send it via FedEx®, and if that isn't fast enough, we fax or email it. From coast-to-coast jet travel to quick-dry nail polish, there is little in our culture that cultivates patience. Small wonder that many people today struggle with short attention spans. Yet God's plan for our lives quite often calls us to wait.

As I read through the Psalms, I am amazed at how many times that annoying word wait appears. I think God is trying to tell us something. But patience is not a task, it is a fruit.

It is *produced in us*, not *performed by us*. We cannot grit our teeth and try real hard and squeeze out patience. Instead, it is manifested through us as *"fruit of the Spirit,"* and often is produced in us through tribulation (James 1:2–4; Romans 5:3). The Christian life, that is, living as God intends, is a life of purpose and power. We experience this "power for living" when we are "filled" (directed and empowered) by the Spirit of God. The problem is that our lives, much like a car metaphorically speaking, have only one steering wheel. If we insist on steering and directing our own lives, then God graciously steps aside, but fortunately He never leaves us (Hebrews 13:5). He is still "resident" in our lives but no longer "president" because He will not force Himself on us.

Often circumstances in our lives demand of us patience. Paul has to sit in Roman custody for two years. Yet the patience he exhibits in this chapter stands in stark contrast to the impatience and flesh we see in Acts 23. The only explanation for the difference between the two is that one is an exhibition of Paul's flesh, and the other is him under the influence of the Holy Spirit. The real issue of patience and of this week's lesson is "who is in the driver's seat of your life?"

Can you think of a time recently when God enabled you to be patient in a challenging circumstance?

In what kinds of situations do you find it the hardest to be patient?

The real issue of patience, and of this week's lesson is "who is in the driver's seat of your life?"

Circle where you spend the most time:

1   2   3   4   5

spirit-filled   self-directed

Christians who characteristically lead a self-directed life do so for one of two reasons— lack of knowledge or lack of belief. They are either uninformed of or have forgotten the abundant life Christ promises. Which is more relevant to your experience and the times when you are not close to the Lord?

Ask yourself this question: "Do I honestly want God to direct my life?" If the answer is yes, then go on; if the answer is no then talk honestly with God about this and ask Him to change your heart. God knows your heart. It is useless to talk spiritually with religious-sounding terminology if your heart is not sincere. If you really don't want God to direct your life, tell Him that, and invite Him to help you deal with that attitude. Often wrong attitudes never change because we never bring them to the One who can change us.

Read Ephesians 4:22–24 and write down what it teaches about how we are to live and the role of the will in this.

In Ephesians chapter 4, Paul relates two main principles of being filled with the Spirit, and he uses figurative language of changing clothes—laying aside the old self and putting on the new self. God does not want His adopted children to be seen wearing filthy garments of their old life. He provides us with new clothes of righteousness. But we are the keepers of our closet, and our will is involved in deciding which clothes we will wear each day. Patience is one of the garments in our new wardrobe, but we must choose to put it on by putting on the "new self." The following explains how we do that.

Laying Aside the Old Self

First, you must confess the general sin of directing your own life. If you have been wearing the old garments of self, then the real problem is not the specific "sins" that creep up, but the general sin of self being in control. Impatience is simply the manifestation of dressing out of the wrong wardrobe.

Next, ask God to reveal any specific sins He wants to deal with and confess them using 1 John 1:9 as a promise. Once we deal with the general sin of running our own life, there will probably be specific individual sins that also need to be dealt with. While a lack of patience may be one of those sins, there are probably plenty of others.

> "...that, in reference to your former manner of life, you lay aside the old self, which is being corrupted in accordance with the lusts of deceit, and that you be renewed in the spirit of your mind, and put on the new self, which in the likeness of God has been created in righteousness and holiness of the truth." (Ephesians 4:22–24)

It is crucial we understand what it means to "confess." The Greek word means "to say the same thing" or "to agree." When we confess our sins, we are agreeing to three things. First, we agree that the action or attitude is wrong. We agree with God's perspective on it. Second, we agree that we are guilty and need to change. Third, we agree that it is forgiven. We choose to see it as Christ does.

We cannot wear the new garment without taking off the old. We must put self aside. But taking off the old garment is not enough. We must also "put on" the new. How do we do this?

Putting On the New Self

The first step to putting on the new garment is to invite Christ to take control of the throne of your life and ask God to fill you with His Holy Spirit. In a word, this step is to "yield."

Second, as an expression of faith, we should thank Him for filling us with His Spirit. We know that it is His will for us to be Spirit-filled because He commands it (Ephesians 5:18). We know according to the promise in 1 John 5:14–15 that when we pray according to His will, He hears us and answers us.

We do not judge whether or not God has filled us with His Spirit by our feelings. We may or may not have an emotional experience. We must walk by faith, not by feelings, and we must trust God to do what He promises.

Why not close out this week's lesson by expressing your faith in God's working in the form of a written prayer to Him...

NOTES

LESSON 11

A DEFENSE FOR THE HOPE WITHIN
ACTS 25—26

You may have heard of the term, "apologetics." It is generally applied to the arena of defending the Christian faith intellectually. While that is certainly a worthwhile pursuit, and often plays an important part in the process of evangelism, intelligent arguments are not the only means of apologetics. In 1 Peter 3:15-16 the Apostle Peter writes, *"but sanctify Christ as Lord in your hearts, always being ready to make a defense to everyone who asks you to give an account for the hope that is in you, yet with gentleness and reverence; and keep a good conscience so that in the thing in which you are slandered, those who revile your good behavior in Christ will be put to shame."* In this passage Peter relates three extremely important, but often neglected, components of evangelism. First, he calls us to *"sanctify Christ as Lord"* in our hearts. Believers whose lives are surrendered to the Lord are letting Him live through them. Jesus is seen in their actions and attitudes. Second, Peter says we are always to be *"ready to make a defense to everyone who asks you to give an account for the hope that is in you."* We must always be ready to personally defend why we believe. Yet this defense is not a debate. It is to be done with *"gentleness and reverence."* Third, we are to maintain a *"good conscience."* In other words, we are to live better lives than the unbelievers around us. The context of this passage is speaking of when believers suffer for doing what is right.

> *"...but sanctify Christ as Lord in your hearts, always being ready to make a defense to everyone who asks you to give an account for the hope that is in you, yet with gentleness and reverence; and keep a good conscience so that in the thing in which you are slandered, those who revile your good behavior in Christ will be put to shame." (1 Peter 3:15-16)*

The Greek word translated *"defense"* in 1 Peter 3:15 is apologia from which we get our word, apologetics. It is used in the book of Acts more than the rest of the New Testament combined, and most of those uses are in Acts 25 and 26. The Greek word actually is a compound word. It is the term *logos*, from which we get our English phrase, "logic." The prefix *apo*, means "from," so when you put the two together you have a word that literally means "from logic." It speaks of reasoning and rationality. Perhaps the greatest insight we gain into the term apologia is from how the apostle Paul uses it. Every time Paul speaks the word, he goes into sharing his own personal testimony of coming to faith in Christ. He defends the reality of Christianity, not simply from reason or argument, but from his own personal experience. One might argue against what is supposed to happen in their lives if they give themselves to Christ, but no one can argue against history—what has already happened. This is why the personal testimony is so important.

Not everyone is gifted with extraordinary intellect. Nor is everyone able to carry on great debate on an intensely intellectual level as a great orator. Most of us would feel unequal to the task were it our responsibility to convince someone by our overwhelming logic of their need for Christ. I am sure there are those rare few who delight in such a challenge, but most of us don't. But that is not the point of *apologia*. Every one of us has a story to tell, and that is the way most of us will make a defense for the hope within us. This week we will see Paul do just that.

DAY 1

A NEW GOVERNOR MEANS A NEW OPPORTUNITY: ACTS 25:1–6

For two years Paul's case has gone nowhere. Felix knows he is innocent, and obviously is in no hurry to send the case to Caesar who will undoubtedly consider it a waste of time. Yet Felix wants friendship with the Jews to make his job of ruling them easier. And of course, Luke also tells us that he hopes to get a bribe from Paul if he waits long enough. But after two years, Felix is replaced by Festus. At least this will get Paul's case some attention. It has become increasingly obvious that Felix is curious about Paul's beliefs, and hopes that if he delays long enough Paul or his friends might come up with a bribe. But Felix is not interested in justice. Yet, to some degree, the same can be said of Paul. He is not motivated by having his named cleared or even by gaining his freedom. What motivates Paul is the chance to witness of the truth to people he will not be around except for his imprisonment. Paul has come to recognize that this is his new mission field. A new governor, to Paul, means a new opportunity to share the good news of Christ.

> *According to Festus, when the chief priests and leading men of the Jews bring their charges against Paul, they are "loudly declaring that he ought not to live any longer." (Acts 25:24)*

📖 Look over Acts 25:1–3 and relate how the Jewish leaders view the change in leadership.

The new governor has only been in the country for three days before the chief priests renew their charges against Paul. Obviously, they are eager to be rid of Paul once and for all. After two years none of their hatred has cooled. The phrase, *"requesting a concession against Paul,"* is a telling one. It reveals first of all that they want this as a favor. Second, it underscores the reality that even they know the charges against Paul are groundless. Were they confident in their case, they would be demanding justice. As it is, justice is the last thing they want. They have no confidence in their chances to win in a court. They are merely looking for another chance to ambush Paul in transit. God is just, and the lack of regard for justice, and even for the due process the Scriptures afford an accused man, reveal how far from God these Jewish leaders are. Remember, by this time most Jews with a true heart for God have already embraced Christ. All that are left are the men who merely use religion to advance their own selfish goals.

📖 According to Acts 25:4–5, what "concession" is Festus willing to give the Jews?

Apparently, Festus has already been warned about this sticky case he is inheriting. No doubt, in his three days at Caesarea, he has read the letter from the Roman commander, Claudius Lysias, and therefore is aware not only of the baseless charges against Paul, but of the plot on his life as well. Festus knows better than to risk moving Paul back to Jerusalem. The only "concession" he offers the Jews is another trial in Caesarea.

📖 Are there any details in Acts 25:6 that strike you as you reflect on it in this context?

IN THEIR SHOES
Festus

Porcius Festus succeeded Felix as governor of Judea in AD 60 and died about two years later. Paul had a hearing before him on false charges by the Jews, and Festus would have released him if not for Paul's appeal to the Emperor (Acts 26:32). The Jewish historian Josephus characterizes Festus as an efficient ruler who did his best to rid the country of robbers.

One would expect that any Roman leader with Jerusalem as one of the cities for which he is responsible sees the need to spend some time there. It is not surprising that Festus visits there after only three days on the job, but it is surprising that he spends so little time there. This seems to be Luke's emphasis with the phrase *"not more than eight or ten days."* When he does return to Caesarea, he immediately brings Paul's case to trial the very next day. Perhaps the reason for his short stay in Jerusalem is a desire to get Paul's case to trial, or it may simply be that he moves fast to appease the Jews.

Festus stands in stark contrast to Felix in his handling of Paul's case. Felix leaves the charges dangling for two years. Festus brings Paul to trial in less than two weeks. Though Paul is probably glad to have some activity on his case, it is most likely the prospect of another opportunity to witness that encourages him most.

DAY 2

ANOTHER TRIAL BUT THE SAME STORY: ACTS 25:7–12

I have a friend who owns an antique tire business. Over the years he has amassed quite a collection of tire molds for vehicles that are no longer manufactured. In fact, he is probably the largest single dealer in the world of such rare tires. Some years ago, a competitor initiated a frivolous lawsuit against him, which on the surface at least, appeared to be motivated by simple jealousy. The charges were baseless, but the case drug on for years. Often, he would share updated details on the case with our Sunday School class and ask for prayer. You could tell that even though he was confident he had done nothing wrong and that in the end he would win the case, it still weighed heavily on him. It was eventually resolved, and thankfully is a closed book for my friend. One can understand how many such lawsuits are settled with payments even when defendants are not guilty of wrongdoing, just to put the whole thing behind them. There is something about unfinished business that has great power to distract us. The apostle Paul would not be human if impatience, frustration, and even worry don't show up once in a while. Yet apart from his display of flesh with Ananias in Acts 23, Paul shows remarkable patience as the years add up on this case. With a new governor, he now gets a new trial. But as we will see today, nothing much else is new.

📖 Compare Acts 25:7 with Paul's last trial in Acts 24:5–6 and write down your thoughts.

After much delay, Paul's trial at last resumes. Though we are not given as specific an account of the charges against Paul, the suggestion is that some accusations have been added. Luke tells us in this trial there are *"many and serious charges against him,"* but in the trial of Acts 24 only four charges are mentioned: being a pest, stirring up dissension among the Jews, being a leader of a sect, and desecrating the Temple. Only the charge of dissension would be thought serious by the Romans. That there are more charges here appears to be irrelevant however, for once again they are charges *"which they could not prove."* There is also no mention of the Jews from Asia being present to bear witness to their accusations. Though the charges may be different, the impact of them is still the same.

📖 What do you learn in Acts 25:8–9 of Paul's response to these charges, and Festus' intentions for the case?

DID YOU KNOW?
Innocent until Proven Guilty

The American judicial concept of "innocent until proven guilty" is based on the Old Testament edict, *"on the evidence of two or three witnesses a matter shall be confirmed"* (Deuteronomy 19:15). In other words, multiple witnesses are needed to confirm guilt. Paul's condemnation by the Jews is in violation of the Law of God, the very authority they take pride in. Like Jewish law, Roman law also required a person to be proven guilty by witnesses. These witnesses had to be present at trial, so Paul's case should have been thrown out.

While it is easy to look at Paul's response as a simple "not guilty" plea, the simplicity says much. By making his defense a blanket statement that he has *"committed no offense either against the Law of the Jews or against the temple or against Caesar,"* Paul is forcing his opponents to prove him wrong. Their silence makes it clear they are unable to do this. Festus recognizes that his job will be easier if he has the support of the Jews, and tries to give them what they ask for, but there is no indication that he believes Paul to be guilty. It is also interesting that Festus asks, rather than orders, Paul to go to Jerusalem for his trial. Were there any real case, Festus would set the terms of trial.

📖 From Acts 25:10–12, identify Paul's response to the request of Festus and the outcome of this particular trial.

Paul is wise enough to see through the guile of the Jewish leaders and probably expects that the plot on his life is still a part of their plans. Though he is not trying to get his case dismissed, neither is he willing to give the Jews another chance to ambush him. He uses his Roman citizenship to protect himself, but also uses his case to keep opportunities coming to him to testify of Christ before the governmental leaders. The fact that Paul boldly states to Festus, *"I have done no wrong to the Jews, as you also very well know,"* shows how weak the case is against him. But this boldness is not disrespect. Notice Paul affirms his submission to the Roman authority by stating his readiness to forfeit his life if indeed he has done anything worthy of such punishment. Paul's appeal to Caesar both protects him from the plots of the Jews and guarantees he will get to Rome.

Not much is said by Luke of this particular trial. Apparently, it is short and to the point. Paul may have wanted to say more of Christ but doesn't try to force it. His confidence, graciousness, and respect for authority, are all the testimony offered in this trial, but they too represent one of the opportunities God affords him to make a defense for the hope within him.

DAY 3

ANOTHER OPPORTUNITY TO TESTIFY: ACTS 25:13–27

After two years of idleness, Paul finds himself in a whirlwind of activity. Perhaps having learned his lesson from the door of opportunity he closed with his fleshly response with Ananias, he is patient and gracious with Festus. As a result, he quickly makes a favorable impression. Providentially, King Agrippa and his wife come to Caesarea for a visit to pay their respects to the new governor, and we find yet another fulfillment of the prophecy that Paul will appear before kings (Acts 9:15). Paul seems to conclude that God has allowed these accusations against him to give him a platform to speak of Christ. He will not give in to striving and try to force doors open, but he is always ready and willing to make a defense for the hope within him. As we see today, God gives him a strategic opportunity to do so.

DID YOU KNOW?
The Evil Legacy of the Herods

Although his relationship with his sister Bernice was scandalous, Herod Agrippa II was not the first of his kinsmen to commit the sin of incest. Herod the Great's granddaughter, Herodias, first married her uncle Herod Phillip, and then while he was still living, married Herod Antipas, another uncle. It is for speaking out against this sinful relationship that John the Baptist was imprisoned and eventually put to death (Mark 6:17–28).

📖 From Acts 25:13, identify the next opportunity God gives Paul to witness before important people. Through a Bible dictionary or online search, find out what you can about these people.

Within a short time of his trial before Festus, Paul is afforded another and even more significant opportunity. As is often the case with a change of political leaders, important dignitaries come to pay their respects. King Agrippa mentioned here is the last of the Herods. His great-grandfather is Herod the Great who murdered the young children of Bethlehem in an effort to kill the new-born Jesus. His great uncle, Herod Antipas, is the king who executed John the Baptist. His father (Agrippa I) made the disciple James a martyr, and tried to put Peter to death, but God took this king's life first. Agrippa II began political life at this point and was given the kingdom of Chalcis by the Emperor Claudius at the young age of 17. Nine years later, he was given the title of king and transferred to the regions his father first ruled over (Batanea, Trachonitis, Auranitis, and Abilene). The Bernice mentioned here is the older sister of Agrippa and is apparently named after her grandmother. Their incestuous relationship was a widely known scandal. Although she briefly marries Polemo, king of Cilicia, she returns to Agrippa and later becomes the mistress of the Roman Emperor Vespasian and his Emperor son, Titus. The dark backdrop of their lives makes Paul's witness to them even more amazing.

📖 Read over Acts 25:14–21 and summarize how Festus represents Paul's case to Agrippa.

The visit of Agrippa and Bernice to Festus is not a short one, and Paul's case probably is not mentioned at first. It is understandable though that Festus brings the matter up, for it represents a difficult problem he inherits from the inept governor Felix. Further, Agrippa is considered by the Romans to be an expert on Jewish matters. Unlike Felix, Festus can report, *"I did not delay,"* and that he has immediately held a formal trial but protects the prisoner as a Roman citizen. Unfortunately, this is clearly not going to resolve the matter. The charges are unsupported by evidence, and even if they had been proven, are not crimes worthy of death. It is also clear that although Luke does not report Paul's mention of Jesus, Festus is aware of Paul's claims of His resurrection. Festus reports his suggested compromise of a trial in Jerusalem, and Paul's appeal to Caesar which makes that impossible. One gains a clear sense that Festus knows Paul is innocent, but as a novice governor, he is unsure how to proceed.

 DID YOU KNOW?
Agrippa's Father's Death

It is ironic that the apostle Paul should appear in trial before Herod Agrippa II in Caesarea. It was in this same city and at the same rostrum Festus presided over at Paul's previous trial only days before that Agrippa's father died, having been judged by God for taking to himself glory meant only for God. Acts 12:23 reports that he was struck dead by an angel and then was eaten by worms.

As you read Luke's narrative in Acts 25:22–27 of the introduction of Paul to Agrippa, make note of all who are in attendance and what Festus indicates as the purpose of this meeting.

Fortunately for Festus, Paul's case holds some interest for Agrippa. The very next day a hearing is convened; most likely in Herod's praetorium. In addition to Agrippa and Bernice, Festus has invited *"the commanders and the prominent men of the city."* Festus communicates not only that the Jews want Paul dead, but he also conveys some of the passion behind that desire, relating that the Jewish leaders have been "loudly declaring that he ought not to live any longer." Festus takes a firm position for Paul's innocence, and mentions that his main purpose for the hearing is having some idea of what to write as the charges when he sends Paul to the Emperor.

It is easy to reflect on these trials from a distance and miss the significance and rarity of such opportunities. Seldom do believers have such a prominent audience before which to testify of Christ. Paul has to be grateful. But another point must be made. God is giving these persons who are so needy of the gospel, a chance to hear a sermon of truth from one of Christianity's greatest spokespersons. Much as God affords a political prominence in modern times to Billy Graham, the apostle Paul in a different way (as a prisoner) gains the ear of the leaders of his day. As we will see tomorrow, he is ready to make the most of the opportunity.

DAY 4

THE MANPOWER OF MISSIONS: ACTS 26:1–32

Everybody loves to hear a story. People quickly get bored with facts and figures and theories and such, but they give their attention freely to a story. That is why a well-thought through presentation of one's own process of coming to faith is far easier to relate and far more engaging to most unbelievers than explaining a series of verses that communicate the plan of salvation. To some, quite often a bunch of Bible verses disengages rather than engages. But to tell one's own story draws people in. It is interesting to notice that if you look at the different times in Acts where Paul shares of his own conversion, he almost never quotes Scripture. Instead, he shares simply but compellingly of his own encounter with Christ. It is also clear, when one compares the different accounts, that the basic content is the same in each, though different points may be emphasized depending on the audience. What this tells us is that in the many quiet hours prison affords, Paul plans and thinks through what he wants to say. He doesn't need to talk a long time, so he reduces his story down to the main essentials. Let's look at how Paul makes a defense for the hope within him.

📖 The first portion of Paul's defense in Acts 26:1–11 relates the kind of person he is before he meets Christ. Go through these verses and summarize the points that stand out to you describing him as a non-Christian.

Apparently, Paul grew up in Jerusalem, the hub of Judaism. We know from our study from previous weeks that his father was a Pharisee, so that makes sense. Like his father, Paul lived strictly according to the Law as a Pharisee. Paul rightly places the resurrection at the center of the Christian faith and points out that this is a belief taught by the Scriptures and treasured by the Pharisees. Paul goes on to relate that as a Pharisee, he thought he needed to *do many things hostile to the name of Jesus of Nazareth.* In this pursuit, Paul put *many of the saints in prisons,* and even cast his vote to put some to death.

He punished them *"often"* in the synagogues, and in his anger *"tried to force them to blaspheme."* Paul was similar to other Pharisees in this regard, but he pursued Christians with even more zeal *"even to foreign cities."* One catches a sense of Paul as very zealous, and of course, he makes the point that he was once antagonistic to that of which he is now convinced.

📖 The second portion of Paul's defense in Acts 26:12–18 relates the process of Paul meeting Christ. Go through these verses and write down the items you consider as key to his conversion.

_____

_____

_____

_____

DID YOU KNOW?
Kick against the Goads

In the agricultural society of Palestine all were familiar with "goads." They were the sharp sticks employed by shepherds or farmers to prod their livestock and motivate them to move in the desired direction. Of course, to be prodded is not comfortable, and sometimes the animals kicked against these prods. What the Lord is saying to Paul is, "Why are you fighting against Me when I am trying to lead you in the right direction?" Paul had a heart for God, but in his zeal, he was not listening to God's conviction about the truth of Christ.

Paul's mention of his journey to Damascus makes it clear that it is not Paul who found the Lord, but the Lord who found him. At midday, Paul and all who traveled with him saw an intensely bright light, and then Paul heard the Lord speak. Imagine what a shock it must have been for Paul to hear the Lord accuse him of persecuting Him. The shock turned to dismay when he realized that the voice is that of Jesus—the very One whose followers Paul was trying to harm. Paul had even more to adjust to when he learned that Jesus was commissioning him as a minister and a witness (one who testifies) of Him. Perhaps the single hardest expectation for Paul to adjust to is the idea that Jesus was sending him to the Gentiles, *"to open their eyes so that they may turn from darkness to light and from the dominion of Satan to God, that they may receive forgiveness of sins and an inheritance among those who have been sanctified by faith in Me."* While it is easy to overlook, the essence of the gospel in Paul's encounter is actually found in the message given to him to take to the Gentiles.

📖 The final portion of Paul's defense in Acts 26:19–23 relates the changes Christ made in Paul's life. As you reflect on these verses make note of how he is different after meeting the Lord.

The first point Paul makes is subtle and easily missed. When he says, *"I did not prove disobedient to the heavenly vision,"* he is saying he obeyed it—he acted on what was revealed and turned his life over to Christ. This decision was demonstrated immediately as instead of taking on the Christians of Damascus, he took their side and began calling Jews and Gentiles all over to *"repent and turn to God, performing deeds appropriate to repentance."* In Paul's case, because of who he was before, there is no greater evidence of his conversion than the fact that he became a minister of the gospel. It is the message Paul carries that caused the Jews to seize him in the Temple and try to put him to death. Paul makes a point of the fact that both Moses and the Prophets foretold of the suffering and resurrection of the Messiah, and that His message is *"both to the Jewish people and to the Gentiles."* There is nothing in his life and ministry that is contrary to the Scriptures.

> *"repent and turn to God, performing deeds appropriate to repentance."*
>
> —the witness of the apostle Paul

📖 Read Acts 26:24–32.

What outcome does Paul hope to have from sharing his own story?

What response does Agrippa make to the opportunity of salvation?

What is Agrippa's overall impression of Paul's message?

The account Luke gives us in Acts 26 of Paul's testimony before Agrippa is one of the fullest explanations we have of his conversion to Christ. It is clear from the statement Paul makes in verse 29 that his main goal is not to defend himself against accusations from the Jews, but to defend his faith in Christ in the hope he might persuade some of his audience. He sees this as an opportunity to witness, not as a trial for himself. In the end, Agrippa is quite impressed with all Paul has to say, and makes the statement: *"In a short time you will persuade me to become a Christian."* Sadly, Agrippa brings the meeting to a close with no decision, and by delaying a decision for Christ it appears he may have avoided it. There is no indication he ever converts to Christianity. It is apparent, however, that he sees Paul as innocent of any crime.

King Agrippa says to Festus, *"This man might have been set free if he had not appealed to Caesar."* Yet being set free is not what Paul is aiming at. His heart is set on Rome, and he hopes to testify there as he has before kings and governors. Peter says that a believer should always be *"ready to make a defense"* for the hope that is within. It is obvious that Paul is ready to make that defense. Because he is ready, God gives him many opportunities to do so.

Day 5

For Me to Follow God

Mark chapter 5 relates a compassionate story of Jesus' miraculous power. After calming the sea for His disciples, they had no sooner arrived on shore than another storm met them in the form of a man possessed with a *"Legion"* of demons. This man dwelled among the tombs, and was so overcome by demons that even chains could not bind him. Day and night, he could be heard screaming in the graveyard or seen gashing himself with stones. Seeing Jesus, he ran up and bowed down before Him; and shouting with a loud voice, he said, *"What business do we have with each other, Jesus, Son of the Most High God? I implore You by God, do not torment me!"* (Mark 5:6b–7). After Jesus had cast the many demons out, the man's life was completely and miraculously changed. Mark speaks of him as *"clothed and in his right mind"* (Mark 5:15). As Jesus prepared to leave the region by boat, the man implored Him that he might travel with Jesus, but interestingly, Jesus refused. Instead, He commanded the man to *"Go home to your people and report to them what great things the Lord has done for you, and how He had mercy on you"* (Mark 5:19). There would come a time for him to be with Jesus, but God had given him a story to tell, and it needed to be told.

> *"Go home to your people and report to them what great things the*
> *Lord has done for you, and how He had mercy on you."*
> (Mark 5:19)

I have often reflected on the spiritual portrait being painted by Jesus at this moment. His sailing to another shore seems almost to foreshadow His ascension and the command He will give to His disciples to *"make disciples of all the nations"* (Matthew 28:19). They will fellowship with Him in heaven, but in the meantime, there is a job to be done. God has given each one of us a story to tell. Sharing what He has done in our lives is so important that it delays our ultimate goal of being with Him for eternity. Peter writes, *"but sanctify Christ as Lord in your hearts, always being ready to make a defense to everyone who asks you to give an account for the hope that is in you"* (1 Peter 3:15). Paul is ready when God gives him the opportunity to make a defense for the hope within him. You and I need to be ready as well. I'd like that to be the application point for this week.

How to Prepare Your Own Story

Your own "defense" for the hope within you ought to be easy to communicate since it is your own story. But to be most effective, sharing your story takes preparation. Peter says we must be "ready." This requires time and forethought to insure we can communicate that story clearly and succinctly. Otherwise, we may ramble or give too much detail for someone who is not where we are spiritually. Paul shares his story in three parts: what he was like before meeting Christ, how he came to know Christ, and the changes in his life since becoming a Christian. Below you will find some thought-provoking questions to help you identify these three aspects of your own spiritual journey. I learned these from training I received and later taught during my days of campus ministry with Campus Crusade for Christ (Cru).

Part 1: What You Were Like before Meeting Christ
(*NOTE: if you came to Christ at a very early age, you may want to focus your story on before, during, and after you first began to walk closely with the Lord.)

What characterized your life? What were your attitudes, emotions, needs and problems?

What did your life revolve around most?

In what ways was your life unsatisfying?

What in your life gave you a sense of security, approval, happiness, and peace of mind?

How did you become dissatisfied with trying to find those things outside the Lord?

Part 2: How You Came to Know Christ

When was the first time you clearly understood the gospel? How did it happen? When were you exposed to true Christianity in someone's life?

What was your initial reaction?

What caused you to take the gospel seriously? Why?

What barriers did you have to overcome in thinking, attitudes, and fears before accepting Christ?

What helped you to overcome those barriers?

Part 3: The Changes in Your life Since Becoming a Christian

What specific changes have you seen Christ make in your attitudes and actions?

How long did it take before you began to notice a difference in your life?

How and why are you different now than before?

How did Christ begin to meet your needs or give you insight about your emotions or problems?

 DOCTRINE
The Hope within Us

What are the main points that make up our own defense of the hope within us?

· what we were like before meeting Christ
· how we come to know Christ
· the changes in our life from becoming a Christian

Begin praying now for God to impress upon you someone you can write a letter to and share your story—an old friend, a distant relative, former co-worker, etc.

As you prepare your story to share with others, here are a few helpful hints to communicate effectively and clearly.

- Illustrate points with examples from your life that non-Christians can relate to.

- Stay away from religious jargon that a non-Christian would have difficulty understanding.

- Make Jesus the issue—not church attendance or morality

- Don't sensationalize your past—that isn't the point of your story

- Limit your story to five minutes or less (most encounters will not give you more time than that)

We normally close out each lesson with a written prayer to the Lord. This week we want to vary that a bit. Instead of writing a letter to the Lord, write your own story in the form of a letter you can send to friends telling your story of faith.

NOTES

LESSON 12

PRISONS BECOME PULPITS
ACTS 27—28

On June 17, 1972, a young security guard working the graveyard shift at the Watergate Hotel, finds a piece of masking tape stuck to the lock of a door as he makes his rounds. After removing the tape, he discovers several more doors have been taped to remain open. Returning to the first door, he finds the tape he removed has been replaced. At 1:47 a.m., Frank Wills telephones police, and at 2:30 a.m., five men are arrested for breaking into the Democratic National Committee head-quarters. One of the biggest scandals in American history is about to be uncovered. Several of those arrested are eventually connected to the Committee to Reelect the President (CREEP). Although President Richard M. Nixon denies knowledge of the break-in, soon the White House is implicated. The scandal, which becomes known as Watergate, will sink the Nixon presidency and take many of its top figures down with it one by one. On August 8, 1974, Nixon becomes the only U.S. President to resign from office.

> *"What gave me my platform for ministry was not my greatest success, but my greatest failure."*
>
> —Charles Colson.
> Serving time as a prisoner for his role in the Watergate scandal—not being an attorney in the White House—is what leads Chuck to the founding of Prison Fellowship International.

A prominent figure in the Watergate scandal is Charles Colson, the White House hatchet man and Special Counsel to President Nixon. Colson is one of the most powerful men in Washington. But because of Watergate he will become a convicted felon with a sentence of 1–3 years in prison. The tragedy will also be the catalyst for his conversion to Christianity. The turning point for Colson is a conversation with Tom Phillips, then president of the huge Massachusetts electronics firm Raytheon and himself a new Christian. Colson sees the change in Phillips and reads the copy of C.S. Lewis' *Mere Christianity* his friend gives him. Within days Colson is a Christian. He never dreamed his brokenness would be redeemed in such a dramatic and far-reaching way. He eventually pleads guilty to crimes related to the Watergate cover-up and gains a vision while he is in prison for the ministry to fellow prisoners he will later establish. Colson will go on to become one of the outstanding Christian spokesmen of our generation.

I once heard Chuck Colson speak on the matter of his conversion and ministry and am gripped by a particular statement. He related he had achieved the pinnacle of success in the eyes of the world. He was special counsel to the President of the United States—the most powerful man in the world. One would think this position would be key to unlocking any door to future success. Yet years later he reflects, "What gave me my platform for ministry was not my greatest success, but my greatest failure." He explains it is not being an attorney in the White House that led to the founding of the ministry called Prison Fellowship International. It is serving time as a prisoner for his role in the Watergate scandal. His White House years were given over to self instead of the Lord. It is only after giving his life to Christ that he finds his purpose in life, and what he initially thought of as his prison eventually becomes his pulpit.

Though Chuck Colson served time in a literal prison, many other believers find themselves figuratively "imprisoned" in a trial of some sort. It may be a relationship trial with an unbelieving spouse or prodigal child. Some find themselves in a health "prison" with a disability or disease. Others face a financial prison. Though the circumstances may vary, the principles are the same. Sometimes God's will takes us to places we don't want to go. We are shackled by an undesirable, yet unchangeable situation. From his Roman imprisonment, the apostle Paul writes in his letter to the Philippian believers, *"Now I want you to know, brethren, that my circumstances have turned out for the greater progress of the gospel, so that my imprisonment in the cause of Christ has become well known throughout the whole praetorian guard and to everyone else"* (Philippians 1:12–13). Paul comes to recognize that what man means to be a prison, God intends to be his pulpit—his place of ministry. Paul ends up preaching some of his greatest sermons from prison. Many of the letters he writes during this time become part of the New Testament. God is able to bring ministry out of mayhem. The same can be true for us. We may not be able to alter our circumstances, but we can put our circumstances on the altar. Once we do, God is able to turn our prison into a pulpit.

DAY 1

A PROMISED JOURNEY BECOMES A PROBLEM: ACTS 27:1–20

The key to an easy life is to be in the center of God's will. So long as you are walking in fellowship with God and are doing His will, you don't have to worry about encountering any problems. At least that is what I understood the television preacher to say. I'm not sure about you, but I have a hard time reconciling such teaching with my own experiences. In fact, there have been times when it seems the opposite is true. Walking with God and doing His will sometimes seems to make life harder instead of easier. Those who teach otherwise obviously haven't spent much time in the Scriptures. Doing the will of God often got the prophets of old in trouble. Some were even killed because of it. Being in the center of God's will meant crucifixion for Jesus. Following God caused all of Jesus' disciples except John to die a martyr's death. It doesn't take much study of the life of Paul to realize that God's will is not always easy for him either. Acts 27 begins with the fulfillment of Festus' promise to send Paul's case to Rome. Unlike with Felix as governor, there appears to be no more delay in the case. Going to Rome is God's will. Paul has long desired it, and God has clearly promised it. But that doesn't mean that getting there is going to be easy. In fact, following the promise brings its own set of problems.

DID YOU KNOW?
Paul's Companions

Acts 27:1 begins with the word "we", letting us know that Luke is traveling with the Apostle Paul. Such references are absent in Acts from 21:18 until now. Paul's imprisonment in Caesarea may have limited their contact during that time, but now Luke is allowed to travel along with him and gives us an eyewitness account of these remaining adventures. Also traveling with them is Aristarchus, the Thessalonian believer. It is unclear if he is simply a traveling companion or is also a prisoner. The letter to the Colossian church that Paul writes once he gets to Rome calls Aristarchus a "fellow prisoner" (Colossians 4:10). In any case, Philemon 1:24 later identifies him as one of Paul's "*fellow workers.*"

📖 Luke's narrative in Acts 27:1–8 reads like a travelogue of the Mediterranean region. Follow Paul's trip on a Bible map and then answer the questions that follow.

Make note of the different people traveling with Paul and their roles in the journey.

What statements in the verses give you the idea that the trip is not going as planned?

Paul is placed with some other prisoners under the charge of a centurion named Julius, presumably with the hundred soldiers under his charge (see 27:32, 37, 42). Also on the journey is Paul's friend Aristarchus. There are no less than fifteen geographical references in these eight verses of Acts, but they represent a fairly straightforward maritime journey from Palestine toward Rome. We can see from the freedoms given Paul in Sidon by the centurion that he is being treated well. Myra (27:5), where they find a ship headed for Rome, is the principle port for the Alexandrian grain ships on their way from Egypt to Rome. Contrary winds (27:4) slow the journey "*many days*" (27:7), and multiple times Luke mentions the difficulty of their travels. The "*Fair Havens*" afford a port of rest, but the calm will be short lived.

📖 As you reflect on the debate of Acts 27:9–12, identify the differing opinions and how the conclusion is reached.

Verse 9 begins with the news that *"considerable time had passed and the voyage was now dangerous."* The weather delays have so slowed their travel that they are nearing winter, the most dangerous time of year to travel, and have more than half their journey still ahead of them. The *"fast"* Luke refers to here is the Day of Atonement, the only mandated fast in the Jewish year, and in AD 59 it occurs on October 5th. Although Paul argues of the dangers if they continue, it is unsurprising that the centurion is "more persuaded" by the sailors than a prisoner. Though the "majority" vote to continue, we will see as the narrative goes on that they should have listened to Paul.

DOCTRINE
Majority Rule

Biblical examples of majority rule in making decisions are rare, but always negative. Here in Paul's journey to Rome, the "majority" overrules his wise counsel to port for winter, and the result is shipwreck. When the twelve spies are sent into the promised land of Canaan (Numbers 13) we are given another example. On returning, their opinion is divided. The majority (10 spies) counsel that the land is unconquerable. Only the minority of Caleb and Joshua have God's will on the matter, as forty years of wandering makes clear. While these examples show grave consequences, they serve as a good reminder that just because the majority support a plan or direction, this does not mean they are right. We should seek counsel in decisions, but instead of simply going with the majority, we should stay sensitive to God and trust Him to quicken our hearts to the right counsel.

📖 Read Acts 27:13–20 and summarize the difficulties they encounter and how bad their circumstances become.

The final vote in the debate seems to be cast by the weather, and with some brief favorable conditions they set sail. Their respite is short-lived however, and a *"violent wind"* catches them and begins to drive the boat out to sea (the word "violent" translated from Gr. *tuphonikos*, from which the English word "typhoon" is derived). The term *"Euraquilo"* that Luke mentions is the common Latin term for a tempestuous and cyclonic northeasterly wind common in the Mediterranean Sea during autumn and winter. It is apparent that the sailors employ every trick in their arsenal, but to no avail. When they begin to *"jettison the cargo,"* it is obvious they are becoming desperate, and when they throw "the ship's tackle overboard," one gets the sense of despair in Luke's summary of verse 20 that *"from then on all hope of our being saved was gradually abandoned."*

It is easy to read such narrative with a sense of detachment, but these are traumatic, life-threatening circumstances that Paul and Luke find themselves in. They represent a serious test of faith. But Paul must keep coming back to the Lord's promise that he will *"witness at Rome also"* (Acts 23:11). His faith is in the promises of God, not in his circumstances.

DAY 2

A CRISIS LETS THE PRISONER BECOME THE LEADER: ACTS 27:21–44

True leadership tends to emerge in crisis. Titles and positions don't mean much in a firefight; what really counts is leadership, and sometimes it comes from unlikely sources. Alvin York is a good example. In the brutal trenches of World War I, on October 8, 1918, York is one of seventeen men dispatched to take command of the Decauville railroad. After misreading a map written in French, the men find themselves behind enemy lines. Surprising a superior German force, they initially surrender to the men. But then, German machine gunners turn on the Americans, and the platoon commander is killed. Few would expect Alvin York, the backward hillbilly from Fentress County, Tennessee, to be the one to step into the void.

DID YOU KNOW?
Alvin York

As a teen in rural Tennessee, Alvin York was known as a "hell-raiser" and nuisance to the community, being a regular at the local bars. In 1914, after one of his best friends was killed in a bar fight, Alvin attended a prayer meeting at the Church of Christ in Christian Union. There he was convicted of the destructive path he was on and turned to Christ. Soon he was teaching Sunday school classes and leading the choir. It was this church's teaching of violence and war being immoral which caused him such conflict after being drafted. In the end, however, he became convinced that some wars are just and necessary. Though too old to fight in World War II, he viewed Hitler as an evil which must be opposed, and traveled the country recruiting volunteers for the war effort.

As a staunch pacifist, York tries to avoid being drafted for the war as a "conscientious objector" but his appeal is rejected. His Camp Gordon trainers are unsure what to make of him, for though he repeatedly speaks of his objection to war, he also distinguishes himself as an outstanding marksman. His company commander eventually convinces York that God sometimes ordains war as moral and necessary. On the fateful day in World War I, when his platoon of 17 has lost more than half its men, it is York who saves the day. His Medal of Honor citation reads, "After his platoon had suffered heavy casualties and 3 other noncommissioned officers had become casualties, Cpl. York assumed command. Fearlessly leading 7 men, he charged with great daring a machine gun nest which was pouring deadly and incessant fire upon his platoon. In this heroic feat the machine gun nest was taken, together with 4 officers and 128 men and several guns." It is not that the war turns Alvin York into a hero. It is rather, that the difficult circumstances of the war reveal the character which is already present. In much the same way, Acts 27 shows us how God uses dire circumstances to show the Roman centurion and everyone else in their company the character of Paul as he steps forward to lead in the midst of their crisis.

📖 Look over Acts 27:21–26 and write out in your own words how Paul encourages and comforts the men.

While it may not be much encouragement for Paul to tell the men they should have listened to him, we should not be too hard on the men for their failure to follow his advice. We must remember that he is a prisoner, and more importantly, he isn't a sailor. Yet these men can take great comfort in knowing that this man of God has a promise from God for them. Not only does Paul reveal that they will all survive, but he also tells them why. The angel reveals, "behold, God has granted you all those who are sailing with you." They will survive because of Paul. There will be consequences; the ship will run aground and be broken to pieces—but they will all survive.

📖 Considering these previous verses along with Acts 27:27–32, identify how the men traveling with Paul have to exercise faith to be able to share in the promised deliverance.

We don't usually think of a sinking ship as a pulpit, but this one Paul travels on becomes one. He preaches truth to the men. He exercises his own faith, trusting the promise God gives, but he also encourages these men to exercise faith in God. When the ship comes close to an island, some of the sailors want to escape, but Paul challenges the Roman soldiers, "*Unless these men remain in the ship, you yourselves cannot be saved.*" They have a decision to make. Will they trust the example of the experienced seamen, or will they put their trust in the words God speaks through this prophet? What a beautiful picture we have of salvation here! These men are promised deliverance by God, but that deliverance is only theirs by faith. They must take Him at His word, and their actions show that they do. Although their faith is focused on temporal deliverance instead of eternal salvation, God is showing them His power, and we can certainly assume that Paul makes clear to them how to have eternal deliverance also. No doubt many of them act to receive the gospel message through Paul's witness.

📖 Through reading Acts 27:33–38, what else do you see of the men's faith in God's words through Paul?

 DID YOU KNOW?
Shipwreck

The 19th century British yachtsman James Smith made a detailed nautical study of Paul's voyage to Rome. Carefully inquiring of veteran navigators of the region, he determined the mean rate of drift for a similar ship in such a storm as about thirty-six miles per day. The depth soundings recorded in Acts 27:28 indicate the ship was passing Koura, a point on the east coast of Malta. He relates, "the distance from Clauda to the point of Koura...is 476.6 miles, which at the rate as deduced...would take exactly 13 days, 1 hour, and 21 minutes." Even more striking, after carefully reckoning the direction of the ship's course from the direction of the wind, from the angle of the ship's head with the wind, and from the lee-way, he goes on: "according to these calculations, a ship starting late in the evening from Clauda would, by midnight on the 14th [day], be less than 3 miles from the entrance of St. Paul's Bay." He admits that calculating so close, "...is to a certain extent accidental, but it is an accident which could not have happened had there been any inaccuracy on the part of the author." (*The Voyage and Shipwreck of St. Paul*, by James Smith, as quoted in *The New International Commentary on the New Testament*, Grand Rapids: Eerdmans, 1971, pp.514–15)

When people hear truth from God, it always comes with a choice of whether or not they will trust Him and trust what He says. That is what faith is all about. Sin is always a result of not taking God at His word. In these verses, Paul repeats the promise he has from God that they will all be spared. But notice how Paul begins to lead the men. Notice not only how he encourages them, but watch how he leads them by his own example. After urging them to eat, he brings out food and thanks God *"in the presence of all."* He leads them in worship, and then he leads them by eating himself. We see yet another glimpse of their faith in God and His promise of deliverance in the fact that *"they themselves also took food."* The last demonstration of faith is perhaps the easiest to miss. When they have eaten enough, Luke tells us, they begin to *"lighten the ship by throwing out the wheat into the sea."* They have already thrown all the ship's cargo overboard (27:18), and even the ship's tackle (27:19), to make the boat lighter. But now, after eating their fill, they throw their food cargo overboard. In trust of the promise of God, they do not expect to be at sea much longer.

📖 Examine Acts 27:39–44 and summarize the climax to their adventure.

After days of storm-tossed fear, the men at last see land. They attempt to beach their vessel, but they lodge instead on a hidden reef, and the vessel is destroyed. That Paul has earned the respect of the Roman centurion is evident by the care he affords him. Miraculously, all two hundred and seventy-six passengers on board make it to land, just as God promised through Paul.

No one in their right mind seeks out hard times; that would be crazy. Yet it is in the crucible of adversity that our character is formed, and more importantly, is revealed. God uses difficult situations to showcase His saints. With trials, He shines a spotlight on His children and allows the world to see the difference He has made in our lives. Paul's calm in the stress of their storm makes him a leader in a place where leadership is desperately needed. From the pulpit of crisis, he is able to preach an unspoken sermon of God's power, care, and grace by the way he lives his life in the midst of that crisis.

DAY 3

THE PRISONER FINDS MORE PULPITS IN HIS JOURNEY: ACTS 28:1–10

Like most children, I watched a lot of television growing up. Of course, that also means I watched plenty of commercials. I can't say that I remember very many of them, but one particular ad campaign is still vividly etched in my conscious memory: an anti-smoking ad with a number of different images but only a four-word script: "Like father, like son." The video clips switch from scene to scene—painting a house, walking down a road, throwing a rock—and in each case, the child does his best to imitate his father. The ad closes with a scene of the son watching intently as the father pulls out a cigarette and lights it. The four-word narrative is identical, except it is delivered in the form of a question instead of a statement: "Like father, like son?" With great clarity the ad drives home the point that others watch what we do and are influenced by our actions or lack of action. Often what they see in us speaks louder than anything we say. Our life preaches many sermons, and though we sometimes might wish it preached a different message, our life speaks volumes about what is really important to us. For one walking with the Lord, it gives an opportunity for Christ to be seen and not just heard about. Though Paul would have liked to avoid shipwreck, the adversity gives him yet another pulpit. Speaking more with his life than his lips, Paul preaches boldly and passionately from this pulpit of the reality of God in his life. Clearly there are many taking notes as he preaches.

> *Speaking more with his life than his lips, Paul preaches boldly and passionately from the pulpit of shipwreck of the reality of God in his life. Clearly there are many taking notes as he preaches.*

📖 As you look over Acts 28:1–2, briefly make note of the new situation Paul and his companions find themselves in.

Weeks of battling an overpowering storm must have been a horrible ordeal for the travelers. Physically weary from laboring day and night, weak from lack of eating and the inevitable battles with seasickness, drenched from battling the waves to get to shore, the group finally reaches land. Only then do they find out where they are—the island of Malta (also called Melita). Fortunately, they are greeted by friendly inhabitants who, in the cold weather of late fall, kindle them a fire and show "*extraordinary kindness.*"

📖 Identify the circumstance of Acts 28:3–6 and how God speaks through it to those present.

Throughout this ordeal, God is placing the apostle Paul on display. Through his life, God is speaking to all who witness how he handles their adversity. In the drama of the bite by the venomous snake, it is easy to miss the activity which puts Paul in that position. He is being a servant. No doubt he is just as wet and cold as the others, but he goes out and gathers a bundle of sticks and puts them on the fire. He is helping to meet practical needs. It really is a simple and small thing, but we would err if we miss the message these menial actions speak to his companions. While he serves by tending the fire, a venomous reptile latches on to Paul's hand. The first thought the inhabitants have is that natural justice catches up with him. No doubt he has already been identified as a prisoner. Though not expressly acknowledging God, they clearly believe in some kind of retribution for evil. But over time, when it becomes obvious that Paul is not going to die, they acknowledge the event as supernatural. The world may not always notice what we do for God, but they quickly see those things God does for us that only He can do.

IN THEIR SHOES
Paul and the Viper

Because of the miracle, this passage has been targeted by critics who prefer a natural explanation. Some suggest Luke fabricates the account to make Paul seem more divine. Others argue that Luke mistakenly identifies the snake as venomous. Neither matches the details of the story. Though the island of Malta has no venomous snakes today, that tells nothing of what one may have encountered two thousand years ago. Both Greek terms used here (*echidna*, v.3, and *therion*, v.4) are commonly used by medical writers to refer to venomous snakes. Further, Luke is a physician, and as Sir William Ramsay notes, "a trained medical man in ancient times was usually a good authority about serpents, to which great respect was paid in ancient medicine" (*Luke the Physician*, Grand Rapids: Baker, 1996, pp.63–64). Finally, the matter is effectively settled by the fact that the natives are expecting Paul to die from the bite.

In what other way does Acts 28:7–10 reveal God speaking to the people through Paul?

Trials and difficult circumstances have a way of intersecting our lives with people we might never meet otherwise. By God's providence, such encounters give us chances to minister to people He wants to reach. Luke introduces Publius as such a person. He apparently is the governor of the island. His good character is reflected in the hospitality he shows these strangers. Luke gives no hint that the man asks for Paul's assistance. Most likely it is Paul who initiates the visit to Publius' father. Showing forth the compassion of the

Lord, he prays for the man, and God heals him. Quickly, word of the miracle spreads, and Paul is able to heal many of the island's sick. Paul's faith is vindicated in the eyes of many unbelievers both by his compassion and by God's power being manifested through him.

One can only imagine what is going through the mind of the Roman centurion and his soldiers. It has to be clear to them that their survival is a blessing from God because they are with Paul. If there are any skeptical of Paul's faith, their hearts are hard indeed if the events on Malta do not remove any remaining doubts. Luke does not dwell on the point, but we will probably meet many of these people in heaven, along with natives from the island. Luke says of them that they *"honored us with many marks of respect; and...supplied us with all we needed."* Even in their departure, the soldiers can see themselves blessed because of Paul. No one likes to live through adversity, but, for the believer, such times bring great opportunities to minister to others and to show what a difference it makes to have Christ in your life. Our prisons quickly become pulpits if we will let them.

DAY 4

"AND THUS WE CAME TO ROME": ACTS 28:11–31

We don't know exactly when Paul first sets his heart on going to Rome, but it makes perfect sense that he would desire it. In his day, the Roman Empire is the dominant world power. The city of Rome is the center of the civilized universe. The Romans are famous for their roads and build the great Appian Way in 312 BC. The French fabulist and poet, Jean de la Fontaine, helped make popular the phrase, "All roads lead to Rome" (Le Juge Arbitre—Fable XII [28, 4]). That is certainly true in Paul's day. It is when he meets Priscilla and Aquila in Corinth (Acts 18:2) in the spring of AD 51 that Paul first learns of the church which God has raised up there. It is in about AD 56, at the end of Paul's time in Ephesus on the third missionary journey (Acts 19:21) that Paul first says he *"must see Rome."* He doesn't realize at that time how he will get there or how long it will take. Near the end of that third journey he writes his letter—the Epistle to the Romans—to the church here and tells them he plans to visit them soon (Romans 1:10). He thinks he will be there in a few months, but years will pass. His arrest in Jerusalem leads to more than two years of imprisonment in Caesarea. It is early in his time there (about June of '57) that God promises Paul, *"you must witness at Rome also"* (Acts 23:11). God will reassure Paul of that reality again on board the ship in the midst of the storm just before the shipwreck in late November of AD 59 (Acts 27:24). With many years and adventures intervening, Paul at last arrives in Rome the following year, and in Acts 28:14, Luke says simply, *"and thus we came to Rome."*

> "All roads lead to Rome"
>
> – Jean de la Fontaine

📖 How does Luke indicate in Acts 28:11–14 that Paul and his shipwrecked friends finally get to Rome?

Paul and the rest of the group end up staying on Malta for three months. On the island they find a ship waiting out the bad weather of winter. Once the season passes, they are able to book passage and complete their journey in uneventful fashion. In Puteoli they are able to connect with some fellow believers and spend an encouraging week with them before traveling the last stage to Rome. After all they have been through; their arrival is noteworthy because of the lack of a great climax. They simply *"came to Rome."*

📖 What does Acts 28:15–16 say are the circumstances that greet Paul when he makes it to Rome?

There must have been plenty of times in these years of difficulty that Paul feels alone. He is only human and has to struggle with uncertainties and doubts. The reassurances from God speak of this reality. But they also speak of Paul seeking the face of God in his uncertainties and doubts. Paul probably wonders what awaits him in Rome. After trials and chains and shipwrecks he may be bracing himself for the worst. I think it is evidence of God's love and care that the first situation Paul has to face in Rome are not trials, but friends. Loving fellow-believers meet him in Puteoli, and more come all the way from the Market of Appius and Three Inns to meet him and his friends. Notice what Luke says of Paul's response: *"when Paul saw them, he thanked God and took courage."* The order here is key: when he sees them, he first thanks God, and then takes courage. They are just what he needs at this moment. Even the Roman guards who have accompanied Paul on this long journey seem to be showing special kindness to him—no doubt in part because of all he has come to mean to them during their travels. Though he is a prisoner, he is *"allowed to stay by himself, with the soldier who was guarding him."* His jail is *"minimum security"* and will allow for him to receive friends.

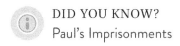

Tradition holds that Paul endured two imprisonments: this first, rather lenient one, and then a second Roman imprisonment in the Mamertine dungeons of Rome. This first imprisonment was something akin to house arrest. Paul was able to live in rented quarters (28:30) and was allowed to receive guests (28:23). It appears that Paul was acquitted and released about two years later (AD 62). Paul's second arrest may have occurred in Troas (see 2 Timothy 1:8, 16; 2:9). It was in the spring of AD 68 that Paul was beheaded during Nero's rule.

📖 Look at Acts 28:17–22 and identify what these verses reveal of the first activities Paul begins to undertake in Rome.

Paul is a veteran of many years of ministry. He has trusted God through three missionary journeys and has been the first to take the gospel to many different locales. In a way, you can call this trip to Rome his "fourth missionary journey." It seems Paul has come to view it that way. In his previous journeys he has developed a pattern of going first to the Jews. Although he can't go to the local synagogue in Rome, he can invite them to come and visit. After only three days, he does just that. Although the Jewish leaders here have heard of the controversy surrounding the message of Jesus, they have heard nothing of Paul's case and hold no bias against him. It is a good place to start his ministry in Rome.

📖 Read Acts 28:23–31 and answer the questions that follow.

How do the Jewish leaders respond to Paul when he shares the gospel with them?

What is Paul's point with the quote from Isaiah?

What stands out to you from Luke's summary in verses 30 and 31?

Not only does it seem like old times when Paul immediately reaches out to the local Jewish community, but it is also reminiscent of the missionary journeys in the response he receives. After spending all day reasoning with them from the Scriptures concerning Jesus, *"Some were being persuaded by the things spoken, but others would not believe."* In Rome, as in every other place, the cross divides the spiritual from the religious. Paul's quote from Isaiah is clearly directed at those who reject his message but may also be to help these who accept it understand why the rest don't. It all comes down to the fact that their hearts have become dull to the Lord. As in other places, Paul will now focus on the Gentiles. Though theoretically in prison, the freedoms given him by the sympathetic Romans allow him to continue *"preaching the kingdom of God and teaching concerning the Lord Jesus Christ with all openness, unhindered."*

> *"Now I want you to know, brethren, that my circumstances*
> *have turned out for the greater progress of the gospel, so that*
> *my imprisonment in the cause of Christ has become well known*
> *throughout the whole praetorian guard and to everyone else,*
> *and that most of the brethren, trusting in the Lord because of my*
> *imprisonment, have far more courage to speak the word of God*
> *without fear." (Philippians 1:12–14)*

The book of Acts closes here. From what we know of other sources, Paul may be in chains, but as he will write to Timothy years later, *"the word of God is not imprisoned"* (2 Timothy 2:9). These years in Rome will be fruitful times. At least four books of the Bible are written by Paul during this Roman imprisonment (Ephesians, Philippians, Colossians, and Philemon). Writing to the Philippians to thank them for their financial support, Paul says of this time, *"Now I want you to know, brethren, that my circumstances have turned out for the greater progress of the gospel, so that my imprisonment in the cause of Christ has become well known throughout the whole praetorian guard and to everyone else, and that most of the brethren, trusting in the Lord because of my imprisonment, have far more courage to speak the word of God without fear"* (Philippians 1:12–14). It is also during this time that he leads Philemon's slave, Onesimus, to Christ (Philemon 1:10). Because Paul trusts God's sovereignty, he looks for and finds God's higher purposes for his difficulties. God allows him to be in chains because the Lord can use that to further the kingdom. If we will trust God's sovereignty over the affairs of our lives, then, like Paul, we will see Him turn our prisons into pulpits.

Day 5

For Me to Follow God

At the end of September in 1992, when my wife was diagnosed with cancer, our immediate assumption was that this was not a ministry but a trial in our lives. Yet we soon learned that many were watching our lives through this time. Both believers and unbelievers among our friends, neighbors, and relatives, as well as among the health care workers and fellow patients we met through the process, were able to see that our faith in Christ made a difference in how we faced the circumstance. The "prison" of a hospital bed became a powerful pulpit from which to preach the good news of Jesus.

I think the key to that transformation—from prison to pulpit—is in our focus. If we focus on ourselves, then we manage our difficulties selfishly. But if we focus on the Lord, He will cause us to focus on others around us who need what we have. Even nonbelievers face trials. I believe that God allows His children to go through the same difficulties as everyone else, so that He can showcase that through faith they do not go through them with hopelessness and despair. But I have learned over the years that sometimes it takes me a while to get to that point.

> *...some of the clearest and most powerful messages come from people who preach with a limp.*

God wants to use our prisons as pulpits, but we are the preachers who must preach the sermons. Sometimes our own pain gets in the way, but I am learning that some of the clearest and most powerful messages come from people who preach with a limp. Perhaps the most important lesson to learn from the book of Acts is not the incredible miracles God performs to manifest His power, but that He is able to take ordinary people and use them to preach His extraordinary message which has the power to change lives. Peter and Paul are human like us. They have to move beyond their own prejudices and problems. They have to deal with their own fleshly attitudes. They hurt and bleed and worry and doubt. But through them, the world is changed. The same can be true of us.

As you reflect on Paul's difficulties and trials, are you able to identify any "prisons" in your own life right now? What are they?

What would you say has been your greatest struggle in dealing with the trials God allows you to go through?

_____

_____

_____

_____

_____

_____

_____

As we reflect on Paul's example in these last few chapters of Acts, some principles emerge which help us to understand practically how he puts himself in a place to be usable to the Lord in his trials. We learn all along that reaching others is already a priority to Paul before his imprisonment begins. We are able to observe Paul accepting his trial as being allowed by the Lord, and not becoming bitter or resentful. Paul knows from Peter's experience, and from his own at Philippi, that God can deliver him from jail if He chooses to though He chooses not to do so here. We also see in very human fashion that Paul has to deal with his own flesh and anger. Giving in to that closes doors of ministry, but laying it aside opens them back up. He is willing to speak openly of his faith when given the chance. In the midst of the storm, he seeks the Lord diligently and receives promises not only for himself, but also for those with him. While they are shipwrecked on Malta, we see him serving others in the menial work of tending the fire. At the governor's house Paul exhibits a compassionate heart by looking in on the man's ailing father and praying for him. After the father is healed, Paul receives those from the island who seek him out and he is used by the Lord to heal them too. Once they finally make it to Rome, Paul looks for chances to minister here with the Jews and even the soldiers who guard him. Paul's prison doesn't automatically become a pulpit. It does so because of a lot of choices that he makes along the way.

As you reflect on these principles from Paul's life that turn his prisons into pulpits, check the ones that you can honestly say are true of you in your own prison.

___ Let reaching others be a priority

___ Accept that the Lord has allowed the trial

___ Lay aside our own fleshly attitudes

___ Speak openly of our faith

___ Seek the Lord diligently during the hard times

___ Be a servant to others in the menial things that need doing

___ Have compassion and pray for the needy around us

___ Receive those God sends to us for help

___ Look for chances to minister

Look back over this list and identify the two or three you most need to work on.

As you bring this week's lesson and your study of the book of Acts to a close, write out a prayer to the Lord and ask Him to turn your prison into a pulpit...

NOTES

LEADER'S GUIDE

TABLE OF CONTENTS

HOW TO LEAD A SMALL GROUP BIBLE STUDY	214
PREPARATION OF THE DISCUSSION LEADER	228
LESSON 1: THE MISSION OF THE CHURCH – ACTS 13—14	230
LESSON 2: THE MESSAGE OF GRACE – ACTS 15:1–35	234
LESSON 3: WHATEVER THE PROBLEM, GOD HAS A SOLUTION - ACTS 15:36—16:40	238
LESSON 4: THE BASIS OF BELIEF - ACTS 17:1–34	242
LESSON 5: JOINING GOD WHERE HE IS WORKING - ACTS 18:1–22	246
LESSON 6: CHANGING THE WORLD - ACTS 18:23—19:41	250
LESSON 7: PASSING THE TORCH – ACTS 20	253
LESSON 8: WHEN GOD'S WILL IS HARD – ACTS 21:1—22:29	256
LESSON 9: THE FALSE SOLUTION OF FOLLOWING OUR FLESH - ACTS 23	260
LESSON 10: THE FRUIT OF PATIENCE- ACTS 24	264
LESSON 11: A DEFENSE FOR THE HOPE WITHIN - ACTS 25—26	268
LESSON 12: PRISONS BECOME PULPITS - ACTS 27—28	272

The best way to become a better discussion leader is to regularly evaluate your group discussion sessions. The most effective leaders are those who consistently look for ways to improve.

But before you start preparing for your first group session, you need to know the problem areas that will most likely weaken the effectiveness of your study group. Commit now to have the best Bible study group that you can possibly have. Ask the Lord to motivate you as a group leader and to steer you away from bad habits.

How to Guarantee a Poor Discussion Group:

1. Prepare inadequately.

2. Show improper attitude toward people in the group (lack of acceptance).

3. Fail to create an atmosphere of freedom and ease.

4. Allow the discussion to wander aimlessly.

5. Dominate the discussion yourself.

6. Let a small minority dominate the discussion.

7. Leave the discussion "in the air," so to speak, without presenting any concluding statements or some type of closure.

8. Ask too many "telling" or "trying" questions. (Don't ask individuals in your group pointed or threatening questions that might bring embarrassment to them or make them feel uncomfortable.)

9. End the discussion without adequate application points.

10. Do the same thing every time.

11. Become resentful and angry when people disagree with you. After all, you did prepare. You are the leader!

12. End the discussion with an argument.

13. Never spend any time with the members of your group other than the designated discussion meeting time.

Helpful Hints

One of the best ways to learn to be an effective Bible discussion leader is to sit under a good model. If you have had the chance to be in a group with an effective facilitator, think about the things that made him or her effective.

Though you can learn much and shape many convictions from those good models, you can also glean some valuable lessons on what not to do from those who didn't do such a good job. Bill Donahue has done a good job of categorizing the leader's role in facilitating dynamic discussion into four key actions. They are easy to remember as he links them to the acrostic ACTS:

*A leader ACTS to facilitate discussions by:

Acknowledging everyone who speaks during a discussion.

Clarifying what is being said and felt.

Taking it to the group as a means of generating discussion.

Summarizing what has been said.

*Taken from *Leading Life-Changing Small Groups* ©1996 by the Willow Creek Association. Used by permission of ZondervanPublishing House.

Make a point to give each group member ample opportunity to speak. Pay close attention to any nonverbal communication (i.e. facial expressions, body language, etc.) that group members may use, showing their desire to speak. The four actions in Bill Donahue's acrostic will guarantee to increase your effectiveness, which will translate into your group getting more out of the Bible study. After all, isn't that your biggest goal?

Dealing with Talkative Timothy

Throughout your experiences of leading small Bible study groups, you will learn that there will be several stereotypes who will follow you wherever you go. One of them is "Talkative Timothy." He will show up in virtually every small group you will ever lead. (Sometimes this stereotype group member shows up as "Talkative Tammy.") "Talkative Timothy" talks too much, dominates the discussion time, and gives less opportunity for others to share. What do you do with a group member who talks too much? Below you will find some helpfulideas on managing the "Talkative Timothy's" in your group.

The best defense is a good offense. To deal with "Talkative Timothy" before he becomes a problem, one thing you can do is establish as a ground rule that no one can talk twice until everyone who wants to talk has spoken at least once. Another important ground rule is "no interrupting." Still another solution is to go systematically around the group, directing questions to people by name. When all else fails, you can resort to a very practical approach of sitting beside "Talkative Timothy." When you make it harder for him (or her) to make eye contact with you, you will create less chances for him to talk.

After taking one or more of these combative measures, you may find that "Timothy" is still a problem. You may need to meet with him (or her) privately. Assure him that you value his input, but remind him that you want to hear the comments of others as well. One way to diplomatically approach "Timothy" is to privately ask him to help you draw the less talkative members into the discussion. Approaching "Timothy" in this fashion may turn your dilemma into an asset. Most importantly, remember to love "Talkative Timothy."

Silent Sally

Another person who inevitably shows up is "Silent Sally." She doesn't readily speak up. Sometimes her silence is because she doesn't yet feel comfortable enough with the group to share her thoughts. Sometimes it is simply because she fears being rejected. Often her silence is because she is too polite to interrupt and thus is headed off at the pass each time she wants to speak by more aggressive (and less sensitive) members of the group.

It is not uncommon in a mixed group to find that "Silent Sally" is married to "Talkative Timothy." (Seriously!) Don't mistakenly interpret her silence as meaning that she has nothing to contribute. Often those who are slowest to speak will offer the most meaningful contributions to the group. You can help "Silent Sally" make those significant contributions. Below are some ideas.

Make sure, first of all, that you are creating an environment that makes people comfortable. In a tactful way, direct specific questions to the less talkative in the group. Be careful though, not to put them on the spot with the more difficult or controversial questions. Become their biggest fan—make sure you cheer them on when they do share. Give them a healthy dose of affirmation. Compliment them afterward for any insightful contributions they make. You may want to sit across from them in the group so that it is easier to notice any nonverbal cues they give you when they want to speak. You should also come to their defense if another group member responds to them in a negative, stifling way. As you pray for each group member, ask that the Lord would help the quiet ones in your group to feel more at ease during the discussion time. Most of all, love "Silent Sally," and accept her as she is—even when she is silent!

Tangent Tom

We have already looked at "Talkative Timothy" and "Silent Sally." Now let's look at another of those stereotypes who always show up. Let's call this person, "Tangent Tom." He is the kind of guy who loves to talk even when he has nothing to say. "Tangent Tom" loves to chase rabbits regardless of where they go. When he gets the floor, you never know where the discussion will lead. You need to understand that not all tangents are bad, for sometimes much can be gained from discussion that is a little "off the beaten path." But diversions must be balanced against the purpose of the group. What is fruitful for one member may be fruitless for everyone else. Below are some ideas to help you deal with "Tangent Tom."

Evaluating Tangents

Ask yourself, "How will this tangent affect my group's chances of finishing the lesson?" Another way to measure the value of a tangent is by asking, "Is this something that will benefit all or most of the group?" You also need to determine whether there is a practical, spiritual benefit to this tangent. Paul advised Timothy to refuse foolish and ignorant speculations, knowing that they produce quarrels. (See 2 Timothy 2:23.)

1) Keep pace of your time, and use the time factor as your ally when addressing "Tangent Tom." Tactfully respond, "That is an interesting subject, but since our lesson is on _____, we'd better get back to our lesson if we are going to finish."

2) If the tangent is beneficial to one but fruitless to the rest of the group, offer to address that subject after class.

3) If the tangent is something that will benefit the group, you may want to say, "I'd like to talk about that more. Let's come back to that topic at the end of today's discussion, if we have time."

4) Be sure you understand what "Tangent Tom" is trying to say. It may be that he has a good and valid point, but has trouble expressing it or needs help in being more direct. Be careful not to quench someone whose heart is right, even if his methods aren't perfect. (See Proverbs 18:23.)

5) One suggestion for diffusing a strife-producing tangent is to point an imaginary shotgun at a spot outside the group and act like you are firing a shot. Then say, "That rabbit is dead. Now, where were we?"

6) If it is a continual problem, you may need to address it with this person privately.

7) Most of all, be patient with "Tangent Tom." God will use him in the group in ways that will surprise you!

Know-It-All Ned

The Scriptures are full of characters who struggled with the problem of pride. Unfortunately, pride isn't a problem reserved for the history books. It shows up today just as it did in the days the Scriptures were written.

Pride is sometimes the root-problem of a know-it-all group member. "Know-It-All Ned" may have shown up in your group by this point. He may be an intellectual giant, or only a legend in his own mind. He can be very prideful and argumentative. "Ned" often wants his point chosen as the choice point, and he may be intolerant of any opposing views— sometimes to the point of making his displeasure known in very inappropriate ways. A discussion point tainted with the stench of pride is uninviting—no matter how well spoken!

No one else in the group will want anything to do with this kind of attitude. How do you manage the "Know-It-All Ned's" who show up from time to time?

EVALUATION

To deal with "Know-It-All Ned," you need to understand him. Sometimes the same type of action can be rooted in very different causes. You must ask yourself, "Why does 'Ned' come across as a know-it-all?" It may be that "Ned" has a vast reservoir of knowledge but hasn't matured in how he communicates it. Or perhaps "Ned" really doesn't know it all, but he tries to come across that way to hide his insecurities and feelings of inadequacy.

Quite possibly, "Ned" is prideful and arrogant, and knows little of the Lord's ways in spite of the information and facts he has accumulated. Still another possibility is that Ned is a good man with a good heart who has a blind spot in the area of pride.

APPLICATION

"Know-It-All Ned" may be the most difficult person to deal with in your group, but God will use him in ways that will surprise you. Often it is the "Ned's" of the church that teach each of us what it means to love the unlovely in Gods strength, not our own. In 1 Thessalonians 5:14, the apostle Paul states, "And we urge you, brethren, admonish the unruly, encourage the fainthearted, help the weak, be patient with all men." In dealing with the "Ned's" you come across, start by assuming they are weak and need help until they give you reason to believe otherwise. Don't embarrass them by confronting them in public. Go to them in private if need be.

Speak the truth in love. You may need to remind them of 1 Corinthians 13, that if we have all knowledge, but have not love, we are just making noise. First Corinthians is also where we are told, "knowledge makes arrogant, but love edifies" (8:1). Obviously, there were some "Ned's" in the church at Corinth. If you sense that "Ned" is not weak or faint-hearted, but in fact is unruly, you will need to admonish him. Make sure you do so in private, but make sure you do it all the same. Proverbs 27:56 tells us, "Better is open rebuke than love that is concealed. Faithful are the wounds of a friend, but deceitful are the kisses of an enemy." Remember the last statement in 1 Thessalonians 5:14, "be patient with all men."

Agenda Alice

The last person we would like to introduce to you who will probably show up sooner or later is one we like to call "Agenda Alice." All of us from time to time can be sidetracked by our own agenda. Often the very thing we are most passionate about can be the thing that distracts us from our highest passion: Christ. Agendas often are not unbiblical, but imbalanced. At their root is usually tunnel-vision mixed with a desire for control. The small group, since it allows everyone to contribute to the discussion, affords "Agenda Alice" a platform to promote what she thinks is most important. This doesn't mean that she is wrong to avoid driving at night because opossums are being killed, but she is wrong to expect everyone to have the exact same conviction and calling that she does in the gray areas of Scripture. If not managed properly, she will either sidetrack the group from its main study objective or create a hostile environment in the group if she fails to bring people to her way of thinking. "Agenda Alice" can often be recognized by introductory catch phrases such as "Yes, but . . ." and"Well, I think. . . ." She is often critical of the group process and may become vocally critical of you. Here are some ideas on dealing with this type of person:

1) Reaffirm the group covenant.
   At the formation of your group you should have taken time to define some ground rules for the group. Once is not enough to discuss these matters of group etiquette.

Periodically remind everyone of their mutual commitment to one another.

2) Remember that the best defense is a good offense.
   Don't wait until it is a problem to address a mutual vision for how the group will function.

3) Refocus on the task at hand.
   The clearer you explain the objective of each session, the easier it is to stick to that
   objective and the harder you make it for people to redirect attention toward their own
   agenda. Enlist the whole group in bringing the discussion back to the topic at hand.
   Ask questions like, "What do the rest of you think about this passage?"

4) Remind the group, "Remember, this week's lesson is about _____."

5) Reprove those who are disruptive.
   Confront the person in private to see if you can reach an understanding. Suggest
   another arena for the issue to be addressed such as an optional meeting for those in
   the group who would like to discuss the issue.

Remember the words of St. Augustine: "In essentials unity, in non-essentials liberty, in
all things charity."

Adding Spice and Creativity

One of the issues you will eventually have to combat in any group Bible study is the
enemy of boredom. This enemy raises its ugly head from time to time, but it shouldn't.
It is wrong to bore people with the Word of God! Often boredom results when leaders
allow their processes to become too predictable. As small group leaders, we tend to do the
same thing in the same way every single time. Yet God the Creator, who spoke everything
into existence is infinitely creative! Think about it. He is the one who not only created
animals in different shapes and sizes, but different colors as well. When He created food,
He didn't make it all taste or feel the same. This God of creativity lives in us. We can trust
Him to give us creative ideas that will keep our group times from becoming tired and
mundane. Here are some ideas:

When you think of what you can change in your Bible study, think of the five senses:
(sight, sound, smell, taste, and feel).

SIGHT:
One idea would be to have a theme night with decorations. Perhaps you know someone
with dramatic instincts who could dress up in costume and deliver a message from the
person you are studying that week.

Draw some cartoons on a marker board or handout.

SOUND:
Play some background music before your group begins. Sing a hymn together that relates

to the lesson. If you know of a song that really hits the main point of the lesson, play it at the beginning or end.

SMELL:
This may be the hardest sense to involve in your Bible study, but if you think of a creative way to incorporate this sense into the lesson, you can rest assured it will be memorable for your group.

TASTE:
Some lessons will have issues that can be related to taste (e.g. unleavened bread for the Passover, etc.). What about making things less formal by having snacks while you study? Have refreshments around a theme such as "Chili Night" or "Favorite Fruits."

FEEL:
Any way you can incorporate the sense of feel into a lesson will certainly make the content more invigorating. If weather permits, add variety by moving your group outside. Whatever you do, be sure that you don't allow your Bible study to become boring!

Handling an Obviously Wrong Comment

From time to time, each of us can say stupid things. Some of us, however, are better at it than others. The apostle Peter had his share of embarrassing moments. One minute, he was on the pinnacle of success, saying, "Thou art the Christ, the Son of the Living God" (Matthew 16:16), and the next minute, he was putting his foot in his mouth, trying to talk Jesus out of going to the cross. Proverbs 10:19 states, "When there are many words, transgression is unavoidable. . . ." What do you do when someone in the group says something that is obviously wrong? First of all, remember that how you deal with a situation like this not only affects the present, but the future. Here are some ideas:

1) Let the whole group tackle it and play referee/peacemaker. Say something like, "That is an interesting thought, what do the rest of you think?"

2) Empathize. ("I've thought that before too, but the Bible says. . . .")

3) Clarify to see if what they said is what they meant. ("What I think you are saying is. . . .")

4) Ask the question again, focusing on what the Bible passage actually says.

5) Give credit for the part of the answer that is right and affirm that before dealing with what is wrong.

6) If it is a non-essential, disagree agreeably. ("I respect your opinion, but I see it differently.")

7) Let it go —some things aren't important enough to make a big deal about them.

8) Love and affirm the person, even if you reject the answer.

Transitioning to the Next Study

For those of you who have completed leading a Following God Group Bible Study, con-gratulations! You have successfully navigated the waters of small group discussion. You have utilized one of the most effective tools of ministry—one that was so much a priority with Jesus, He spent most of His time there with His small group of twelve. Hopefully yours has been a very positive and rewarding experience. At this stage you may be look-ing forward to a break. It is not too early however, to be thinking and planning for what you will do next. Hopefully you have seen God use this study and this process for growth in the lives of those who have participated with you. As God has worked in the group, members should be motivated to ask the question, "What next?" As they do, you need to be prepared to give an answer. Realize that you have built a certain amount of momentum with your present study that will make it easier to do another. You want to take advan-tage of that momentum. The following suggestions may be helpful as you transition your people toward further study of God's Word.

- Challenge your group members to share with others what they have learned, and to encourage them to participate next time.

- If what to study is a group choice rather than a church-wide or ministry-wide decision made by others, you will want to allow some time for input from the group members in deciding what to do next. The more they have ownership of the study, the more they will commit to it.

- It is important to have some kind of a break so that everyone doesn't become study weary. At our church, we always look for natural times to start and end a study. We take the summer off as well as Christmas, and we have found that having a break brings people back with renewed vigor. Even if you don't take a break from meeting, you might take a breather from homework—or even get together just for fellowship.

- If you are able to end this study knowing what you will study next, some of your group members may want to get a head start on the next study. Be prepared to put books in their hands early.

- Make sure you end your study with a vision for more. Take some time to remind your group of the importance of the Word of God. As D. L. Moody used to say, "The only way to keep a broken vessel full is to keep the faucet running."

Evaluation

Becoming a Better Discussion Leader

The questions listed below are tools to assist you in assessing your discussion group. From time to time in the Leader's Guide, you will be advised to read through this list of evaluation questions in order to help you decide what areas need improvement in your role as group leader. Each time you read through this list, something different may catch your attention, giving you tips on how to become the best group leader that you can possibly be.

Read through these questions with an open mind, asking the Lord to prick your heart with anything specific He would want you to apply.

1. Are the group discussion sessions beginning and ending on time?

2. Am I allowing the freedom of the Holy Spirit as I lead the group in the discussion?

3. Do I hold the group accountable for doing their homework?

4. Do we always begin our sessions with prayer?

5. Is the room arranged properly (seating in a circle or semicircle, proper ventilation, adequate teaching aids)?

6. Is each individual allowed equal opportunity in the discussion?

7. Do I successfully bridle the talkative ones?

8. Am I successfully encouraging the hesitant ones to participate in the discussion?

9. Do I redirect comments and questions to involve more people in the interaction, or do I always dominate the discussion?

10. Are the discussions flowing naturally, or do they take too many "side roads" (diversions)?

11. Do I show acceptance to those who convey ideas with which I do not agree?

12. Are my questions specific, brief and clear?

13. Do my questions provoke thought, or do they only require pat answers?

14. Does each group member feel free to contribute or question, or is there a threatening or unnecessarily tense atmosphere?

15. Am I allowing time for silence and thought without making everyone feel uneasy?

16. Am I allowing the group to correct any obviously wrong conclusions that are made by others, or by myself (either intentionally to capture the group's attention or unintentionally)?

17. Do I stifle thought and discussion by assigning a question to someone before the subject of that question has even been discussed? (It will often be productive to assign a question to a specific person, but if you call on one person before you throw out a question, everyone else takes a mental vacation!)

18. Do I summarize when brevity is of the essence?

19. Can I refrain from expressing an opinion or comment that someone else in the group could just as adequately express?

20. Do I occasionally vary in my methods of conducting the discussion?

21. Am I keeping the group properly motivated?

22. Am I occasionally rotating the leadership to help others develop leadership?

23. Am I leading the group to specifically apply the truths that are learned?

24. Do I follow through by asking the group how they have applied the truths that they have learned from previous lessons?

25. Am I praying for each group member?

26. Is there a growing openness and honesty among my group members?

27. Are the group study sessions enriching the lives of my group members?

28. Have I been adequately prepared?

29. How may I be better prepared for the next lesson's group discussion?

30. Do I reach the objective set for each discussion? If not, why not? What can I do to improve?

31. Am I allowing the discussion to bog down on one point at the expense of the rest of the lesson?

32. Are the members of the group individually reaching the conclusions that I want them to reach without my having to give them the conclusions?

33. Do I encourage the group members to share what they have learned?

34. Do I encourage them to share the applications they have discovered?

35. Do I whet their appetites for next week's lesson discussion?

Getting Started

The First Meeting of Your Bible Study Group

Main Objectives of the First Meeting: The first meeting is devoted to establishing your group and setting the course that you will follow through the study. Your primary goals for this session should be to . . .

- Establish a sense of group identity by starting to get to know one another.

- Define some ground rules to help make the group time as effective as possible.

- Get the study materials into the hands of your group members.

- Create a sense of excitement and motivation for the study.

- Give assignments for next week.

BEFORE THE SESSION

You will be most comfortable in leading this introductory session if you are prepared as much as possible for what to expect. This means becoming familiar with the place you will meet, and the content you will cover, as well as understanding any time constraints you will have.

Location—Be sure that you not only know how to find the place where you will be meeting, but also have time to examine the setup and make any adjustments to the physical arrangements. You never get a second chance to make a first impression.

Curriculum—You will want to get a copy of the study in advance of the introductory session, and it will be helpful if you do the homework for Lesson One ahead of time. This will make it easier for you to be able to explain the layout of the homework. It will also give you a contagious enthusiasm for what your group will be studying in the coming week.

You will want to have enough books on hand for the number of people you expect so that they can get started right away with the study. You may be able to make arrangements with your church or local Christian Bookstore to bring copies on consignment. We would encourage you not to buy books for your members. Years of small group experience have taught that people take a study far more seriously when they make an investment in it.

Time—The type of group you are leading will determine the time format for your study. If you are doing this study for a Sunday school class or church study course, the time constraints may already be prescribed for you. In any case, ideally you will want to allow forty-five minutes to an hour for discussion.

WHAT TO EXPECT

When you embark on the journey of leading a small group Bible study, you are stepping into the stream of the work of God. You are joining in the process of helping others move toward spiritual maturity. As a small group leader, you are positioned to be a real catalyst in the lives of your group members, helping them to grow in their relationships with God. But you must remember, first and foremost, that whenever you step up to leadership in the kingdom of God, you are stepping down to serve. Jesus made it clear that leadership in the kingdom is not like leadership in the world. In Matthew 20:25, Jesus said, "You know that the rulers of the Gentiles lord it over them, and their great men exercise authority over them." That is the world's way to lead. But in Matthew 20:26–27, He continues, "It is not so among you, but whoever wishes to become great among you shall be your servant, and whoever wishes to be first among you shall be your slave." Your job as a small group leader is not to teach the group everything you have learned, but rather, to help them learn.

If you truly are to minister to the members of your group, you must start with understanding where they are, and join that with a vision of where you want to take them. In this introductory session, your group members will be experiencing several different emotions. They will be wondering, "Who is in my group?" and deciding "Do I like my group?" They will have a sense of excitement and anticipation, but also a sense of awkwardness as they try to find their place in this group. You will want to make sure that from the very beginning your group is founded with a sense of caring and acceptance. This is crucial if your group members are to open up and share what they are learning.

DURING THE SESSION

GETTING TO KNOW ONE ANOTHER

Opening Prayer—Remember that if it took the inspiration of God for people to write Scripture, it will also take His illumination for us to understand it. Have one of your group members open your time together in prayer.

Introductions—Take time to allow the group members to introduce themselves. Along with having the group members share their names, one way to add some interest is to have them add some descriptive information such as where they live or work. Just for fun, you could have them name their favorite breakfast cereal, most (or least) favorite vegetable, favorite cartoon character, their favorite city or country other than their own, etc.

Icebreaker—Take five or ten minutes to get the people comfortable in talking with each other. Since in many cases your small group will just now be getting to know one another, it will be helpful if you take some time to break the ice with some fun, nonthreatening discussion. Below you will find a list of ideas for good icebreaker questions to get people talking.

____ What is the biggest risk you have ever taken?

____ If money were no object, where would you most like to take a vacation and why?

____ What is your favorite way to waste time?

____ If you weren't in the career you now have, what would have been your second choice for a career?

____ If you could have lived in any other time, in what era or century would you have chosen to live (besides the expected spiritual answer of the time of Jesus)?

____ If you became blind right now, what would you miss seeing the most?

____ Who is the most famous person you've known or met?

____ What do you miss most about being a kid?

____ What teacher had the biggest impact on you in school (good or bad)?

____ Of the things money can buy, what would you most like to have?

____ What is your biggest fear?

____ If you could give one miracle to someone else, what would it be (and to whom)?

____ Tell about your first job.

____ Who is the best or worst boss you ever had?

____ Who was your hero growing up and why?

DEFINING THE GROUP: 5–10 MINUTES
SETTING SOME GROUND RULES

There are several ways you can lay the tracks on which your group can run. One is simply to hand out a list of suggested commitments the members should make to the group. Another would be to hand out 3x5 cards and have the members themselves write down two or three commitments they would like to see everyone live out. You could then compile these into the five top ones to share at the following meeting. A third option is to list three (or more) commitments you are making to the group and then ask that they make three commitments back to you in return. Here are some ideas for the types of ground rules that make for a good small group:

Leader:

____ To always arrive prepared

____ To keep the group on track so you make the most of the group's time

____ To not dominate the discussion by simply teaching the lesson

____ To pray for the group members

____ To not belittle or embarrass anyone's answers

____ To bring each session to closure and end on time

Member:

____ To do my homework

____ To arrive on time

____ To participate in the discussion

____ To not cut others off as they share

____ To respect the different views of other members

____ To not dominate the discussion

It is possible that your group may not need to formalize a group covenant, but you should not be afraid to expect a commitment from your group members. They will all benefit from defining the group up front.

INTRODUCTION TO THE STUDY: 15–20 MINUTES

As you introduce the study to the group members, your goal is to begin to create a sense of excitement about the Bible characters and applications that will be discussed. The most important question for you to answer in this session is "Why should I study _____?" You need to be prepared to guide them to finding that answer. Take time to give a brief overview of each lesson.

CLOSING: 5–10 MINUTES

Give homework for next week. In addition to simply reminding the group members to do their homework, if time allows, you might give them 5–10 minutes to get started on their homework for the first lesson.

Key components for closing out your time are a) to review anything of which you feel they should be reminded, and b) to close in prayer. If time allows, you may want to encourage several to pray.

PREPARATION OF THE DISCUSSION LEADER

I. Preparation of the Leader's Heart

A. Pray. It took the inspiration of the Holy Spirit to write Scripture, and it will require His illumination to correctly understand it.

B. Complete the Bible Study Yourself

1. Prayerfully seek a fresh word from God for yourself. Your teaching should be an overflow of what God taught you.

2. Even if you have completed this study in the past, consider using a new book. You need to be seeking God for what He would teach you this time before looking at what He taught you last time.

3. Guard against focusing on how to present truths to class. Keep the focus on God teaching you.

II. Keeping the Big Picture in Sight

One value of discussion: It allows students to share what God's Word says.

A. Looking back over the homework, find the one main unifying truth. There will be a key emphasis of each day, but all will support one main truth. Keep praying and looking until you find it (even if the author didn't make it clear).

B. Begin to write questions for each day's homework. Do this as you go through the study.

1. Consider key passage(s) for the day and ask questions of the text. For example, use the 5 Ws and an H (Who, What, When, Where, Why, and How): What was Jesus' main point? What is the context here? Do you see any cultural significance to this statement? How did this person relate to... (God? His neighbor? An unbeliever? The church? etc.)

2. Don't ask, "What do you think" questions unless it's "What do you think GOD is saying...?" It's easy to slip into sharing opinions if we don't carefully guide students to consider what God says. What I think doesn't matter if it differs from what God thinks.

3. Ask application questions as well. For example, "What steals our joy?" "How are we like these Bible characters?" "How can we learn from _____'s lessons so that we don't have to learn it the hard way?" "How can I restore/protect my _____ (joy, faith, peace...)?" Consider making a list where you write answers to "So what?" questions: So, what does this mean to me? How do I put this truth into practice?

4. Include definitions, grammar notes, historical/cultural notes, cross references, and so forth, from your own study. Go back over your notes/questions and add/delete/re-write after further prayer and thought. Go through your notes again, highlighting

(underlining, color coding, whatever works for you) what you believe is MOST important. This will help when time gets cut short. It will also jog your memory before moving to next day's homework,

III. Leading the Discussion

A. Begin with prayer

1. Consider varying the method - this will help to remind the group that we pray not as habit but as needy children seeking our loving Father Who teaches us by His Spirit.

2. If having a time of prayer requests, consider ways to make it time effective and to avoid gossip disguised as a prayer request. Time management is a way you can serve the group.

B. Start the Study with Review—Briefly review context of the study (or have a student come prepared to do it). This keeps the group together for those joining the study late or who've missed a week. This also serves as a reminder since it's been a week or so since your previous study session.

C. Go through the study questions day by day.

1. You may offer a "unifying theme" of study or ask if students can identify a theme.

2. Follow the Holy Spirit. Remember that you can't cover everything from every day. As you prepare, highlight any notes He leads you to consider as being most important.

3. Watch your time! When you are leading a group Bible study, you enter into a different dimension of the physical realm. Time moves at a completely different pace. What is 20 minutes in normal time flies by like 5 minutes when you are in the speaking zone.

4. Manage the questions raised by students and consider their value to the whole group within time constraints. Turn any questions raised back to the group.

5. Whether you make application day by day (probably best) or make application at end, be sure to allow time for students to name ways to put knowledge into practice.

IV. Evaluation

1. After 1-2 days, evaluate how the lesson went.

2. Thank God—thank Him for using His Word in all participants' lives and ask Him to guard the good seed planted!

V. Begin Preparation for the Next Lesson

Lesson #1 - The Mission of the Church – Acts 13:1—14:28

Memory Verse: Acts 1:8

"But you will receive power when the Holy Spirit has come upon you;
and you shall be My witnesses both in Jerusalem, and in all Judea and Samaria, and
even to the remotest part of the earth.

BEFORE THE SESSION

- Be sure you have read through the introductory material and that you are seeking to apply the principles yourself. The more impact the Word makes in your heart the more enthusiasm you will communicate.

- Spread your homework out rather than trying to cram everything into one afternoon or night. You may want to use this as your daily quiet time.

- As you study, write down any good discussion questions you think of as they come to mind.

- Be transparent before the Lord and before your group. We are all learners – that's the meaning of the word "disciple."

WHAT TO EXPECT

It seems by the examples we see today that the average local congregation is much better at "doing" church than at "being" the church. Many local bodies go through the motions of all the programs and activities they have always done, but have lost focus on their ultimate goals. Expect both encouragement and challenge to come from this week's lesson. There may be a mixture of vision of what could be and frustration at what is. You will need to lead your group to honestly evaluate without becoming critical and judgmental. Make sure you bring their focus toward personal responsibility and action, helping to guard them from trying to apply the truths to others instead of themselves.

THE MAIN POINT

The main point to be seen in the lesson on the mission of the church is that as the body of Christ, we are called to His mission: *"...to seek and to save that which was lost"* (Luke 19:10).

DURING THE SESSION

OPENING: 5–10 MINUTES

Opening Prayer – You or one of your group members should open your time together in prayer.

Opening Illustration – In rescuing His people from Egypt, God gave the Jews a vision and a mission. Their vision was the Promised Land and their mission was to be the people of God and point others to Him. He performed great miracles in changing Pharaoh's mind to let them go. He parted the Red Sea and let them walk through on dry land. Yet during the forty days Moses was up on the mountain getting the Ten Commandments, we see these same people reverting to pagan idol worship and rebelling against God. Think about that. It took them less than forty days to lose vision. We need to realize the importance of keeping a sense of God's vision for us as the church. As we will see in this week's lesson, there are many practical applications to be drawn for today from the mission outreach of the early church.

DISCUSSION: 30 MINUTES

Main Objective in Day One: Day One focuses on the reality that the labor of ministry takes laborers. Below are some possible discussion questions for the Day One discussion. Check which questions you will use.

___ As you looked at the list of leaders in Acts 13:1 what stood out to you?

___ How do you think your church would handle it if God suddenly called two of your top leaders to the mission field?

___ What principles did you see with the call of Barnabas and Paul that relate to us today?

___ Why do you think the guys chose the route they did on the first missionary journey?

Main Objective in Day Two: A vision for missions is not just recognizing what needs to be done. Day two focuses on the methods and strategies we see employed here. Check which discussion questions you will use for Day Two.

___ What principles did you observe in verses 5 and 6?

___ Have you encountered any opposition as you communicate your faith?

___ Did anything in particular stand out to you from Paul's opposition?

___ What applications can you glean from Paul's response to his opposition?

Main Objective in Day Three: The focus in Day Three is on the message we need to bring to others. Check which discussion questions for Day Three you might use.

___ What do you consider to be the main points of the gospel?

___ How do you see those points expressed in Paul's message?

___ Is there anything in Paul's presentation that surprised you?

___ What applications did you see in the end of Paul's message?

Main Objective in Day Four: Day Four takes a look at the importance of taking the message of Christ to where it is needed. In addition to any discussion questions that may have come to your mind in your studying, the following suggested questions may prove beneficial to your group session:

___ What stood out to you from the different responses to the gospel recorded here?

___ Do you see different responses today than those Paul experienced?

___ What similarities do you find today with the responses of Paul's day?

___ How did the missionaries follow up the responses of their outreach? Do we do a good job of that today?

Day Five – Key Points in Application: The most important application from our study this week is to recognize the need to take the gospel to others. Check which discussion questions you will use for Day Five.

___ In what ways do you identify with Chuck Swindoll's illustration of the lifesaving station?

___ As you honestly reflect on your church or ministry, are your victories in the present or mostly in the past?

___ What would you say are your church's greatest weaknesses in the area of world missions?

___ What application points do you sense the Lord calling you to?

CLOSING: 5–10 MINUTES

Summarize – Restate the key points highlighted in the class.

Preview – Take just a few moments to preview next week's lesson.

Encourage the group to be sure to do their homework.

Pray – Close in prayer.

TOOLS FOR GOOD DISCUSSION

Some who are reading this have led small group Bible studies many times. Here is an important word of warning: experience alone does not make you a more effective discussion leader. In fact, experience can make you less effective. You see, the more experience you have the more comfortable you will be at the task. Unfortunately, for some that means becoming increasingly comfortable in doing a bad job. Taking satisfaction with mediocrity translates into taking the task less seriously. It is easy to wrongly assert that just because one is experienced, that he or she can successfully "shoot from the hip" so to speak. If you really want your members to get the most out of this study, you need to be dissatisfied with simply doing an adequate job and make it your aim to do an excellent job. A key to excellence is to regularly evaluate yourself to see that you are still doing all that you want to be doing. We have prepared a list of over thirty evaluation questions for you to review from time to time. This list of questions can be found on pages 222–223 in this Leader's Guide. The examination questions will help to jog your memory and, hopefully, will become an effective aid in improving the quality of your group discussion. Review the evaluation questions list, and jot down below two or three action points for you to begin implementing next week.

ACTION POINTS:

1.

2.

3.

Lesson #2—The Message of Grace – Acts 15:1–35

Memory Verse: Galatians 2:21

"I do not nullify the grace of God for if righteousness comes by the works of the Law, Christ died needlessly."

BEFORE THE SESSION

- Remember that your goal is not to teach the lesson, but to facilitate discussion.

- Make sure your own heart is right with God. Be willing to be transparent with the group about your own life experiences and mistakes. This will make it easier for them to open up.

- Don't be afraid of chasing tangents for a while if the diversions capture the interest of the group as a whole, but don't sacrifice the rest of the group to belabor the questions of one member. Trust God to lead you.

- You may want to keep a highlight pen handy as you study to mark key statements that stood out to you.

WHAT TO EXPECT

You need to recognize that legalism is just as much an issue today as it was in Paul's day. Be prepared for questions and perhaps even disagreement. Keep focused on the main point that we cannot fulfill the Law in our own strength and that is what makes grace so attractive. Help your group see that the Christian life is not simply about morality, but a personal relationship with God which changes our morality. Expect that your group not only needs to understand grace, but also that there are errors in both directions. Legalism is wrong, but so is using grace as an excuse for license to sin. It is important that they grasp the concept that the Christian life is not me trying hard to be like Jesus, but rather, me yielding myself to Christ's control and allowing Him to live through me by His Spirit. No doubt, all in your group will have experienced their own share of failure and frustration as they tried to live the Christian life in their own efforts. They will want to share their own stories as time allows. Expect that this will be a very motivating lesson with lots of interest.

THE MAIN POINT

The main point of this week's lesson is to focus in on the impact of the Jerusalem Council on clarifying the message of grace and where the Law of Moses fits for us today.

DURING THE SESSION

OPENING: 5–10 MINUTES

Opening Prayer – You or one of your group members should open your time together in prayer.

Opening Illustration – In Romans 6 Paul is explaining the concept of grace to some very confused believers. His points address some of the key misconceptions people have about grace. In Romans 5:20 he makes the point that *"where sin increased, grace abounded all the more."* In other words, there is always more grace than enough grace for our sin. He addresses misconception #1 in Romans 6:1 with the question, *"What shall we say then? Are we to continue in sin so that grace may increase?"* Some say more sin means more grace so sin all the more. *"May it never be!"* Paul states emphatically (6:2). Christ died to set us free from sin, not to make us sin more (6:6). In Romans 6:15 Paul reveals a second misconception: *"Shall we sin because we are not under law but under grace?"* Some use grace to say that sinning doesn't matter. *"May it never be!"* is again his response. In Romans 7:7 Paul brings up misconception #3: *"What shall we say then? Is the Law sin?"* In other words, if grace is right does that make law wrong? Again he exclaims, *"May it never be!"* Law is not wrong, but it has no power to change us. It can only reveal our need for a Savior. The Law is not our problem, but rather, our problem is our inability to keep the Law. There are many misconceptions about the message of grace, but there is also great hope to be found there. In Romans 8:1-2 Paul expresses the liberation of grace, saying, *"Therefore there is now no condemnation for those who are in Christ Jesus. For the law of the Spirit of life in Christ Jesus has set you free from the law of sin and of death."* Hallelujah!

DISCUSSION: 30 MINUTES

Once your group gets talking you will find that all you need to do is keep the group directed and flowing with a question or two or a pointed observation. You are the gatekeeper of discussion. Don't be afraid to ask someone to elaborate further or to ask a quiet member of the group what they think of someone else's comments. Time will not allow you to discuss every single question in the lesson one at a time. Instead, make it your goal to cover the main ideas of each day, and help the group to personally share what they learned. You don't have to use all the discussion questions. They are there for your discretion.

Main Objective in Day One: In Day One, the central objective of the study is to introduce the problem from the Jews when Gentiles started becoming Christians. Below, check any discussion questions that you might consider using in your group session.

___ What was controversial in the teaching of the men from Judea?

___ What stands out from the attempts to resolve the disagreement?

___ Why do you think this was such a problem?

___ What are some modern ways we see a battle between grace and law?

Main Objective in Day Two: In Day Two, we see Peter's speech and the impact it has on the debate. Below, check which discussion questions you will use for Day Two..

___ Why was Peter a good person to speak to this matter?

___ What did you consider to be the main points in Peter's sermon?

___ How do you see the tone of the meeting changing after Peter speaks?

___ What else did you learn from the Scriptures we looked up in Day Two?

Main Objective in Day Three: Day Three gives us a look at the resolution of the problem as the leaders came to agreement. Look over the discussion-starter questions below to see if any are applicable to your group.

___ What stood out to you from James' Old Testament defense of Peter's points?

___ Why do you think James wanted them to abstain from the things he mentioned?

___ How do you think the verdict relates to us today?

___ Did anything else stand out to you in the letter the mother church sent?

Main Objective in Day Four: Day Four shows us some of the response and results as the report is brought back to the Gentile churches. Review the discussion question list below, and choose any that you feel are good questions for your session.

___ How did the Antioch believers receive James' letter?

___ Why do you feel it was helpful that Barsabbas and Silas went with Paul?

___ What stood out to you from what you studied as the main priorities in ministry?

___ Do you think the message of grace is communicated clearly today?

Day Five – Key Points in Application: The most important application point from our study this week begins with our own understanding of grace and then with helping others understand it. Some good application questions from Day Five include...

___ Where would you place yourself on the spectrum between law and grace?

___ Did this lesson clear up any misunderstandings for you about grace?

___ Were there any evidences of being a "closet legalist" that you could identify with personally?

___ Are there any "pluses" you tend to add to the message of Christ?

CLOSING: 5–10 MINUTES

Summarize—Review the main objectives for each day.

Remind them that living a victorious Christian life is not attained when we try hard to be like Jesus, but only when we surrender our lives to God and let Him work through us.

Preview—Take a few moments to preview next week's lesson. Encourage your group members to complete their homework.

Pray—Close in prayer.

TOOLS FOR GOOD DISCUSSION

Bill Donahue, in his book, The Willow Creek Guide to Leading Life-Changing Small Groups (©1996 Zondervan Publishing House), lists four primary facilitator actions that will produce dynamic discussion. These four actions are easy to remember because they are linked through the acrostic method to the word, ACTS. You will profit from taking time to review this information in the "Helpful Hints" section of **How to Lead a Small Group Bible Study**, which can be found on page 214 of this book.

Lesson #3—Whatever the Problem, God Has the Solution - Acts 15:36—16:40

Memory Verse: James 1:5

"...if any of you lacks wisdom, let him ask of God, who gives to all generously and without reproach, and it will be given to him."

BEFORE THE SESSION

- Pray each day for the members of your group. Pray that they spend time in the Word, grasp the message God wants to bring to their lives, and that they surrender to what God is saying.

- Thoroughly prepare for your group session—don't procrastinate!

- As you go through the study, jot down any ideas or questions you want to discuss. Those, along with the suggested questions listed throughout this Leader's Guide, can personalize the discussion to fit your group. Think of the needs of your group and look for applicable questions and discussion starters.

- Remain ever teachable. Look first for what God is saying to you.

- Be prepared to be transparent and open about what God is teaching you. Nothing is quite as contagious as the joy at discovering new treasures in the Word.

WHAT TO EXPECT

Every life has difficulty. The only fellow with all his troubles behind him is a school bus driver. In the midst of life we will often encounter situations that are challenging. Expect that those in your group will have their share of challenges going on right now. This gives an opportunity for immediate application and should be an encouragement to all as we recognize how practical and relevant this week's lesson is. Keep bringing them back to the main point. Help them to see this principle that God has a solution for each problem we face. More importantly, help them take the next step of looking to God for solutions to their own problems.

THE MAIN POINT

The main point to be seen in this lesson is two important realities – there will be problems in ministry, and God always has a solution for those problems.

DURING THE SESSION

OPENING: 5–10 MINUTES

Opening Prayer—Remember the Lord is the Teacher and wants us to depend on Him as we open the Scriptures. Ask Him to teach you as you meet together.

Opening Illustration—It was lunar mission Apollo 13 that popularized the phrase, "Houston, we have a problem. This trip to the moon started out as a routine repeat of previous missions, and went largely unnoticed by the masses and the media. That is, until major mechanical problems quickly transformed Apollo 13 into a drama that gripped our whole nation. Damage to the spacecraft not only forced the astronauts to abandon plans to walk on the moon, but placed their ability to return to earth in serious jeopardy. The eventual triumph of returning these men to earth was not as a result of solving one problem but of systematically tackling a myriad of problems that arose one after another. The key to solving many of those problems was the very man who was intended to be on the mission but was replaced at the last minute because he had been exposed to an illness and they feared he might possible take sick while in flight. His expertise and training on the ground proved crucial to being able to solve some of the most challenging problems the men encountered. While a triumph of human ingenuity and effort, the help of Houston is no comparison to the resource we have in God. Because He is all-knowing, He always has the best solution. Because He is all-powerful, He is always able to apply it. We have access to this limitless resource when we contact our "mission control" and declare, "God, I have a problem."

DISCUSSION: 30 MINUTES

Keep the group directed along the main point of the power of God. You may have a pointed observation that helps sharpen the focus of the group. Encourage some to elaborate further on a key point or ask a quiet member of the group what they think of someone's comments. Watch the time, knowing you can't cover every single question in the lesson. Seek to cover the main ideas of each day and help the group to personally share what they have learned.

Main Objective in Day One: In Day One, the main objective is for you and your study group to grasp the problem of Paul and Barnabas' disagreement and to see the results of God's solution. Check which discussion questions you will use from Day One.

___ Why do you think these two spiritual men had such disagreement?

___ What was the result of their conflicting burdens?

___ How do you think the lives of Paul and Mark and Timothy would have been different without the disagreement?

___ What else stands out to you from God's solution?

Main Objective in Day Two: Day Two focuses on the problem Paul ran into of confusion on where to minister. The following questions may serve as excellent discussion starters for your group session:

___ How do you think Paul knew what the Spirit was saying to him?

___ What extra help was found in the Macedonian vision?

___ What meaning do you find in the phrase "we concluded"?

___ What stood out to you from Paul's start at ministry in Philippi?

Main Objective in Day Three: Day Three introduces us to the problem Paul encountered of persecution. Check which discussion questions you will use from Day Three.

___ Why do you suppose Paul decided to cast the demon out of the servant girl?

___ What motive do you see as the root behind Paul's opponents?

___ Why do you think God allowed Paul to receive such opposition?

___ Did anything stand out to you from the actions against Paul?

Main Objective in Day Four: In Day Four, we look at the contrast between Paul's circumstances and his response, and at God's solution. Check which discussion questions you will use from Day Four.

___ What stood out to you from the attitude and actions of Paul and Silas in jail?

___ Where do you think the Philippian jailer and his family would have heard the gospel without Paul's imprisonment?

___ Have you ever heard anyone use this passage to suggest that our salvation guarantees that of our family?

___ Did anything specific grab your attention when you considered Paul's time in Philippi?

Day Five – Key Points in Application: The most important application point for this week's study is that God has a solution for the problems He allows in our lives, and may have a greater purpose even in the problems themselves. Below, select a question or two for your Day Five discussion.

___ What is the main thing you learned from looking at this passage?

___ Have you ever encountered a disagreement like Barnabas and Paul's?

___ What are some problems you are facing that we need to ask God for a solution to?

___ Did anything else grab you this week?

CLOSING: 5–10 MINUTES

Summarize—Restate the key points the group shared. Review the objectives for each of the days found in these leader notes.

Remind—Using the memory verse, remind the group of the importance of a greater view of God.

Ask them to share their thoughts about the key applications from Day Five.

Preview—Take a few moments to preview next week's lesson. Encourage your group to do their homework and to space it out over the week.

Pray—Close in prayer.

TOOLS FOR GOOD DISCUSSION

One of the people who show up in every group is a person we call "Talkative Timothy." Talkative Timothy tends to talk too much and dominates the discussion time by giving less opportunity for others to share. What do you do with a group member who talks too much? In the "Helpful Hints" section of **How to Lead a Small Group Bible Study** (p. 214), you'll find some practical ideas on managing the "Talkative Timothy's" in your group.

Lesson #4—The Basis of Beliefs - Acts 17:1-34

Memory Verse: Acts 17:26-27

"He made from one man every nation of mankind to live on all the face of the earth, having determined their appointed times and the boundaries of their habitation, that they would seek God, if perhaps they might grope for Him and find Him, though He is not far from each one of us."

BEFORE THE SESSION

- Be sure to do your own study far enough in advance so as not to be rushed. You want to allow God time to speak to you personally.

- Don't feel that you have to use all of the discussion questions listed below. You may have come up with others on your own, or you may find that time will not allow you to use them all. These questions are to serve you, not for you to serve.

- You are the gatekeeper of the discussion. Do not be afraid to "reel the group back in" if they get too far away from the subject of the lesson.

- Remember to keep a highlight pen ready as you study to mark any points you want to be sure to discuss.

- Pray each day for the members of your group—that they spend time in the Word, grasp the message God wants to bring to their lives, and that they surrender to what God is saying.

WHAT TO EXPECT

Everyone operates from some kind of world view, and the mistake most of us make is to wrongly believe that everyone else looks at the world the same way we do. In this lesson expect that the concept of world view may or may not be familiar to your group members. Make sure they leave with at least an understanding of this concept even if they don't fully understand or agree with the different categories of world view we discuss this week.

THE MAIN POINT

The main point to be seen in this lesson is that in the Apostle Paul's ministry we learn that though the message of Christ is unchanging, the methods we use to present Him must be adapted to the world view of those we are trying to reach.

DURING THE SESSION

OPENING: 5–10 MINUTES

Opening Prayer—Remember that if it took the inspiration of God for people to write Scripture, it will also take His illumination for us to understand it. Have one of the members of your group open your time together in prayer.

Opening Illustration—On September 11, 2001 four planes were hijacked by radical extremists from the terrorist group Al Qaeda and converted into weapons. Two were crashed into the World Trade Center and one was flown into the Pentagon, while the fourth plane crashed in a field in Pennsylvania. In all nearly 3,000 people were killed as America was rudely inducted into the community of terrorist victims. For most Americans the actions of these hijackers were incomprehensible. We cannot understand the "why" or "how" of such horrific violence against non-military targets. Yet these men saw themselves as patriot warriors in a justified cause. Their actions were consistent with and acceptable to their world view. Clearly their view of the world is vastly different than ours, yet in varying shades there are large portions of the world population that look at life through the eyeglasses of Islam. To reach them with the good news of Christ requires that we understand how their thinking differs from ours, and demands that we begin with where they are rather than where we want them to be. The same application is true as we reach out to those from any world view different from our own)

DISCUSSION: 30 MINUTES

Once your group gets talking, you will find that all you need to do is keep the group directed and flowing with a question or two or a pointed observation. You are the gate-keeper of discussion. Don't be afraid to ask someone to elaborate further ("Explain what you mean, Barbara?") or to ask a quiet member of the group what they think of someone else's comments ("What do you think, Dave?"). Time will not allow you to discuss every single question in the lesson one at a time. Instead, make it your goal to cover the main ideas of each day and help the group to share what they learned personally. You don't have to use all the discussion questions. They are there for your choosing and discretion.

Main Objective in Day One: Day One focuses on introducing Paul's ministry to the Thessalonians and their world view of Rationalism. Below, check which discussion questions you will use from Day One.

___ What stood out to you from Paul's approach to reach out to the Thessalonians?

___ Why do you think he spent so much time "reasoning", "explaining" and "giving evidence"?

___ Why do you think the same message is often met with such conflicting responses?

___ What are some strengths of Paul's approach here and some challenges this type of thinking presents?

Main Objective in Day Two: Day Two studies the different mindset Paul encountered in the city of Berea. Check which discussion questions you will use from Day Two.

___ Why do you think Luke calls the Bereans "more noble minded" than the Thessalonians?

___ What are some strengths of the way they approached truth that we can learn from?

___ Why do you suppose many (but not all) of the Bereans responded positively?

___ Did anything else stand out to you in Day Two?

Main Objective in Day Three: In Day Three, we focus in on the very different world view Paul found in the city of Athens. In addition to any discussion-starter questions that you may have in mind, the following questions may also prove useful to your group time.

___ Have you ever experienced your spirit being provoked as Paul's was in Athens? Why?

___ What are some of the changes to be seen in Paul's evangelistic strategy here compared to his ministry elsewhere?

___ What are the similarities and differences of the thinking in Athens with unbelievers here today?

___ What mistakes could Paul have made if he didn't understand the different thinking in Athens?

Main Objective in Day Four: In Day Four, we examine how Paul built a bridge between where the Athenians were coming from and the message of Christ. Below, place a checkmark next to the questions that you feel are worthy of mention in your session. Or you may want to place ranking numbers next to each question to note your order of preference.

___ How did Paul make use of their own culture to build a bridge to the gospel?

___ Why do you think Paul started with Creation instead of with Christ?

___ What are some examples of Paul confronting the weaknesses in their way of thinking?

___ What do you consider to be the strongest points in Paul's argument?

Day Five—Key Points in Application: The most important application point your group can glean from the lesson on the basis of belief is the importance of understanding how others think before we try to persuade them to our way of thinking. Examine the question list below, and decide if there are any that fit your group discussion for the Day Five application time.

___ What is the dominant world view you grew up with?

___ How has your world view changed because of your faith in Christ?

___ Who are some people you think of that you associate with the three world views of this lesson?

___ What are some creative ways you can build bridges to people with different views of the world?

CLOSING: 5–10 MINUTES

Summarize—Restate the key points that were highlighted in the class. You may want to briefly review the objectives for each of the days found at the beginning of these leader notes.

Focus—Using this lesson's memory verse, focus on the heart that Jesus wants us to have

Ask the members of your group to reveal their thoughts about the key applications from Day Five.

Preview—Take a few moments to preview next week's lesson.

Pray—Close in prayer.

TOOLS FOR GOOD DISCUSSION

As mentioned earlier, there are certain people who show up in every discussion group. Last week we looked at "Talkative Timothy." Another person who is likely to show up is "Silent Sally." She doesn't readily speak up. Sometimes, her silence is because she doesn't yet feel comfortable enough with the group to share her thoughts. Other times, it is simply because she fears being rejected. Often, her silence is because she is too polite to interrupt and thus is headed off at the pass each time she wants to speak by more aggressive (and less sensitive) members of the group. In the "Helpful Hints" section of How to Lead a Small Group Bible Study (p. 216), you'll find some practical ideas on managing the "Silent Sally's" in your group.

Lesson #5—Joining God Where He Is Working - Acts 18:1-22

Memory Verse: Acts 18:6

"...when they resisted and blasphemed, he shook out his garments and said to them, 'Your blood be on your own heads! I am clean. From now on I will go to the Gentiles.'"

BEFORE THE SESSION

- Resist the temptation to do all your homework in one sitting or to put it off until the last minute. You will not be as prepared if you study this way.

- Make sure to mark down any discussion questions that come to mind as you study. Don't feel that you have to use all of the suggested discussion questions included in this leader's guide. Feel free to pick and choose based on your group and the time frame with which you are working.

- Remember your need to trust God with your study. The Holy Spirit is always the best teacher, so stay sensitive to Him!

WHAT TO EXPECT

Most in your group will know something about the missionary journeys of Paul, but many will have looked at them only as history instead of instruction. You will need to keep reminding them to look for the life lessons that are woven into the stories Luke chooses to include. Expect that even if they are already familiar with Paul's ministry in Corinth, they may have missed this underlying theme of moving to where God is at work. Many in your group will have a concept of service and ministry, but more likely than not, they will have sometimes seen it simply as working hard for God rather than letting Him work through them. Make sure they see the difference between received ministry and achieved ministry and have a sense of how to connect with the ministry the Lord is initiating.

THE MAIN POINT

The main point to be seen in this lesson is that true ministry is not what we do for God, but what God initiates for us and then does through us.

DURING THE SESSION

OPENING: 5–10 MINUTES

Opening Prayer—Remember that if it took the inspiration of God for people to write Scripture, it will also take His illumination for us to understand it. Have one of the members of your group open your time together in prayer.

Opening Illustration—Most people have heard of Welch's Grape Juice and related products. But few know the story behind the man who started the company and why. Welch was a young man devoted to his faith in Christ and committed to taking the gospel to the far reaches of the world. He had his sights set on a career in missions, but to his great disappointment, poor health prevented the mission agencies from accepting him. Finally, he gave up on the dream of going to the world but decided that if he could not go, he would stay behind and make as much money as he could to give to the cause of Christ. Where God was working in his life wasn't where he planned or expected, but when he joined God where He was working, Welch's life and business prospered and the phenomenal success of his business resulted in millions of dollars being directed to the cause of world evangelization. The most important measure of successful ministry is not how much we do, how hard we work at it, or how long we serve. The measurement that matters is how well we aligned ourselves with the work God wanted for us, and whether we aligned ourselves with Him so He could accomplish that work through us.

DISCUSSION: 30 MINUTES

Remember that your job is not to teach this lesson, but to facilitate discussion. Do your best to guide the group to the right answers, but don't be guilty of making a point someone else in the group could just as easily make.

Main Objective in Day One: Day One focuses on the principle that Paul was led in ministry to the different cities and didn't just make plans on his own. Below, check which discussion questions you will use from Day One.

___ Why do you suppose Paul left Athens when he did?

___ Do you think Priscilla and Aquila were already Christians when they met Paul? Why?

___ From your perspective is it better to be a "tent-maker missionary" than to be supported by others?

___ What things stood out to you from Paul's willingness to work and support himself?

Main Objective in Day Two: Day Two studies the problem of Jews rejecting Jesus and Paul's moving on to the Gentiles. Check which discussion questions you will use from Day Two.

___ What do you think were some of the benefits of Paul being able to work full-time at ministry?

___ What stood out to you from those who did respond positively to Christ in Corinth?

___ Why do you think Paul needed a vision to reassure him about ministry in Corinth?

___ Did Day Two raise any questions for you?

Main Objective in Day Three: Day Three takes a look more specifically at the striving of those who opposed Paul in Corinth. Review the questions below, and see if any are suitable to your group discussion on Day Three.

___ Why do you think so many of those who were supposed to be followers of God missed what He was doing through Paul?

___ What did the Jews hope to gain by their legal arguments against Paul?

___ What stands out to you from how the case against Paul was resolved?

___ Why from your perspective was the reaction of the Jews to the verdict so strong?

Main Objective in Day Four: In Day Four, we see the importance of a heart that seeks God's will in finding real ministry. Check which discussion questions you will use from Day Four.

___ What do you suppose was the purpose behind Paul keeping a Nazarite vow at this point?

___ How do you see the principle of the Nazarite vow applying to us today?

___ Why do you suppose Paul didn't stay on in Ephesus when there was obvious spiritual interest?

___ How do we keep the value of "if God wills" in our life planning and labors?

Day Five—Key Points in Application: The important thing to see out of Day Five is the focus on how important it is to let God guide us in ministry instead of just trying to help Him out as we think best. Decide on some discussion-starter topics for the application section of Day Five. The following questions are suggested questions that you may want to use for your discussion:

___ Where are some places you see God working around you right now?

___ What can you do to join God in what He is doing?

___ What are some steps of faith you need to take to be part of His work?

___ What are some evidences of striving and trying to make something happen that you see in your life or in the actions of others around you.

CLOSING: 5–10 MINUTES

Summarize—Go over the key points of the lesson.

Remind them that living a victorious Christian life is not attained when we try hard to be like Jesus, but only when we surrender our lives to God and let Him work through us.

Ask them what they think are the key applications from day five

Preview—Take a few moments to preview next week's lesson. Encourage them to be sure to complete their homework.

Pray—Close in prayer.

TOOLS FOR GOOD DISCUSSION

Hopefully your group is functioning smoothly at this point, but perhaps you recognize the need for improvement. In either case, you will benefit from taking the time to evaluate yourself and your group. Without evaluation, you will judge your group on subjective emotions. You may think everything is fine and miss some opportunities to improve your effectiveness. You may be discouraged by problems you are confronting when you ought to be encouraged that you are doing the right things and making progress. A healthy Bible-study group is not one without problems but is one that recognizes its problems and deals with them the right way. At this point in the course, as you and your group are nearly halfway-completed with the study, it is important to examine yourself and see if there are any mid-course corrections that you feel are necessary to implement. Review the evaluation questions list found on pages 222-223 of this book, and jot down two or three action points for you to begin implementing next week. Perhaps you have made steady improvements since the first time you answered the evaluation questions at the beginning of the course. If so, your improvements should challenge you to be an even better group leader for the final seven lessons in the study.

ACTION POINTS:

1.

2.

3.

Lesson #6—Changing the World (One Place at a Time)
Acts 18:23—19:41

Memory Verses: Acts 19:20

"So the word of the Lord was growing mightily and prevailing."

BEFORE THE SESSION

- Remember the Boy Scout motto: BE PREPARED! The main reason a Bible study flounders is because the leader comes in unprepared and tries to "shoot from the hip."

- Make sure to jot down any discussion questions that come to mind as you study.

- Don't forget to pray for the members of your group and for your time studying together. You don't want to be satisfied with what you can do—you want to see God do what only He can do!

WHAT TO EXPECT

I believe that all true Christians long to see the world following God. Yet most I meet don't seem to really believe that it will happen. Some I would suppose it they were honest, struggle with trusting that it can happen. The main reason for our doubts is not that we disbelieve God, but that we do not believe in ourselves and in the church's ability to accomplish the mission of the Great Commission. For most, this struggle with belief is based on the fact that we have never seen God radically change a single community. Expect that your group will need help conceptualizing seeing the world change, and will benefit from considering the possibility on the level of their own communities. Encourage them to reflect on all that changed in Ephesus as a result of the gospel's impact.

Main Point: The main point to be seen in this lesson is that although it takes time to change the world, God's Word is able to do just that, one place at a time.

DURING THE SESSION

OPENING: 5–10 MINUTES

Opening Prayer—Remember to have one of your group members open your time together in prayer.

Opening Illustration—This week you might consider trying a different approach to "hooking" your group's interest into the theme of this lesson. Start by asking "What do most people think it will take to change the world or a particular country?" Look for answers like military power, political influence, large financial resources, mass media, etc. If these aren't mentioned, you might suggest them. Next, ask "which of these resources did Paul and the early church have?" Obviously not much, yet what they did have was the power of God accessed through prayer, and the life-changing power of the gospel. With these, they changed the world. Help your group to realize that although the church doesn't have military power or political influence, we still have the resources necessary to make a difference and see our community change.

DISCUSSION: 30–40 MINUTES

Remember to pace your discussion so that you will be able to bring closure to the lesson at the designated time. You are the one who must balance lively discussion with timely redirection to ensure that you don't end up finishing only part of the lesson.

Main Objective in Day One: In Day One, the main objective is to explore how the work at Ephesus began and how God used Priscilla and Aquila to further prepare Apollos for ministry. Check which discussion questions you will use from Day One.

___ Why do you think God prevented Paul from ministering in Phrygia before now?

___ How do you suppose Apollos didn't know about the resurrection?

___ What is the right and the wrong way to come along side someone like Apollos?

___ Were there any particulars that stood out to you from Apollos' ministry in Corinth?

Main Objective in Day Two: In Day Two, we look at the ministry of Paul coming into Ephesus behind Apollos and clarifying the gospel to the disciples he found there. Choose a discussion question or two from the Day Two list below.

___ Do you think these men Paul found were Christians yet?

___ What stood out to you most from the way Paul handled the incomplete faith of these men?

___ What did you see of Paul's approach to ministry in Acts 19:8–10?

___ Can you think of a particular location where you could honestly say *"everyone heard the word of the Lord"*?

Main Objective in Day Three: Day Three introduces us to the different ways God worked to validate the gospel message and to cause people to take it seriously. Decide on some discussion-starter questions for your session on detours. Below, are some possible discussion questions for you to consider.

___ Why do you think God was doing "extraordinary miracles" in Ephesus?

___ How do you see the encounter with the sons of Sceva and the demon serving to validate the gospel message?

___ What do you think it takes for a believer to be known to the demonic realm?

___ What do the evidences of changed lives at Ephesus show us about the gospel's impact there?

Main Objective in Day Four: In Day Four, we take some time to learn about the continued prospering of the church in spite of opposition. Check which discussion questions you will use from Day Four.

___ What do you think was really driving the opposition to Paul and the church?

___ Why do you think people react differently in the emotion of a crowd than they would by themselves?

___ How would you imagine things would have turned out if Paul had gone into the mob and tried to speak?

___ Do you believe that opposition is a negative thing? Why or why not?

Day Five—Key Points in Application: The most important application point out of Day Five is that we personalize the lessons from God's working at Ephesus and look with eyes of faith on our own communities. Below, check any discussion questions that are best suited to your group for application.

___ What are some practical things you learned this week that will help you have a vision for reaching others?

___ Do you have a passion for the work of the gospel in a particular country?

___ How do the principles of targeted ministry and critical mass relate to you and your church or ministry?

___ What other applications did you see in this week's lesson?

CLOSING: 5–10 MINUTES

Summarize—Restate the key points.

Remind those in your group that living a victorious Christian life is not attained when we try hard to be like Jesus, but only when we surrender our lives to God and let Him work through us.

Preview—Take a few moments to preview next week's lesson.

Pray—Close in prayer.

TOOLS FOR GOOD DISCUSSION

As discussed earlier, there are certain people who show up in every discussion group that you will ever lead. We have already looked at "Talkative Timothy" and "Silent Sally." This week, let's talk about another person who tends to show up. Let's call this person "Tangent Tom." He is the kind of guy who loves to talk even when he has nothing to say. Tangent

Tom loves to "chase rabbits" regardless of where they go. When he gets the floor, you never know where the discussion will lead. You need to understand that not all tangents are bad. Sometimes, much can be gained from discussion "a little off the beaten path." But these diversions must be balanced against the purpose of the group. In the "Helpful Hints" section of **How to Lead a Small Group** (p. 216), you will find some practical ideas on managing the "Tangent Toms" in your group. You will also get some helpful information on evaluating tangents as they arise.

Lesson 7—Passing the Torch – Acts 20:1–38

Memory Verse: Acts 20:28

"Be on guard for yourselves and for all the flock, among which the Holy Spirit has made you overseers, to shepherd the church of God which He purchased with His own blood."

BEFORE THE SESSION

Try to get your lesson plans and homework done early this week. This gives time for you to reflect on what you have learned and process it mentally. Don't succumb to the temptation to procrastinate.

Make sure you keep a highlight pen handy to highlight any things you intend to discuss, including any questions that you think your group may have trouble comprehending. Jot down any good discussion questions that come to your mind as you study.

Don't think of your ministry to the members of your group as something that only takes place during your group time. Pray for your group members by name during the week that they would receive spiritual enrichment from doing their daily homework. Encourage them as you have opportunity.

WHAT TO EXPECT

Most people in your group will probably have heard bits and pieces of Paul's missionary journeys, but few will have studied the details of his life and ministry revealed in Acts. Expect that most will not have connected the different geographical references in this chapter into a coherent theme. Expect that some may still not see the connection between the locations here and the common ground Luke's references here share. Remind them that in each case, this is the last visit Paul makes to the city in question. Help them to see that the whole chapter focuses on the process of Paul passing the torch of ministry to those leaders God has raised up after him to continue the work.

THE MAIN POINT

The main point to be seen in this lesson is that changes in leadership are both natural and required as well as healthy if done right.

OPENING: 5–10 MINUTES

Opening Prayer—It would be a good idea to have a different group member each week open your time together in prayer.

Opening Illustration—On March 30, 1981, President Ronald Reagan fell victim to an assassination attempt as he left the Washington Hilton Hotel in Washington, D.C. Six shots were fired by John Hinckley striking the President and three other men (Presidential Press Secretary James Brady, Secret Service Agent Timothy McCarthy, and Metropolitan Police Officer Thomas Delahanty) with explosive bullets called "Devastators." It was not immediately public knowledge that Reagan had been hit, and took still longer for word to come out that his injury was serious and even life-threatening. His bullet-punctured lung had collapsed, and in surgery Doctors would drain over seven pints of blood from his chest cavity as they removed the bullet which miraculously had not exploded. For a short time, there was apparent confusion about the state of the Government. With Vice President Bush rushing out of Austin, Tex., to fly back to the Capital, Cabinet officers gathered in the White House situation room. At 4:14 P.M., citing, incorrectly, rules for Presidential succession, a visibly strained Secretary of State Alexander M. Haig declared he was "in charge." In reality though, the Government was little altered, as Mr. Bush touched down at Andrews Air Force Base at 6:30 P.M., to gracefully assume the duties but not the powers of the Presidency. You see, the founding fathers had enough wisdom and forethought to put in place a plan for exactly who would take over the leadership of the country in the event that a change had to be made quickly. In an even greater way, we can have confidence that God has a plan for every time there must be a passing of the torch of leadership in the church. This week we see this process in action as Paul says goodbye to churches he loved and had led.

DISCUSSION: 30–40 MINUTES

A key objective in how you manage your discussion time is to keep the big picture in view. Your job is not like a schoolteacher's job, grading papers and tests and the like, but more like a tutor's job, making sure your group understands the subject. Keep the main point of the lesson in view, and make sure they take that main point home with them.

Main Objective in Day One: In Day One the main objective is to look at Paul's departure from Ephesus, Macedonia and Greece and how he says goodbye. Start thinking now about what discussion starters you will use in your session. Review the question list below. Perhaps there is a question or two below that might be essential to your group time.

___What sort of things do you suppose Paul would have included in his final "exhortation" to these places he visits?

___Why do you think Jesus instructed His followers to leave a town when persecution arose?

___How do you think the congregations of Macedonia felt about saying goodbye to Paul?

___Why do you suppose such a larger contingent accompanied Paul on his trip to Jerusalem?

Main Objective in Day Two: In Day Two, we look at Paul's farewell service at Troas. Check which discussion questions you will use from Day Two.

___Why do you suppose Paul stayed behind for a few extra days?

___What do you think about the early church's practice of gathering on Sunday instead of the traditional Jewish Sabbath on Saturday?

___What stood out to you from the narrative of the boy's fall from the window?

___Did anything else in particular grab your attention from Day Two?

Main Objective in Day Three: Day Three focuses us in on Paul's time with the Ephesian elders and specifically his review of his ministry with them. Take a look at the discussion question list below to see if any are applicable to your group session.

___What did you learn by tracing Paul's travels on the map?

___What leadership principles do you see in the example Paul set in ministry?

___Paul considered his "course" as more important than even his life. Do you have a sense of the course God has for you?

___What are some things that sidetrack us from finding and following our course?

Main Objective in Day Four: Day Four examines the advice Paul has for the Ephesian elders as he passes the torch of leadership to them. Choose some discussion starters for your group session.

___What stood out to you from Paul's instructions to the leaders in Ephesus?

___Why do you suppose many churches today do not have elders as a leadership role like we see modeled here?

___Why was it important for the elders to guard themselves first instead of the flock?

___What did you learn from the exhortations Paul gives as he passes the torch?

Day Five—Key Points in Application: The focus of Day Five is to move us into evaluating applications to us today in the development and deployment of leaders in the church. Below, check any discussion questions that you might consider using for your application time.

___What sort of things do you feel our group does well in meeting the ongoing need for leaders?

___Where do you feel we most need to improve?

___What are some practical ways we can give present leaders the honor they ought to have?

___What is the biggest application point you observed this week?

CLOSING: 5–10 MINUTES

- **Summarize**—You may want to read "The Main Point" statement at the beginning of the leader's notes.

- **Preview**—If time allows, preview next week's lesson. Encourage your group to complete their homework.

- **Pray**—Close in prayer.

TOOLS FOR GOOD DISCUSSION

One of the issues you will eventually have to combat in any group Bible study is the enemy of boredom. This enemy raises its ugly head from time to time, but it shouldn't. It is wrong to bore people with the Word of God! Often boredom results when leaders allow their processes to become too predictable. As small group leaders, we tend to do the same thing in the same way every single time. Yet God the Creator, who spoke everything into existence is infinitely creative! Think about it. He is the one who not only created animals in different shapes and sizes, but different colors as well. When He created food, He didn't make it all taste or feel the same. This God of creativity lives in us. We can trust Him to give us creative ideas that will keep our group times from becoming tired and mundane. In the "Helpful Hints" section of How to Lead a Small Group (pp. 219–20), you'll find some practical ideas on adding spice and creativity to your study time.

Lesson 8—The Sovereign Hand of God in Ministry - Acts 8

Memory Verse: Proverbs 16:9

"The mind of man plans his way, But the LORD directs his steps."

BEFORE THE SESSION

- Your own preparation is key not only to your effectiveness in leading the group session, but also in your confidence in leading. It is hard to be confident if you know you are unprepared. These discussion questions and leader's notes are meant to be a helpful addition to your own study, but should never become a substitute.

- As you do your homework, study with a view to your own relationship with God. Resist the temptation to bypass this self-evaluation on your way to preparing to lead the group. Nothing will minister to your group more than the testimony of your own walk with God.

- Don't think of your ministry to the members of your group as something that only takes place during your group time. Pray for your group members by name during the week that they would receive spiritual enrichment from doing their daily homework. Encourage them as you have opportunity.

WHAT TO EXPECT

Every life is punctuated with situations that require wisdom and direction. God could have just given us a road map and told us to find our own way, or only given us our minds, making us dependent on our logic, but instead, He has chosen to give us a guide—His Spirit living in us. He does not want us to reject our own logic, but at the same time, we cannot lean only on that. In all these different and dramatic situations of Acts 8, the common denominator is the sovereign hand of God making use of circumstances and guiding His saints to those hungry for the gospel. Expect that your students will see each of the different situations, but not necessarily grasp the connection between them right away. Lead them toward the theme of God's sovereign working and guiding.

THE MAIN POINT

The main point in this lesson is that just because something is God's will, that doesn't necessarily mean that it will be easy.

DURING THE SESSION

OPENING: 5–10 MINUTES

Opening Prayer—A good prayer with which to open your time with is the prayer of David in Psalm 119:18, "Open my eyes, that I may behold Wonderful things from Thy law." Remember, if it took the illumination of God for men to write Scripture, it will take the same for us to understand it.

Opening Illustration—In the garden of Gethsemane we are given a glimpse of our Lord's humanity as He wrestles in prayer, making ready for what the day ahead will hold. His fervency is manifested as His sweat became like drops of blood. Jesus recognized that God's will would be hard. In Gethsemane He prayed, *"Father, if You are willing, remove this cup from Me; yet not My will, but Yours be done"* (Luke 22:42). Even for our Lord there was that moment when He wrestled with God's will being difficult. Yet we see a reflection of Jesus' prayer this week when Paul convinces those with him that even though chains await him in Jerusalem, it is God's will for him to go. They respond, *"The will of the Lord be done"* (Acts 21:14). If we know something is God's will, and God's will is all that we want, then we move forward even if it is hard. Our hearts need to be "not My will, but Yours be done."

DISCUSSION: 30–40 MINUTES

Remember to pace your discussion so that you don't run out of time to get to the application questions in Day Five. This time for application is perhaps the most important part of your Bible study. It will be helpful if you are familiar enough with the lesson to be able to prioritize the days for which you want to place more emphasis, so that you are prepared to reflect this added emphasis in the time you devote to that particular day's reading.

Main Objective in Day One: In Day One, the main objective is to use the opposition of Paul's friends to his going to Jerusalem to highlight the difference between a godly opinion and God's will. Choose a discussion question or two from the Day One list below.

___ What stood out to you when you traced Paul's journey on the map?

___ What was the gist of the message Paul kept hearing everywhere he stopped?

___ How do you reconcile the disciples at Tyre telling Paul "through the Spirit" not to go to Jerusalem with his confidence it was God's will?

___ Are there any other thoughts from Day One that you would like to discuss?

Main Objective in Day Two: We learn in Day Two some of the specific challenges Paul faced with concerns from some of the believers in Jerusalem. Check which discussion questions you will use from Day Two.

___ What do you sense was the feeling of the Church leadership at Jerusalem toward Paul?

___ How do you think the rumors about Paul got started among the Jewish believers in Jerusalem?

___ What do you think of the church leaders' proposal for Paul?

___ Do you think Paul did the right thing in following their advice?

Main Objective in Day Three: Day Three introduces us to the unfolding fulfillment of the prophecies of about Paul's visit and how following the leaders' advice contribute to his problems. In addition to any discussion questions you may have in mind for your group session, the following questions below may also be useful:

___ From what you know of Acts so far, where do you think the opposition to Paul at the Temple started from?

___ How do you think the crowd could get so agitated over an accusation that was false?

___ What happened when the Roman authorities got involved in the commotion surrounding Paul?

___ What stood out to you from Paul's handling of the situation as it unfolds?

Main Objective in Day Four: In Day Four, our study focuses on the reaction of the crowd to the truth Paul was trying to share with them. Place a checkmark next to the discussion question you would like to use for your group session. Or you may want to place a ranking number in each blank to note your order of preference.

___ What ways did you see Paul building a bridge to his audience?

___ What stood out to you from Paul's account of his actual conversion?

___ What are some of the evidences that Paul's live had been changed through his conversion experience?

___ Why do you think these Jews had such a hard time accepting the gospel message?

Day Five—Key Points in Application: The main goal of Day Five is to seek to put these truths about handling God's will when it is hard. Check which discussion questions you will use from Day Five.

___ Can you think of some examples where you have found God's will to be hard?

___ How do you normally respond when following God's leading becomes hard?

___ What are some examples in Scripture or your experience when God's leading didn't really make sense logically?

___ What other applications did you see from this week?

CLOSING: 5–10 MINUTES

- **Summarize**—You may want to read "The Main Point" statement at the beginning of the leader's notes.

- **Preview**—If time allows, preview next week's lesson. Encourage them to be sure and do their homework.

- **Pray**—Close in prayer.

TOOLS FOR GOOD DISCUSSION

From time to time, each of us can say stupid things. Some of us, however, are better at it than others. The apostle Peter had his share of embarrassing moments. One minute, he was on the pinnacle of success, saying, "You are the Christ, the Son of the Living God" (Matthew 16:16), and the next minute, he was putting his foot in his mouth, trying to talk Jesus out of going to the cross. Proverbs 10:19 states, "When there are many words, transgression is unavoidable. . . ." What do you do when someone in the group says something that is obviously wrong? First of all, remember that how you deal with a situation like this not only affects the present, but the future. In the "Helpful Hints" section of How to Lead a Small Group (p. 220), you'll find some practical ideas on managing the obviously wrong comments that show up in your group.

Lesson 9—The False Solution of Following Our Flesh - Acts 23:1–35

Memory Verse: 1 Peter 2:23

"while being reviled, He did not revile in return; while suffering, He uttered no threats, but kept entrusting Himself to Him who judges righteously."

BEFORE THE SESSION

- Pray each day for the members of your group—that they spend time in the Word, grasp the message God wants to bring to their lives, and that they surrender to what God is saying.

- Be sure you have searched the Scriptures carefully for each day's lesson.

- While preparing for this lesson, read through the discussion questions on the following pages, and select which questions you will use.

- Remain ever teachable. Look first for what God is saying to you. This will help you in relating to some of the situations your group members may be facing as they are seeking to make an impact on those around them.

WHAT TO EXPECT

The concept of "received" ministry has been mentioned often and was dealt with pretty thoroughly in Acts 18 (Lesson 5). In many ways this lesson presents the opposite truth by showing the results of trying to "achieve" something in one's own efforts instead of receiving something God has initiated. Although most in your group probably already have some familiarity with Paul's ministry in the book of Acts, few will have studied chapter 23 closely enough to have recognized the outburst of Paul's flesh. This is one of the challenges of studying biblical narrative. It simply reports what happened rather than spelling out what was right or wrong. For many, the recognition that this hostility and closed door for ministry was as a result of Paul failing, rather than due only to the closed minds of the Jews will be novel, and perhaps a bit unsettling at first. Remind them that one of the beauties of Scripture is that it presents an honest portrait of its heroes, showing their failures as well as their successes. Help them to see the benefit of not keeping Paul on a pedestal, as it helps us to identify our own humanity with what we see of his.

THE MAIN POINT

The main point to be seen in the lesson on Acts 23 is the fact that both non-Christians and Christians can try to "achieve" ministry, but that God does not allow it to prosper in the end.

DURING THE SESSION

OPENING: 5–10 MINUTES

Prayer—Remember to ask the Lord for His wisdom. He has promised to guide us into the truth.

Opening Illustration—One of the dark times in Israel's history is reflected in the early chapters of 1 Samuel. Shortly after Samuel was appointed as prophet, Israel went into battle with the Philistines and was badly beaten (see 1 Samuel 4-6). After reflection, the elders concluded, "Maybe we will do better if we take the Ark of the Covenant with us into battle." God was not their first thought, but rather, an afterthought, and though they now had a prophet who could help them seek God, he was not included in this decision. It was an idea from man, rather than from God – definitely not "received." The result was disastrous. In the first battle four thousand died without the ark. With the ark, 30,000 were slaughtered and the ark was taken by the Philistines. Instead of joining God and letting him lead, Israel came up with their own idea and asked God to bless it. They tried to use God like a lucky rabbit's foot. But things didn't go much better for the Philistines either. Like the movie, "Raiders of the Lost Ark," where Hitler thought the Ark of the Covenant could help him in war, the Philistines tried to use God in the same way as Israel had. Instead of help thought, the ark brought plague and problems. They quickly concluded that they wanted no part of Israel's ark, and placed it on a new cart and sent it back unmanned to Israel. Like Israel, they learned the hard way that "achieved" doesn't work. The ark stayed put for decades. But finally God placed David as king, and when he went into battle with the Philistines, he sought the Lord and followed the direction he "received" from God, leading to victory. But even David was not immune to striving. After his victory, he decided it would be a good thing to bring the ark back to Jerusalem (see 2 Samuel 6). But what is the most efficient way to do this? David takes an idea from the Philistines and puts the ark on a cart for the journey. Half-way their, the ark is tipped and Uzzah is struck dead for placing his hands on the holy throne of God. But the real problem wasn't Uzzah's hand. The whole incident never would have happened if David had followed the "received" instructions God gave Moses for the moving of the ark. It was never to be carried by cart—that was employing Philistine philosophy instead of God. He made it clear in the giving of the Law that the ark was always to be carried by priests on poles. It was slow, but it was God's will. David speeding things up with a cart in the end didn't help out God like he thought it would. Man-initiated plans or fleshly energy may seem like solutions, but in the end they never are.

DISCUSSION: 30–40 MINUTES

Select one or two specific questions to get the group started. Keep the group directed along the main point. By this point in the course (Week 9), you know the talkative and the quiet. Continue to encourage each member in the importance of his or her input. Some of the greatest life lessons we ever learn may come from someone who has said very little up to this point.

Main Objective in Day One: In Day One, the main objective is to show how the fleshly actions of the high priest incited Paul to respond out of the flesh as well. Review the question list below, and decide upon some discussion starters for your group session.

___ Why do you think the high priest took such offense at Paul claiming a clear conscience?

___ What was right in Paul's answer to Ananias? What was wrong?

___ How good is Paul's excuse for his response to the high priest?

___ What do you think were the ministry consequences of Paul's fleshly actions here?

Main Objective in Day Two: Day Two focuses on how Paul draws the attention away from his fleshy response. Check which discussion questions you will use from Day Two.

___ How did Paul use the differences between the competing factions in the Sanhedrin to deflect the attention away from himself?

___ As you look at the two groups in the Sanhedrin, who would be some similar groups in the body of Christ today?

___ What was the ultimate outcome of Paul's strategy?

___ How do you see Paul's vision relating in this context?

Main Objective in Day Three: Day Three introduces us to yet another example of flesh in the vow the Jewish assassins make to kill the Apostle Paul. Some good discussion questions for Day Three include . . .

___ What exactly is the cause these forty men take up and how committed are they to it?

___ What stands out to you from how the plot was discovered?

___ Why do you think the Roman commander took the plot against Paul so seriously?

___ Did anything else stand out to you from Day Three?

Main Objective in Day Four: Day Four examines the Roman commander's counter-plan to protect Paul and looks at it from the vantage point of God's sovereignty. Check which discussion questions you will use from Day Four.

___ What all did the Roman commander do to insure Paul's protection?

___ What do you see in the commander's letter about his view of the accusations against Paul?

___ Did any particular details grab you as you studied Paul's trip to Caesarea?

___ What stands out to you from the end of the journey?

Day Five—Key Points in Application: The most important application point in this lesson is to recognize the many different examples of flesh that Luke weaves together to make his underlying point, and to learn from the mistakes of others the impotency of flesh. Below, are some suggestions for discussion questions. Feel free to come up with your own questions as well.

___ What are some examples you have seen of flesh causing problems and bringing negative consequences?

___ In which areas do you struggle with what the study calls "squeeze-out" flesh?

___ What kind of situations did you think of where "help-out" flesh shows up?

___ Of these two kinds of flesh, which would you say you struggle with more?

CLOSING: 5–10 MINUTES

Summarize—Restate the key points the group shared. Review the objectives for each of the days found at the beginning of these leader notes.

Focus—Using the memory verse (2 Corinthians 5:17), focus the group on the fact that Christianity is not us trying hard to be good people, but God changing us.

Ask them to express their thoughts about the key applications from Day Five.

Encourage—We have finished nine lessons. This is no time to slack off. Encourage your group to keep up the pace. We have three more lessons full of life-changing truths. Take a few moments to preview next week's lesson. Encourage your group members to do their homework in proper fashion by spacing it out over the week.

Pray—Close in prayer.

TOOLS FOR GOOD DISCUSSION

The Scriptures are replete with examples of people who struggled with the problem of pride. Unfortunately, pride isn't a problem reserved for the history books. It shows up just as often today as it did in the days the Scriptures were written. In your group discussions, you may see traces of pride manifested in a "know-it-all" group member. "Know-It-All Ned" may have shown up in your group by this point. He may be an intellectual giant, or he may be a legend only in his own mind. He can be very prideful and argumentative. If you want some helpful hints on how to deal with "Know-It-All Ned," look in the "Helpful Hints" section of How to Lead a Small Group Bible Study (p.217–18).

Lesson 10—The Fruit of Patience - Acts 24:1–27

Memory Verses: Galatians 5:22–23

"But the fruit of the Spirit is love, joy, peace, patience, kindness, goodness, faithfulness, gentleness, self-control; against such things there is no law."

BEFORE THE SESSION

- Never underestimate the importance of prayer for yourself and for the members of your group. Ask the Lord to give your group members understanding in their time in the Word and to bring them to a new level of knowing Him.

- Spread your study time over the week.

- Remember to mark those ideas and questions you want to discuss or ask as you go through the study.

- Be sensitive to the needs of your group. Be prepared to stop and pray for a member who may be facing a difficult struggle or challenge.

WHAT TO EXPECT

This lesson stands on its own, but is best appreciated when viewed in contrast to the previous lesson on "The False Solution of Following Your Flesh." The patience exhibited by Paul is very different than his fleshly impatience in Acts 23. You will want to briefly remind them of last week's lesson so they can make this connection. Expect that all will have struggled at some point with a lack of patience, and will have many personal experiences to relate as you discuss the topic of patience. You will not want to discourage this, but you will need to manage it for two reasons. Although you desire interaction and discussion, you want to cover the text and not just chat. Secondly, you want to insure that talking about the problem doesn't take so much time that you don't adequately cover the solution. Be grateful for personal sharing, but emphasize the need for brevity and keep bringing the focus back to the lesson.

THE MAIN POINT

The main point to be seen in the lesson is that patience is part of the fruit of the Spirit, and it is manifested through us when Christ is in control of our lives.

DURING THE SESSION

OPENING: 5–10 MINUTES

Opening Prayer—Have one of the group members open the time with prayer.

Opening Illustration—Joseph is one of the most remarkable characters of the Old Testament. He went from being his father's favorite, to being his brothers' worst enemy.

He went from being thrown into a pit, to being sold as a slave. He went from faithful service to false accusation and wrongful prison, and he waited there for God to show some justice. Finally, after years of waiting, he was able to interpret the dream of one of the king's servants. He asked the servant to remember him and his case to the king, but the servant forgot. For two more years Joseph sat in that jail, cruelly sold as a slave by his own brothers, wrongfully accused by his master's wife, falsely imprisoned by the man he had served faithfully, and now, forgotten by the man he comforted and helped. Only in God's strength could he have had the patience to keep waiting and hoping. Yet finally, God delivered him and prospered his way more than anyone could have imagined. Chances are that in each of our lives there will be circumstances which demand patience. We will have that patience we need if we are filled with the Spirit of God. Patience is a fruit He produces in us.

DISCUSSION: 30–40 MINUTES

Select one or two specific questions to get the group started in discussion. Continue to encourage each member in the importance of his or her insights and input.

Main Objective in Day One: Day One looks at Paul's accusers making their case against him to the governor, Felix. Good discussion starters for Day One include . . .

___ What do you think was going through Paul's mind as he waited for his trial to begin?

___ How do you think Felix received the flattery given him by the Jewish attorney?

___ What stands out to you most from the accusations leveled against Paul?

___ Did anything in particular grab you out of the way Tertullus closed out the case against Paul?

Main Objective in Day Two: In Day Two, the main objective is to consider Paul's response to the charges made against him. Below are some suggested questions for your discussion on Day Two. Which questions will you use for your group session?

___ What impresses you most as you look at the manner in which Paul handles responding to the charges?

___ How strong do you think his defense is in logic and merit?

___ Who do you think Paul was most speaking to when he addressed his involvement what they called a sect?

___ Do you think Paul's main goal is to prove his innocence?

Main Objective in Day Three: In Day Three, the main objective is to look at the contrast in how Paul relates to the high priest compared to last week. What discussion questions do you plan to use for Day Three? Below are some suggestions.

___ What stood out to you when you compared the opening statements of Paul from the two different situations?

___ Why do you think Paul emphasized the connection between his actions and the Mosaic Law?

___ Why do you think the Jews from Asia didn't come to this trial?

___ How do you think Paul did at defending himself here?

Main Objective in Day Four: Day Four zeros in on the results of the trial and the details of Paul's time in Caesarea. Check which questions you will use for your discussion on Day Four.

___ Why do you suppose Felix allowed the Jews no rebuttal and put the case off?

___ What do you think Felix's impression was of Paul and the case against him?

___ How spiritually interested do you think Felix really was?

___ What sort of things were getting in the way of Felix moving toward the Lord?

Day Five—Key Points in Application: The most important aspect of each lesson is taking the time to seek to apply the truths to our own lives. Make sure you save time for this important part. Select a discussion question or two from the list below.

___ Can you think of a time when God enabled you to be patient in a challenging circumstance?

___ In what kinds of situations do you find it the hardest to be patient?

___ What stood out to you most from looking at Ephesians 4:22–24?

___ Do you feel like you understand practically what it means to do what Paul instructs us to do?

CLOSING: 5–10 MINUTES

Summarize—Review the key points the group shared. You may want to review "The Main Point" statement for this lesson. Also, ask your group to express their thoughts about the key applications from Day Five

Focus—Using the memory verse, focus the group on the miracle of salvation.

Preview—Take a few moments to preview next week's lesson.

Pray—Close in prayer.

So, group leaders, how have the weeks of this study been for you? Have you dealt with anyone in your group called "Agenda Alice?" She is the type that is focused on a Christian "hot-button" issue instead of the Bible study. If not managed properly, she (or he) will either sidetrack the group from its main study objective, or create a hostile environment in the group if she fails to bring people to her way of thinking. For help with "Agenda Alice," see the "Helpful Hints" section of **How to Lead a Small Group Bible Study** (pp. 218–19).

Lesson 11—A Defense for the Hope Within - Acts 25:1—26:32

Memory Verse: 1 Peter 3:15–16

"But sanctify Christ as Lord in your hearts, always being ready to make a defense to everyone who asks you to give an account for the hope that is in you, yet with gentleness and reverence; and keep a good conscience so that in the thing in which you are slandered, those who revile your good behavior in Christ will be put to shame."

BEFORE THE SESSION

- Pray for your group as they study through this week's lesson.

- Spread your study time over the week. This is like a large meal. You need time to chew each truth and digest it fully.

- Remember to jot down those ideas and questions you want to discuss or ask as you go.

WHAT TO EXPECT

Every person has a story to tell, and one of the most effective ways any of us can share the reality of Christ with others is by telling our own story. This week's lesson on "A Defense for the Hope Within" gives us our fullest look at the conversion of the Apostle Paul and how he used his story in evangelism. Expect that as your group members compare Paul's testimony with their own, some will feel that they don't have much of a story to tell. They may feel that theirs is not dramatic enough to be interesting. Make sure that you address this. What you want to make sure they see is that while a dramatic story may be entertaining, there are far more people that can relate with growing up religious but not understanding what it means to have a personal relationship with Christ. Help them make the connection that the main point of any testimony is not how bad we were, but Christ and the difference He makes. Remind them that in every audience there will be someone who can relate more to them than to a drug addict or murderer.

THE MAIN POINT

The main point to be seen in the lesson is that when Christ does a work in our hearts, we have a story to tell others that helps evangelism to happen naturally.

DURING THE SESSION

OPENING: 5–10 MINUTES

Opening Prayer—Have one of the group members open the time with prayer.

Opening Illustration—Normally I encourage you to make use of an opening illustration as a hook to gain your group's attention and interest. This time, perhaps the best illustration will be a personal one. Why not BRIEFLY share your own personal testimony of coming to the Lord. Another option if you are not comfortable with this, or if you think it would be an encouragement to someone else, is to ask another group member to share their testimony. If you go this route, make sure you give them ample time to prepare, and that you emphasize the need for them to be brief (no more than 3-5 minutes) so as to allow time to discuss the lesson.

DISCUSSION: 30–40 MINUTES

When leading small group discussion, the most important temptation to avoid is doing most of the talking yourself. See yourself as the referee, always putting the ball back into play. Don't view yourself as the star player who always takes the shot. Your group will learn more from self-discovery than they will from anything else. If you guide the discussion properly, they will not realize how much you are directing the flow of discussion. It will seem to them as if they have been having a natural conversation. As you trek through the lesson, seek to keep the main point the main point. Emphasize what you clearly know and understand. Then you can move on to the things that are not as clear as the Lord gives you time and insight.

Main Objective in Day One: In Day One, the main objective is to see the renewal of Paul's case when a new governor takes over. In addition to any discussion questions you may have in mind, the list of questions below may also contain useful discussion-starter ideas.

___ What would you suppose the Jewish leaders were hoping to gain from their being a new governor?

___ Why do you think they still felt so passionately about trying to be rid of Paul?

___ Why would Festus be hesitant to give in to the request of the leaders?

___ Did anything else stand out to you from Day One?

Main Objective in Day Two: In Day Two, we examine Paul's first trial before the new governor, Festus. Check which discussion questions you will use from Day Two.

___ Did you learn anything new by comparing Paul's statement here with his previous meeting with the high priest?

___ What do you see in Paul's response to the charges against him?

___ Why do you think Festus asked Paul to go to Jerusalem for trial instead of ordering it?

___ What was the response of Paul to the request?

Main Objective in Day Three: In Day Three, we are exposed to the visit to Festus by King Agrippa and Bernice. Below, are some suggested discussion starters for you to consider.

___ What do you think Festus' attitude was to the visit by Agrippa and Bernice?

___ Did you learn anything interesting about them by looking at any other resources?

___ What grabs you most as you consider Festus' representation of Paul's case?

___ Why do you think so many prominent people took an interest in being at Paul's hearing?

Main Objective in Day Four: Day Four's main objective is to focus on the content of Paul's defense as he shares his testimony before these prominent people. Check any questions that are applicable for your Day Four-discussion time.

___ What aspects of Paul's life before meeting Christ does he emphasize to this audience?

___ What stands out to you as key in Paul's account of his conversion?

___ What do you consider to be the important things Paul identifies as changes in his life after meeting Christ?

___ Did any particular things catch your attention from Agrippa's response to Paul?

Day Five—Key Points in Application: The most important application point in this lesson is that we recognize how effective and important a tool our own testimony is when we have the chance to share Christ with others. Check which discussion questions you will use to help focus the applications from Day Five.

___ Were you able to give some thought to organizing your own story to share with others?

___ Were there any areas you struggled with communicating your heart?

___ What are some benefits to having this prepared beforehand instead of just winging it?

___ Did the Lord impress you with anyone you should send a testimony letter to?

CLOSING: 5–10 MINUTES

Summarize—Restate the key points the group shared.

Focus—Focus the group again on the fact that we cannot love as we should or lay aside our prejudices in our own strength. Remind them it must be done by His power, wisdom, and grace.

Ask them to share their thoughts about the key applications from Day Five.

Preview—Take a few moments to preview next week's lesson. Encourage your group members to do their homework in proper fashion by spacing it out over the week.

Pray—Close in prayer.

TOOLS FOR GOOD DISCUSSION

Well, it is evaluation time again! You may be saying to yourself, "Why bother evaluating at the end? If I did a bad job, it is too late to do anything about it now!" Well, it may be too late to change how you did on this course, but it is never too late to learn from this course what will help you on the next. Howard Hendricks, that peerless communicator from Dallas Theological Seminary, puts it this way: "The good teacher's greatest threat is satisfaction—the failure to keep asking, 'How can I improve?' The greatest threat to your ministry is your ministry." Any self-examination should be an accounting of your own strengths and weaknesses. As you consider your strengths and weaknesses, take some time to read through the evaluation questions list found in How to Lead a Small Group Bible Study on pages 222–23. Make it your aim to continue growing as a discussion leader. Jot down below two or three action points for you to implement in future classes.

ACTION POINTS:

1.

2.

3.

Lesson 12—Prisons Become Pulpits - Acts 27:1—28:31

Memory Verse: Philippians 1:2

"Now I want you to know, brethren, that my circumstances have turned out for the greater progress of the gospel."

BEFORE THE SESSION

- You will certainly need to pray for your group as they walk through this last lesson in the study. Never underestimate the importance of prayer for yourself and for the members of your group. Pray for each of them by name.

- Spread your study time over the week.

- Remember to mark those ideas and questions you want to discuss or ask as you go through the study. Add to those some of the questions listed below.

- Be sensitive to the working of the Spirit in your group meeting, ever watching for ways to help one another truly follow God.

WHAT TO EXPECT

One of the most important principles to grasp in drawing out application from this last lesson is the definition of a "prison." Most will never serve time in jail, but all will find themselves at one time or another in a figurative prison—a place they didn't choose which is negative, maybe even painful, and from which they cannot escape. The central point of this lesson is that Paul's prison became his figurative "pulpit"—his place of ministry, from which he communicates truth to others. Expect that some will have difficulty at first identifying their own circumstances as prisons of sorts. If you can help them make that connection, you will go a long way toward helping them apply the lesson to their own lives. There is an underlying assumption here that not all will preach or be pastors, but all are called to be ministers. Some may preach sermons by the example they set rather than the information they teach or preach. If you can help each person in your group see themselves as a minister and their own trials as prisons, then they too can see their prisons become pulpits.

THE MAIN POINT

The main point to be seen in this lesson is that rather than keeping him from his ministry, Paul's prison actually enhanced his ministry and even became his ministry.

DURING THE SESSION

OPENING: 5–10 MINUTES

Opening Prayer—Psalm 119:18 says, "Open my eyes, that I may behold wonderful things from Thy law." Ask the Lord to open your eyes as you meet together. Have one of the group members open the time with prayer.

Opening Illustration—Joni Erickson Tada is a dynamic Christian spokesperson with a world-wide ministry of lecturing, writing, and radio programs. But her ministry is founded on a personal tragedy. As a teenager, she was swimming at a lake one day and had an accident. She dove into water she believed to be deeper than it was. Her head struck bottom and her neck was broken. In a moment, she became a paraplegic. She went through stages of fear, anger, false hope, and despair. But eventually she came to accept the prison of her wheelchair. As she trusted God with her trial and grew in her faith, her attitude became one of hope instead of hopelessness. Concluding that God had known long before she did what would happen, and that His plan and purpose for her life included her wheelchair, she began to try to make the most of her life and times. She began to paint and draw, holding the brush or pen in her mouth. After writing her story down in a book simply called Joni, her recognition and influence began to grow. Offers to speak came in. Other books were written. She began a daily radio program and started an international ministry to the handicapped. Without realizing it, she turned the prison of her wheelchair into her pulpit. As we will see in this week's lesson, the Apostle Paul set an example of this powerful principle: God can use us wherever we are and whatever our trial is if we will let Him be in control of our hearts.

DISCUSSION: 30–40 MINUTES

Select one or two specific questions to get the group started. This lesson on prisons offers many application points in which to look at how each of us is following (or faltering in following) God. Remember to look for those "Velcro" points where members can see something that applies to their own lives. Encourage them to share the insights the Lord has shown them during the week.

Main Objective in Day One: In Day One, the main objective is to introduce the surprise difficulties Paul and his companions began to encounter on their way to Rome. Place a checkmark next to the suggested discussion questions that you would like to use in your group session. Or you may want to use ranking numbers and rank the questions in preferential order.

___ Did anything stand out to you from those accompanying Paul?

___ What phrases in these verses show you things weren't going well on their journey?

___ Why do you perceive that Paul's concerns were not acted on by the leaders of the trip?

___ What do these verses reveal about how bad their circumstances were?

Main Objective in Day Two: In Day Two, the main objective is to look at how Paul was leading in the midst of the difficulties. Check which discussion questions you will use from Day Two.

___ How did you see Paul encouraging and comforting those on board?

___ Did you see evidence of the men trusting God through Paul's words and their response?

___ How many different ways do you suppose Paul was used to reveal God to these men?

___ What stood out to you from the end of the boat ride?

Main Objective in Day Three: Day Three continues to focus on Paul's journey and focuses in on how his actions were used to speak of the truth of God. Some good discussion questions for Day Three include. . .

___ What do you suppose Paul and his group were feeling in those first few verses of the chapter?

___ How does the snakebite fit into what God was doing with Paul?

___ How did Paul's healing of all those people impact those on the island?

___ How do you think it and the islanders' responses impacted those traveling with Paul?

Main Objective in Day Four: In Day Four, the main objective is to introduce Paul's arrival at last in Rome. Select a discussion question or two from the list of questions below.

___ How did Paul and his friends finally get to Rome?

___ What were the circumstances that greeted Paul in Rome?

___ What do his actions say about how he viewed his time there?

___ Did anything in particular grab you from the response of the Jews or the summary of Paul's time in Rome?

Day Five—Key Points in Application: The most important application point seen in this lesson is to recognize the principle of prisons becoming places of ministry. Check which discussion questions you will use to help focus the applications from Day Five.

___ Are you able to identify any "prisons" in your own life right now? What are they?

___ What would you say has been your greatest struggle in dealing with the trials God has allowed you to go through?

___ Did the list of principles from what Paul did offer any encouragement to you in your own difficulties?

___ Did it give you some direction of things you need to do?

CLOSING: 5–10 MINUTES

Summarize—Restate the key points the group shared. Review the main objectives for each of the days found in these leader notes.

Focus—Using the memory verse, direct the group's focus to the reality that God wants us to pray for each other.

Ask the group to express their thoughts about the key applications from Day Five.

Pray—Close your time in prayer by thanking the Lord for the journey He has led you on over the past twelve weeks.

TOOLS FOR GOOD DISCUSSION

Congratulations! You have successfully navigated the waters of small group discussion. You have finished all twelve lessons in this study, but there is so much more to learn, so many more paths to take on our journey with the Lord, so much more to discover about what it means to follow Him. Now What? It would be wise for you and your group to not stop with this study. In the front portion of this leader's guide (in the "Helpful Hints" section of How to Lead a Small Group Bible Study, p. 221), there is information on how you can transition to the next study and share those insights with your group. Encourage your group to continue in some sort of consistent Bible study. Time in the Word is much like time at the dinner table. If we are to stay healthy, we will never get far from physical food, and if we are to stay nourished on "sound" or "healthy" doctrine, then we must stay close to the Lord's "dinner table" found in His Word. Job said it well, "I have not departed from the command of His lips; I have treasured the words of His mouth more than my necessary food" (Job 23:12).

When you purchase a Bible or book from **AMG Publishers, Living Ink Books,** or **God and Country Press,** you are helping to impact the world for Christ.

How? AMG Publishers and its imprints are ministries of **AMG International,** a Gospel-first global ministry that meets the deepest needs – spiritual and physical – while inspiring hope, restoring lives and transforming communities. Profits from the sale of AMG Publishers' books are poured into AMG International's worldwide ministry efforts.

For over 75 years, AMG International has leveraged the insights of local leaders and churches, who know their communities best to identify the right strategies to meet the deepest needs. AMG's methods include child and youth development, media evangelism, pastor training, church planting, medical care and disaster relief.

To learn more about AMG International and how you can partner with the ministry through your prayers and financial support, please visit **www.amginternational.org**.

AMG INTERNATIONAL | MEETING THE DEEPEST NEEDS